FROM THE FJORDS TO THE NILE

Essays in honour of Richard Holton Pierce on his 80th birthday

edited by

Pål Steiner, Alexandros Tsakos and Eivind Heldaas Seland

ARCHAEOPRESS ARCHAEOLOGY

ARCHAEOPRESS PUBLISHING LTD
Gordon House
276 Banbury Road
Oxford OX2 7ED

www.archaeopress.com

ISBN 978 1 78491 776 0
ISBN 978 1 78491 777 7 (e-Pdf)

Cover image: Aswan 1970. Photo by Richard Holton Pierce

Printed in England by Holywell Press, Oxford
This book is available direct from Archaeopress or from our website www.archaeopress.com

Contents

Preface iii

Nubians move from the margins to the center of their history 1
László Török

Potsherds on the grave. On burial traditions in the Renk area, South Sudan 19
Else Johansen Kleppe

Reconstructing a codex with the Coptic Encomia on Apa Victor 36
Alexandros Tsakos

Bridging Gaps: Archaeological sources and resources in museums 41
Saphinaz-Amal Naguib

'Egypt and the recalcitrant Pharaoh.' Origin and function of a biblical motif 48
Kåre Berge

A 'Sayings Gospel' attested at Nag Hammadi 57
Einar Thomassen

Chaotic mothers and creepy shadows. Metaphors of procreation and vision in *On the Origin of the World* (NHC II, 5) 64
Ingvild Sælid Gilhus

Liquid Images and the poetics of vision in ancient Greece 72
Jørgen Bakke

Umm Gumyāna and the *Zār* 88
Richard Johan Natvig

Trade and religion in the Central Sahara. The Ibāḍīs and Kawar 98
Knut Vikør

Fluidité et fixité dans les néotextes numériques 109
Daniel Apollon

Fieldwork in Dorginarti. From the archive of Pierce's family.

Preface

On October 24th 2015, Richard Holton Pierce celebrated his 80th anniversary. It was an occasion for friends and colleagues to come together for a conference reflecting his wide research interests, 'From River to Sea through Desert and Text', at the University of Bergen.

Richard H. Pierce has spent his life at the university. He obtained his PhD in Egyptology at Brown University in 1963, after which he worked as an epigrapher and field supervisor in Sudanese Nubia. Pierce was engaged at Brown as an instructor in Egyptology from 1964 to 1966, and then as a fellow in classical Greek at the University of Bergen, where he was also given a professorship in Egyptology in 1971. In a short but significant period at the University of Khartoum in 1976 as Visiting Professor of Archaeology (acting also as chairman of the department) he directed surveys in the Shilluk region of South Sudan.

Richard Holton Pierce is primarily an Egyptologist with profound knowledge of all the phases of the Egyptian language from hieroglyphics to Coptic, as well as Latin, Greek and Arabic. He works with traditional Egyptological fields, in particular demotic papyrology and inscriptions. Perhaps it is characteristic that among his contributions stands out a work that has become not only a standard reference, but also a vital handbook for students of a field that has profited much from Pierce's work, Nubiology: the seminal work *Fontes Historiae Nubiorum, Textual Sources for the History of the Middle Nile Region between the Eighth century BC and the Sixth century AD*, compiled in four volumes in collaboration with Tormod Eide, Tomas Hägg and László Török.

However, Egyptology is a marginal field in Norway. Thus, Pierce's long-standing engagement with Egypt and Nubia has been accompanied by interest in other areas often considered peripheral by students of the ancient world. Pierce has offered his competences to an array of students and scholars in a wide variety of fields, from classical philology to art history and digital humanities. His knowledge and interests extend beyond Egypt's geographical and historical borders. He has been involved in extensive fieldwork in Egypt and Nubia. He and his wife participated in the Aswan High Dam campaign. But he is also among the very few people in the world to have conducted archaeological research in South Sudan. Since the 1990s he has collaborated with the Department of Biology at the University of Bergen in studies of the longue durée of the cultural landscape of the Eastern Desert.

Most importantly, Pierce established and expanded collections of material relating to regions such as the Eastern Desert of Egypt and Sudan, the Aksumite and Early South Arabian civilizations, and the Red Sea and Indian Ocean in the pre-Islamic period. This has provided Bergen with an infrastructure for the study of these 'people without history' that has enabled several major research projects and a substantial body of scholarship from a corner of the world that arguably has few comparative advantages for the study of these regions.

Many have profited from Pierce's long-standing and passionate engagement with university life. In fact, he translated this experience into inspiration for research that he offered unreservedly to his students and colleagues. Also typical of Pierce has been his effort to make knowledge available in the most up-to-date form possible; hence his devotion to digital humanities, deriving undoubtedly from his way of visualizing research through endless diagrams that can be found in his personal archive.

Perhaps it is this amazingly rich repository of a life's devotion to finding out not only what we know but also (or even mainly) how we get to know it that is Pierce's most important contribution to future generations – a repository that the University of Bergen is determined to manage and promote, together with the very rich collection of publications that Pierce either ordered through the libraries or bought himself and donated to his academic home in Bergen.

Pierce has acted as co-supervisor, in many cases informally and institutionally unrecognized, for a large number of research students in archaeology, classics, Egyptology, religion, history, statistics and linguistics, several of whom have contributed to this book. Colleagues who ask for advice are never turned down. Beneficiaries will recall how manuscripts are returned with markups and comments, with different colours for sources or data, statements and arguments, references to scholarship and so on. These have proved to be important lessons in reading as well as writing academic texts to many of his students, as no unreferenced or unfounded statement would go through the process unnoticed. The sometimes less-than-perfect English of Norwegian and other non-native speakers is patiently corrected and improved, references provided to scholarship and source material that the author might have overlooked. Ideas for how arguments and perspectives could be developed are suggested. This takes place in a manner that leaves the author feeling good about his or her work even in light of the shortcomings that have been pointed out. In this way, Pierce has contributed and continues to contribute to the quality and internationalization of Norwegian research not only within his own field, but also within subjects that fall within his wide field of interest.

The Conference

On October 26th, friends and colleagues of Richard Holton Pierce gathered at the University of Bergen to celebrate the day with the conference 'From River to Sea through Desert and Text'. Reflecting the breadth of Pierce's research interests, the conference was sectioned under three main headings: 'Along the river', 'The desert and the sea' and 'Papyri, books and the Internet'. A number of the talks are presented in this book. Besides the papers found in this volume, presentations at the conference were given by colleagues in a range of fields in which Pierce has been engaged. Topics rcovered the archaeology of the Red Sea hills by Gábor Lassány, the climate of the Eastern Desert by Knut Krzywinski, tree cultivation in the Eastern Desert by Gidske Andersen, Bronze Age contacts across the Red Sea by Nils Anfinset, the incorporation of societies along the Nile in the Bronze Age by Henriette Hafsaas Tsakos, the modern economic history of Sudan by Anders Bjørkelo, explorers of the Syrian Desert by Jørgen C. Meyer, and qualitative and quantitative textual criticism by Odd Einar Haugen, and the senet game by Espen Aarseth.

Nubians move from the margins to the center of their history

László Török
Hungarian Academy of Sciences

THE STUDY OF THE KINGDOM OF KUSH BEFORE AND AFTER THE *FONTES HISTORIAE NUBIORUM*

> [R]eaders should be aware that the case is not closed.
> (Burstein 2003: 142)[1]

For a whole decade between 1991 and 2000, I was a participant in the *Fontes Historiae Nubiorum* project where I had the privilege of working together with Richard Holton Pierce, Tormod Eide and our late friend Tomas Hägg.[2] I remember the many hours we spent together working on the *Fontes Historiae Nubiorum* (*FHN* I-IV) as some of the most stimulating and blissful I have experienced as a student of Nubian history. 'Throughout the nineties we have published one large volume of texts, translations, [philological and historical] comments and bibliography every second year, ending up with page 1375.'[3] The four volumes present all textual sources of the history of the Middle Nile Region from the eighth century BC to the sixth century AD that were available up to 1998. Ever since the publication of Volume I, the *Fontes* have continued to give momentum to the study of ancient Kush and support the process in the course of which 'Nubians move from the margins to the center of their history and become its principal actors' (Burstein 2003: 142).

As a beginner in Nubian Studies in the 1960s, I could turn for a modern general history of the Middle Nile Region to Anthony Arkell's *A History of the Sudan* (1955), to some chapters in Sir Alan Gardiner's *Egypt of the Pharaohs* (1961) or to Walter Emery's *Egypt in Nubia* (1965). I read Arkell's fatalistic portrayal of post-New Kingdom Nubia with bewilderment:

> the [E]gyptianized kingdom [of Kush was] running gradually downhill to a miserable and inglorious end. There were interludes of prosperity when contact with the outside world was free and friendly, and new inspiration and energy (the effect of new ideas from outside) were infused into the kingdom. (Arkell 1955: 138)

The vision of an ancient African kingdom's total dependence on ideas borrowed from outside was first outlined one generation earlier by George Andrew Reisner (Manuelian 1999), the founding father of twentieth century Nubian Studies.[4] Reisner reconstructed the history of the Middle Nile Region in terms of archaeological cultures identified with different peoples. He described 'progressive' periods, which he connected to the influx or domination of the superior Hamitic race, that is, of Egypt. The progressive periods alternated with periods of political and cultural decline, which Reisner (1919) explained as a consequence of the immigration of Negroid peoples from the interior of Africa.[5] Reisner (1919; 1920a) declared that Kushite society was ethnically stratified, consisting of a native aristocracy, an Egyptian professional middle class and a native proletariat. He also postulated that the Twenty-Fifth Dynasty was of foreign, Libyan, origin (Reisner 1919: 247; cf. Dunham and Macadam 1949; Griffith 1922: 68f.).[6] After excavating the Kushite royal cemeteries of El Kurru (Dunham 1950), Nuri (Dunham 1955), Gebel Barkal

[1] R. H. Pierce on the interpretation of an often-discussed passage (lines 9-12) in Piankhy's Great Triumphal Stela, FHN I: 113.
[2] The way for the project was prepared by their 'Greek, Latin, and Coptic Sources for Nubian History' published between 1979 and 1984 in the Sudan Text Bulletin; see Eide *et al.* (1979; 1980; 1984).
[3] For the genesis of the project, see Hägg (2004: 14f.).
[4] For the study of ancient Nubia before Reisner, see Török (2011).
[5] Reisner (1923: 16) also argued that '[t]he tradition of Egypt became fixed as the traditions of [Kush]. This is the basis on which rests the whole history of the culture of [Kush]. The civilization was Egyptian, not native, and the subsequent history is one of loss, not of gain, of the gradual fading of the traditions of the arts and crafts and of the knowledge of the Egyptian language and the sacred texts'.
[6] Eduard Meyer (1928: 38ff.) believed that the Twenty-Fifth Dynasty directly descended from the family of the High Priests of Amun of Thebes. Cf. Budge (1928: 25f.); Drioton and Vandier (1936: 513).

(Chapman and Dunham 1952; Dunham 1957) and Meroe (Dunham 1957), the temples of Napata (Dunham 1970) and the elite cemeteries at Begarawiya West and South (Dunham 1963), he drew an 'episodic', i.e., ethnically, politically and culturally discontinuous, history of Kush. His general conclusion was that

> 'Wretched Nubia' was at first a part of Egypt. After the First Dynasty it was only an appendage of the greater country, and its history is hardly more than an account of its use or neglect by Egypt. (Reisner 1910: 348)

As for Sir Alan Gardiner, he explained the Kushite rulers' success in a patronizing manner by their 'fresh blood' and 'deep devotion to Pharaonic tradition' (1935: 219), and rejected Reisner's theory of their Libyan origins (1961: 340). Gardiner (1935: 219) remarked with obvious disdain that

> [f]or those whose life is devoted to the study of Egyptian texts it is somewhat humiliating to find that some of the most interesting hieroglyphic inscriptions are not really Egyptian at all, but emanate from the Nubian kings of alien descent[.]

When writing his *Egypt in Nubia*, Walter Emery was already confronted with the unexpected richness and complexity of the finds made in the first years of the UNESCO Nubian campaign. Nevertheless, his work did not go beyond Reisner's episodic history, and according to Adams (1977: 4) he too described

> a series of disconnected scenes performed by different actors. If there was any thread of continuity in his picture of Nubia, it was an Egyptian and not an indigenous one.

The archaeological discoveries made by the UNESCO Nubian Campaign between 1959 and 1969 (Adams 1992; Trigger 1994; Vercoutter 1995; Török 1995b; 1997a: 20ff.) prompted the self-definition of Nubian Studies as a new branch of knowledge that is not an appendage to any other discipline. Arriving from a wide variety of epistemological backgrounds, the post-Campaign generation of Nubian scholars set out interdisciplinary agendas. Radicals of the generation turned against the 'uncritical acceptance of Egyptological assumptions and their incorporation into new work' (Morkot 2003: 152). The result was frequently an uncritical rejection of essential methods and information deriving from the study of the very civilization that was, in some way or other, omnipresent in ancient Nubia. A more important, lasting result of the Nubian Campaign was the resolute shift from Reisner's 'episodic' history to William Adams' 'continuous narrative of the cultural development of a single people' (Adams 1977: 5). Adams' model of ethnic and cultural continuity was based almost entirely on archaeological sources, however. The evidential unbalance of Adams' magisterial *Nubia: Corridor to Africa* (1977) reminded his readers of the necessity of a coordinated treatment of material and textual sources.[7] As a result, from the 1980s several groundbreaking studies were published on various historical problems.[8] Returning to the Reisnerian image of the interface of Egyptian and Nubian culture, several authors dealt with the nature of the New Kingdom domination and with Nubia's 'Egyptianization'.[9] Torgny Säve-Söderbergh (1991), Lana Troy (Säve-Söderbergh and Troy 1991), Robert Morkot (1991; 1995), Stuart Tyson Smith (1995; 1997; 2003) and others argued that the administration (Reisner 1920b; Habachi 1979; Gasse and Rondot 2003; Mahfouz 2005; Müller 2013)[10] introduced in Nubia was not a colonial system (cf. Adams 1984: 36-71; for a different approach, see Kemp (1978)) excluding mutual benefit (cf. R.J. Horvath 1972; Frandsen 1979; Säve-Söderbergh and Troy 1991: 10 ff.; Smith 1995; 2003; Kemp 1997). To recall the basic facts, the conquered territory was placed under the authority of a viceroy with the title 'King's Son', beginning with Thutmose IV 'King's Son of Kush'. It was divided into two administrative units, viz., Wawat between the First and Second Cataracts and Kush between the Second and Fourth Cataracts. A 'Deputy of the

[7] Not without extremism: Török (1987).

[8] For an initial coordination of the archaeological and textual evidence in the study of Kushite cultures, see Hintze and Hintze (1966). See further the essays presented by Priese, Hintze and Trigger in Hochfield and Riefstahl (eds) 1978. For more explicit attempts at a neo-historical approach, see Desanges (1978), Török (1977; 1984; 1986; 1987; 1988a 1988b 1989; 2002), O'Connor (1993) and cf. Burstein (2000; 2003).

[9] For the New Kingdom conquest of Nubia, see Trigger (1976), Zibelius-Chen (1988), Smith (1995), Bryan (2000), Smith (2003) and Bonnet (2004a; 2004b).

[10] For further literature, see also Török 2009: 171 ff.

King's Son' administered them each.[11] Nubia was incorporated into the Egyptian redistributive system in such a way that the conquered native political structures were integrated into the political and economic administration together with their chiefs and elite (cf. Morkot 1991; 1995; 2000: 69 ff.; Török 2009: 157-283). The substructure of production and local redistribution was to a large extent based on the social structure of the indigenous pre-conquest polities. The authority of the territorial princes extended over special tasks such as the maintenance of order in the native communities, the collection and delivery of the tribute, and the maintenance of temples of 'Nubian' gods (Kemp 1978; Frandsen 1979; Säve-Söderbergh and Troy 1991; Morkot 1991; 2000: 81 ff.; Török 2009: 263 ff.).[12] They were regarded as vassals of the pharaoh. The annual delivery of the Nubian tribute was a feast of mutual legitimation (Smith 2003: 184 ff.). On the whole, the involvement of the native elite decreased rather than increased the costs of domination. The mediatory position of the princes between the Egyptian overlords and the native communities secured the possibility of the latter to preserve much of their traditions and resulted in different degrees of Egyptianization in the different social milieus (Török 2009: 263 ff.). The recurrent rebellions of Irem, an Upper Nubian chiefdom,[13] give an idea of the risks of the system and the dimensions of the native princes' playfield.

The decline of the late Ramesside state in the first half of the eleventh century BC brought about the withdrawal of Egypt (Leahy 1990; Jansen-Winkeln 1992: 22-37; 1995; J. van Dijk 2000). The Egyptian professional class and its literacy disappeared together with the viceregal administration (cf. Török 2009: 288 ff. and the literature cited there; and see Dodson (2012: 139 ff.) and Müller (2013)). The towns as elements of the Egyptian political and economic structure collapsed, but as settlements they were not necessarily depopulated (cf. Spencer 2012: 21-28; Spencer, Woodward and Macklin 2012; Spencer, Stevens and Binder 2014: 88 ff.). The majority of the Kushite urban centres would develop at sites of New Kingdom temple-towns. The next three centuries saw two opposed processes: first, the rapid disintegration of the viceregal realm into smaller native polities, and then their reintegration into one vast polity extending from the Fourth Cataract region to Lower Nubia.

Elite and 'middle-class' cemeteries started in the late New Kingdom and used up to the Twenty-Fifth Dynasty period and beyond demonstrate the continuity of indigenous traditions, which were amalgamated with Egyptian elements during the New Kingdom domination. I refer especially to Debeira East (Säve-Söderbergh *et al.* 1989) in Lower Nubia north of the Second Cataract and to Sanam (Lohwasser 2012), El Kurru (Dunham 1950) and Hillat el-Arab (Liverani 2004; Vincentelli 2006) in Upper Nubia. Robert Morkot also calls our attention to

> the importance of a continuous tradition of kingship/rulership in Kush that can be traced back to the A-Group phase (pre-3000 BCE)

arguing that

> such a continuous tradition (which was exploited by Egyptians during the New Kingdom) (...) resulted in the emergence of independent states and power holders soon after the Egyptian withdrawal (Morkot 2001: 246).

The spatial distribution of the cemeteries of the post-New Kingdom period (Williams 1990; 1992; cf. Török 2009: 285 ff.) indicates that the native polities emerging after the Egyptian withdrawal were mostly

[11] For the administration of New Kingdom Nubia, see Säve-Söderbergh (1941); Habachi (1979); Gasse and Rondot (2003); Török (2009: 169 ff); Müller (2013).

[12] Contrarily, Redford suggests that 'The coming of the empire meant the imposition of an administration from without in which Nubians had no special place, and local autonomy was the exception rather than the rule' (Redford 2004: 44).

[13] The Irem of New Kingdom texts seems to have been identical to the Yam appearing in Old Kingdom evidence; see Zibelius (1972: 78 ff., 84 f.) According to Priese (1974: 7-41), Kemp (1983 129 f.) and Goedicke (1988), Irem may be located in the Kerma region. The identification of the Kerma region as the site of Yam-Irem should be preferred to the location of Irem in the northern Butana (i.e., the northern part of the 'Island of Meroe') suggested by O'Connor (1987: 99-136) and Darnell (1986: 17-23), which was also accepted in Török (1997a: 94 f). For the princes of Irem, see also Zibelius-Chen (1988: 77 f.), Morkot (2000: 73, 89 f.) and Török (2009: 166 ff.).

identical to the subordinate territorial/political units of viceregal Nubia.[14] A wide range of imported objects discovered at the cemeteries mentioned a moment ago indicates increasing contacts between the successor polities and the establishment of trade and gift exchange with Egypt and with African regions (Török 1997a: 109 ff.; 2009: 298 ff.; and see Kendall 1999a).

Reintegration started from a post-New Kingdom polity in the Dongola-Napata Reach.[15] It was ruled by a line of princes who resided at El Kurru in the neighbourhood of Napata in a walled settlement (cf. Kendall 1999a: 47 ff.; Emberling and Dann 2013: 43 ff., Fig. 1). Reisner carried out some sondages at the settlement site, but these remained unpublished.[16] The El Kurru chiefdom owed its leading role to its direct access to gold-producing areas and to its geographical situation that secured control over the caravan route(s) connecting Egypt with the interior of Africa. Its princes were buried in a necropolis close to their residence first in tumulus, then in tumulus-on-mastaba (?) and finally in pyramid-on-mastaba tombs. From Piankhy onwards, the kings and queens of the Twenty-Fifth Dynasty would also be buried in pyramid tombs in the same necropolis (Dunham 1950). Notwithstanding recurrent doubts (Edwards 2004: 118 ff.), we may conclude from this that the Twenty-Fifth Dynasty kings considered themselves, and probably were in fact, descendants of the El Kurru princes.

I cannot enter here the debate about the dating of the El Kurru cemetery. As a logical working hypothesis I continue to rely on its 'long chronology'[17] according to which the first prince was buried in the first quarter of the tenth century BC, i.e., some 60 or 70 years after the Egyptian withdrawal.[18] In terms of the 'long chronology' there were 12 generations of princes buried at El Kurru between the first quarter of the tenth and the middle of the eighth century BC. Only the princes of the eleventh and twelfth generations, Alara (*Ỉrwrw*, Zibelius-Chen 2011: 63 ff.) and Kashta (*Kꜣštꜣ*, Zibelius-Chen 2011: 261 f.),[19] are known by name.

The 'Long Chronology' of the Ancestral Cemetery at El Kurru

tomb	*owner*	*estimated dates BC*
Ku. Tum. 1	prince	*c.* 995-975
Ku. Tum. 4	prince	*c.* 975-955
Ku. Tum. 5	prince	*c.* 955-935
Ku. Tum. 2	prince	*c.* 935-915
Ku. Tum. 6	prince	*c.* 915-895
Ku. 19	prince	*c.* 895-875
Ku. 14	prince	*c.* 875-855
Ku. 13	prince (?)	*c.* 855-835
Ku. 11	prince	*c.* 835-815
Ku. 10	?	*c.* 815-795
Ku. 9	Alara	*c.* 795-775
Ku. 8	Kashta	*c.* 775-755

[14] An alternative to this scenario was suggested by Robert Morkot (2001: 246) who argued that by the late Ramesside period the Upper Nubian region between the Third and Fourth Cataracts was already under the control of native princes: Egypt 'withdrew in the face of rising indigenous powers'. While it cannot be decided how nominal it was, viceregal control is attested at Napata in the reign of Rameses IX (1125-1107 BC), and it remained intact in Lower Nubia until the reign of Rameses XI. The withdrawal from Nubia occurred in parallel with the withdrawal from Palestine (cf. Redford 1992: 289 ff.).

[15] For the emergence of the Kingdom of Kush, see also Zibelius-Chen (1996: 195-217).

[16] For recent fieldwork at El Kurru, see Emberling and Dann (2013) and Emberling *et al.* (2015).

[17] 'Long' chronologies were suggested by Kendall (1982), Ali Hakem (1988: 240 ff.) and Török (1997a: 88 ff., 109 ff.; 1999; 2009: 298 ff.). For the 'short chronology' of the El Kurru cemetery and of the El Kurru chiefdom, see Kendall (1999a; 1999b). Morkot (2000: 142 ff.; 2003: 161 ff.) argues two alternative models. The first is that the cemetery comprised two groups of graves, the earlier dating from the period of the New Kingdom domination and representing the indigenous chiefdom in the region, and the later, after a hiatus, including the burials of the kings of Kush. The second model is based on a radical reduction of the dates for the New Kingdom (cf. James *et al.*, 1991: 204 ff.).

[18] The 'long chronology' of El Kurru received further support from the study by Budka (2014) of the ceramic finds connected to pot-breaking ceremonies from Ku. Tum. 6 and Ku. 19. With reference to recently found parallels from Abydos/Umm el-Qaab, Budka (2014: 651) concludes that '[t]he sherds from Abydos are safely dated to the Libyan Period, in particular to the late 10th and 9th centuries (*c.* 950-800 BC) (...) Thus, the parallels from Abydos could also support a date of the [El] Kurru pieces within Török's 'long' chronology of the cemetery' (cf. also Dodson 2012: 142 f.).

[19] The current interpretation of the name as 'The Kushite' is contested by Vinogradov (2003-2008).

The 12 burials present an archaeological narrative recounting the slow, inner-directed process of the El Kurru chiefdom's political and cultural transformation into a kingdom in the course of which the traditional native tomb types and mortuary rites were amalgamated with, rather than replaced by, elements of contemporary Egyptian mortuary religion.[20] From the early ninth century BC onwards the tombs were complemented with an offering niche or a small mortuary cult chapel and enclosed within a walled precinct. An advanced stage of the reintegration of the post-New Kingdom polities was reached around the middle of the ninth century BC when the round tomb superstructure was replaced by a rectangular pyramid-on-mastaba superstucture.[21] The new type was modelled on the Eighteenth Dynasty period tombs of the indigenous princes of Teh-khet in Lower Nubia.[22] The enclosed princely tomb with its mortuary cult chapel functioned as a place of ancestor cult and played an essential role in the process of establishing a religious image of political continuity (Török 1999).

In the 'mythical history' of Kush as it was formulated under the reign of Taharqo, Alara appears as a king and dynasty founder who concluded a covenant with Amun of Kawa.[23] In terms of the covenant the god raised up the descendants of Alara's sister as kings (*nsw.w*) in return for their commitment to him.[24] Thanks to recent excavations at Kawa and Napata[25] we now know that Alara's devotion to Amun of Kawa was part of the revival of the New Kingdom temple cults of the two great Nubian gods of Kush, viz., Amun of Kawa and Amun of Napata.

Similarly to Alara, his successor Kashta[26] (*c.* 775-755 BC) also plays the role of the founder of the kingdom and appears in Kushite historical memory as a perennial source of royal legitimacy. In the late fifth century BC, King Irike-Amannote would receive from Amun of Kawa 'long life like Alara' and 'every land South, North, West and East like Kashta'.[27] In the fourth century BC, King Nastasen visited Alara's birthplace on his coronation journey to Napata where the god confers 'the power of King Pi(ankh)y-Alara' on him.[28] Associating themselves with Alara and Kashta, Irike-Amannote and Nastasen connected their kingship to the very beginnings of the 'mythical history' of Kush.

At one point of his regency Kashta dedicated a stela at Elephantine to the gods of the First Cataract[29] on which he bears the Egyptian royal title *nsw-bity*, 'King-of-Two-lands' and the Throne name *Ny-M3ʿt-Rʿ*, 'He who belongs to Re's Order'.[30] The latter name was modelled on the Throne name of the Twelfth Dynasty pharaoh Amenemhat III (Beckerath 1984: 66 XII.6), who established Egypt's southern frontier at Semna after his predecessor Senusret III conquered Lower Nubia (*FHN* I: 43 ff.). The adoption of a name associated with the Middle Kingdom conquest of Nubia proclaimed nothing less than the political programme of a reversal of history.

In Karl Jansen-Winkeln's (2003: 157 f.) view, the El Kurru princes became involved in Upper Egyptian matters during the warlike conflicts that started in Year 11 of Takeloth II,[31] i.e., around 850 (Kitchen 1995) or 823 BC (Dodson 2012: 192), and lasted to the beginning of the reign of Osorkon III, i.e., around 787 (Kitchen) or 791 BC (Dodson). The latter date is very close indeed to the inception of Alara's reign in Nubia.[32] We also know that Kashta's daughter Amenirdis (I) was adopted as God's Wife of Amun Elect

[20] For the different readings of the narrative, see Kendall (1982: 21 ff.), Ali Hakem (1988: 240 ff.), Kendall (1999a) and Török (2009: 304 ff.).

[21] Ku. 13; for its description see Kendall (1999a: 25 ff.).

[22] For the Debeira cemetery, see Säve-Söderbergh and Troy (1991: 182 ff., Figs 44, 45); see also Török (2009: 263 ff.).

[23] For Alara's memory, see the different interpretations in Zibelius-Chen (1997: 86 ff.), Vinogradov (1999), Jansen-Winkeln (2003), Blöbaum (2006: 140 ff.) and Török (2009: 314 ff.).

[24] Stelae of Taharqo from Kawa, Khartoum 2678, *FHN* I No. 21 lines 16-20; Khartoum 2679, *FHN* I No. 24 lines 23-25.

[25] For the pre-Piankhy Kushite temple-building activities at Napata (temple B 800 nucleus, attributed to Alara, and temple B 800-first, attributed to Kashta), see Kendall (2002; 2014).

[26] *FHN* I No. 3.

[27] Graffito inscription on the east wall of the hypostyle, Kawa, Temple T. *FHN* II No. 71, columns 54 and 116, respectively.

[28] Berlin 2268, *FHN* II No. 84, lines 8, 15-16. For the name form *P-(ʿnḫ)-3l3rʿ*, see Zibelius-Chen (2011: 66 ff.).

[29] Cairo JE 41013, Leclant (1963); *FHN* I No. 4.

[30] For the orthography of *M3ʿt* in the name, see Bonhême (1987: 173) and Török (in: *FHN* I 43 f.).

[31] Chronicle of Prince Osorkon, inscribed on the Bubastite Portal at Karnak. See Caminos (1958), Jansen-Winkeln (2007: 161-68 [20.7], 186-96 [22.21]) and Ritner (2009: 348-377).

[32] The last attested holder of the title ‚King's Son of Kush' was Pamiu, the consort of a daughter of Takeloth III (Kitchen: 764-757 BC, Dodson: 768-753 BC) (Aston and Taylor 1990: 147 f.). According to Jansen-Winkeln (2003: 158 note 51), there was no actual competence behind the title.

by Shepenwepet I, the reigning God's Wife of Amun,[33] daughter of the Theban Twenty-Third Dynasty king Osorkon III. By this adoption Kashta was 'legitimated' in a most ingenious manner as ruler in Upper Egypt. His reception at Thebes can hardly be interpreted as anything other than an attempt made by the Theban Twenty-Third Dynasty[34] at the curbing of Egypt's political fragmentation. It remains unknown, however, whether Kashta's entry was initiated by Thebes and prepared by diplomatic negotiations or whether it was preceded by a demonstration of Kushite military power. Only so much is certain, i.e., that Kushite units would be stationed in Upper Egypt by the early reign of Kashta's direct successor, Piankhy.[35]

In the discussion following one of the papers presented in June 2015 at the Münster conference *Prayer and Power. The God's Wives of Amun in Egypt during the First Millennium BC*,[36] Professor Angelika Lohwasser referred to her ongoing study of a text, which may to some extent lift the blanket of fog over the beginnings of Kushite presence in Egypt. The text in question is the much-quoted Sandstone Stela found by Reisner at his excavation of the great Amun temple at Napata.[37] As is well known, the Son of Re name of the king who erected the stela was erased both in the lunette scene and in the main text, of which only a part of the first six lines is preserved. In the lunette scene the king is shown[38] before Amun of Napata, who presents him with the Red Crown of Lower Egypt and the cap crown of Kush. His Horus, *Nebty*, Golden Horus and Throne names can be read on the first line of the main text. The Horus name *K3-nḫt Ḫꜥ-m-Npt*, 'Strong Bull appearing[39] in Napata' (Blöbaum 2006: 366), is a paraphrase of *K3-nḫt Ḫꜥ-m-W3st*, 'Strong Bull appearing in Thebes', i.e., the Horus name of Nubia's New Kingdom conqueror, Thutmose III,[40] whose great triumphal stela from Year 47[41] could be studied at Napata.[42] The *Nebty* and the Golden Horus names: *W3ḥ-nsyt mi-Rꜥ-m-pt*, 'Whose kingdom endures like Re's in heaven' and *Dsr-ḫꜥ sḫm-pḥty*, 'Whose appearances are holy, whose might is powerful' (Blöbaum 2006: 367), respectively, are similarly paraphrases of names of Thutmose III as they had been inscribed on his great stela seven centuries earlier.

Considering first Thutmose III, and after some hesitation, Reisner (1931: 89 ff.) attributed the stela to Piankhy.[43] His hypothesis entered the literature, also including the *Fontes*, as a fact. In Angelika Lohwasser's view, however, the erased Son of Re name can by no means be reconstructed as Piankhy. Besides pondering an attribution to Thutmose III, which is inspired doubtless by the titulature, she also considers that the erased name can be reconstructed as Alara or Kashta. I cannot resist the urge to speculate about the effect of this possibility on our image of the emergence of the Double Kingdom of Egypt and Kush.[44]

I quote the dialogue of the god with the king in the lunette scene of the Sandstone Stela in Professor Pierce's translation (*FHN I*: 57):

> THE ORACLE OF AMUN-RE OF NAPATA
>
> 'I said of you (while you were still) in your mother's womb
> that you were to be ruler of Egypt (*ḥḳ3 n Kmt*)
> I knew you in the semen, while you were in the egg,
> that you were to be lord.

[33] For the issue, see the literature quoted in *FHN* I No. 4; Ayad (2009); cf. Yoyotte (1961).

[34] To be distinguished from Manetho's Twenty-Third Dynasty, cf. Aston and Taylor (1990); Leahy (1990: 186 ff.) and Dodson (2012: 113 ff.).

[35] Cairo 48862; 47086-47089, Great Triumphal Stela line 8, Grimal 1981; *FHN* I No. 9; Jansen-Winkeln (2009).

[36] Westfälische Wilhelms-Universität Münster, 25-27 June 2015.

[37] Khartoum 1851, *FHN* I No. 8; cf. Gozzoli (2009: 51 ff.). For a description and a recent photograph, see W. V. Davies in Welsby and Anderson (2004: 162 f. Cat. 146).

[38] The original raised relief figure of the king was erased and replaced at a later time by a smaller sunk relief figure.

[39] I.e. crowned.

[40] *FHN* I Nos 5, 8, line 1.

[41] MFA 23.733, URK IV 1227-1243, 8; Cumming (1982: 1 ff.); Klug (2002: 193 ff.); Gozzoli (2009: 59 ff.).

[42] The name may also contain an allusion to the regency of the Twenty-Third Dynasty, however: namely, Alara's and Kashta's contemporary, Osorkon III, bore the Horus name 'Strong Bull appearing in Thebes' (Beckerath 1984: 105 XXIII.4).

[43] The problem of the attributions suggested so far (Thutmose III, Alara, Kashta) will be discussed in a forthcoming publication by Angelika Lohwasser and Anne Sörgel.

[44] For the literature on the beginnings of Kushite rule in Upper Egypt, see Priese (1970), Jansen-Winkeln (2003: 156 ff.), Exell and Naunton (2007: 98 ff.) and Dodson (2012: 113 ff.).

I made you receive the Great (Double) Crown [of Egypt] (...)
it is I who decreed (the kingship) to you
(so) who shall share it with you? (...)
No other (can) decree (who is to be) a king (*nsw*).
It is I that grants kingship to whomever I will.'

SPEECH OF KING

Amun of Napata has granted me to be ruler of every foreign country.
He to whom I say, 'You are chief (*wr*)!', he is to be chief.
He to whom I say, 'You are not king!', he is not king.
Amun in Thebes has granted me to be ruler of Black-land [Egypt].
He to whom I say, 'Make (your formal) appearance (as king)!' he shall make (his) appearance.
He to whom I say, 'Do not make (your formal) appearance (as king)!', he does not make (his) appearance.
(As for) every one to whom I grant my favor, there is no way to seize his town
(even though) it is not in my hand.
Gods make a king, men make a king,
(but) it is Amun that has made me.

The dialogue presents a political structure, which, at first sight, may look like a discourse on New Kingdom domination in Nubia as viewed from the aspect of the conqueror. But this resemblance is illusory: the terminology speaks clearly against it. As aptly stated by Jeremy Pope (2014: 280), the masterfully formulated text portrays Kushite rule in Egypt as 'superordinate to the Libyan [period] system of provincial *wr.w* [chiefs, chieftains] and *nsw.w* [kings]'. Assuming that Lohwasser's study proves the attribution of the Sandstone Stela to Alara or Kashta, we may conclude that by the first quarter of the eighth century BC the ruler of Kush possessed excellent information about the actual political situation and the conditions of legitimate rule in Egypt. The formulation of the inscription does not leave much doubt, either, that it was first-hand information. He was not merely in contact with the Theban Twenty-Third Dynasty, he was actually present in Upper Egypt and felt prepared to do as the oracle of Amun of Napata[45] had ordered him, namely, to extend his rule over the whole of Egypt.

A dating to '[regnal] year 3' in the preserved part of the main text (Priese 1970: 25) introduced a now lost report starting with the words *iw.ntw r ḏd n ḥm=f*, '[One] came [to say to His Majesty]',[46] a standard formula introducing various types of narratives in the Egyptian 'king's novel', first of all accounts of wars (cf. Hermann 1938; Jansen-Winkeln 1993; Loprieno 1996; Hofmann 2004).[47] The lunette scene points in the latter direction: Amun presents the king with the skullcap-crown of Kush with *one* uraeus and the Red Crown of Lower Egypt. Since the skullcap-crown with *one* uraeus may appear in lieu of the Upper Egyptian White Crown,[48] in the lunette scene it may well have referred to the king's actual rule over Upper Egypt. The Red Crown, however, may hardly indicate more than the god's *promise* that he will make the king successful in Lower Egypt too. In the opinion of Robert Morkot,[49] the text on a granite stela fragment from Napata, now in Berlin,[50] is from the record of a Kushite king's journey to Egypt in his fourth regnal year. The king attends the Opet festival in Thebes, after which his army encounters the 'army of the Land

[45] For the role of the oracle of Amun in Kushite royal investiture, see Török (1997a: 216 ff., 241 ff., 268 ff.), and cf. Graefe (1971: 137 ff.) and Römer (1994: 142 ff.).
[46] *FHN* I No. 8 main text line 6.
[47] For the king's novel genre in Kushite texts, see Török (2002: 342 ff.).
[48] Russmann (1974: 29). I cannot follow Timothy Kendall in supposing the White Crown, simulated the shape of Gebel Barkal' (Kendall 2002: 49; cf. T. Kendall: Egypt and Nubia, in: Wilkinson (ed.), 2007: 401-416, 410 f.).
[49] Kind oral communication, Münster, June 27, 2015.
[50] Berlin 1068, *FHN* I No. 10.

of North', [*m*]*šꜥ n p*(*ꜣ*) *tꜣ mḥw*, that is, the army of some Lower Egyptian power. Morkot attributes the text to Kashta, and not to Piankhy, as was suggested by Priese (1970: 28 f.) and by the editors of the *Fontes*. But even if the inscription fragment records Kashta's actual presence in Lower Egypt, this presence was temporary at the most (Cf. Pope 2014: 258 ff.).

Kashta's successor, Piankhy, assumed the Throne name *Wsr-Mꜣꜥt-Rꜥ*, 'Re is One whose Order is strong'. Thus, he appropriated the Throne name of Takeloth III of the Theban Twenty-Third Dynasty (Payraudeau 2009). Takeloth III's Theban regency started in the early years of Kashta's reign and ended sometime in the early years of Piankhy. We know about Takeloth's successor, Rudamun, that he left Thebes in Piankhy's early reign (Dodson 2012: 113 ff.). He, as well as his successors, Peftjauawybast and Iuput II, resided now as *nsw.w*, kings, in Herakleopolis in Middle Egypt (Naunton 2010: 125) but, until the end of the Twenty-Fifth Dynasty, descendants of their dynasty continued to live in Thebes and were buried there (Aston and Taylor 1990; cf. Naunton 2010: 126).

The moving of the Twenty-Third Dynasty from Thebes to Herakleopolis indicates that the establishment of the Kushite control of Upper Egypt that started with the adoption of Amenirdis I as heiress to the God's Wife was now accomplished. Rudamun and his successors remained allies, or rather vassals, of Piankhy, similarly to numerous kings and chiefs in Middle and Lower Egypt. Sais in the western Delta emerged, however, as a rival, and its ruler Tefnakht expanded his power first over the western Delta and the area of Memphis and then made advances towards Middle Egypt (Kahn 2006; 2009). In his 19th regnal year, *c*. 736 BC, Piankhy received the news at Napata that Tefnakht had besieged Herakleopolis. Soon he also learnt that another ally of his, viz., Nimlot of Hermopolis, had defected to Tefnakht. The ensuing events were recorded on Piankhy's Great Triumphal Stela erected at Napata in Year 21, *c*. 734 BC.[51] First, Piankhy's troops stationed in Upper Egypt were sent north to recapture Hermopolis. Then the king dispatched an army from Kush with orders to let the enemy concentrate his forces. After celebrating at Napata the rites of the New Year, Piankhy led personally an army to Egypt. Reaching Thebes he celebrated there the Opet festival of Amun, after which he directed the campaign from one victory to another. As a result, the majority of the local rulers of Middle and Lower Egypt, except for the western Delta, became his vassals.

The Great Triumphal Stela presents a detailed discourse on the political geography and power relationships of the Double Kingdom of Kush and Egypt. The nuances of political hierarchy are explained with the help of devices that may appear indirect to us but that were direct enough for contemporaries. The first device is not textual. Namely, the lunette scene (Grimal 1981: Pls I, V) provides a pictorial summary of the outcome of the events. We see on the left Amun of Napata enthroned with Mut standing behind him and Piankhy before him, all facing right. In front of Piankhy, Nimlot, king of Hermopolis, leads up a horse. He is shown shaking a sistrum in order to pacify Piankhy and the divine couple. Nimlot is accompanied by his queen, who is shown with her right arm raised in a gesture of adoration. In the lower register are the figures of Osorkon IV, king of Bubastis, Iuput II, king of Leontopolis and Peftjauawybast, king of Herakleopolis, kissing the ground in front of Piankhy. Behind the group of the deities and Piankhy, in two registers, are the prostrate figures of the hereditary prince (*iry-pꜥt*) Peteese and the chiefs (*ḥꜣty-ꜥ*) of the Libyan Ma Patjenfy, Pemui, Akanosh and Djedamenefankh, kissing the ground. It is the lunette relief that first alerts the reader of the inscription that Piankhy's chief adversary was in fact Nimlot, not Tefnakht. The latter gives his oath of allegiance by message, not personally, and retains his independence. He is absent from the lunette scene.[52]

The other device is terminological. The hierarchical structure of the government, (re-)established as a result of the campaign, is indicated in a subtle manner by the phraseology of the text in which the title *n*(*j*)*swt*, 'king', is employed not only for Piankhy but also for Nimlot, Osorkon IV, Iuput II and

[51] Cairo 48862; 47086-47089, Grimal (1981); *FHN* I No. 9; Jansen-Winkeln (2009).

[52] In the stela text, Tefnakht comes forward as a protagonist from the evil's mythical sphere in *indirect reports* – even his surrender is told in the same indirect story-within-the-story manner – while Nimlot is directly present in it in the same manner as he is in the lunette relief. On Nimlot's significance see Kessler (1981: 232 ff.).

Peftjauawybast. By contrast, the terms *n(j)swt-bity*, 'king of Upper and Lower Egypt', *pr-ꜥꜣ*, 'Pharaoh' and *ḥm=f*, 'His Majesty', remain reserved for Piankhy (Grimal 1981: 248 ff.).

Both the Sandstone Stela and the Great Triumphal Stela depict a government and an administration that are radically different from the New Kingdom state. As pointed out by Karen Exell and Christopher Naunton (2007: 102), first of all 'it is not possible to speak of a 'court''. It also becomes clear that the Double Kingdom had no central capital. The move of the royal residence from Napata to Memphis under Shabaqo[53] does not replace the regional centres. It adds one to them. At the local level, the Double Kingdom was governed and administered by local rulers – here the model was the Kushite rule over Twenty-Third Dynasty Thebes. While the Sandstone Stela presents a theological formulation of the governance of the Double Kingdom, the Great Triumphal Stela provides two clear-cut, pragmatic snapshots of Egypt, the first taken just before Piankhy's campaign, the second just after its conclusion. The actual significance of the two inscriptions comes to light in its full complexity in Jeremy Pope's 2014 monograph on *The Double Kingdom under Taharqo* (Pope 2014), a seminal work pioneering a new historical approach to the Twenty-Fifth Dynasty.

In agreement with Christopher Naunton (Naunton 2000; 2004; 2010; cf. Exell and Naunton 2007), Pope (2014: 279, cf. 278) observes that

> [a]t Thebes, the Kushite house left in place much—if not all—of the civil administrative elite (...) and forged marriage alliances with the local aristocracy[.]

Pope also further argues in Exell and Naunton's (2007: 104) line of reasoning, according to which

> [the Kushite] pharaoh was (...) content to leave the mundane business of running the country to those individuals and systems already in place[.]

Expanding his research over the entire territory of the Double Kingdom, Pope (2014: 278) demonstrates that in Middle Egypt the Twenty-Fifth Dynasty

> not only countenanced officials of Saite affinity but may actually have utilized the intermarriages of such tribal lineages as a valuable means of regional integration across the Double Kingdom. Instead of replacing local aristocracies with centralized institutions, the Kushites appear to have used links between the former as a substitute for the latter.

In conclusion, Pope (2014: 278) states that

> [s]imilar strategies were employed in variable combinations in Lower Egypt, Middle Egypt, [and] Upper Nubia[.]

In the core region of the Double Kingdom, that is, in the Dongola-Napata Reach,

> [a]uthority appears (...) to have been dispersed across a number of kin groups; there is (...) little pyramidal hierarchy of governmental positions; (...) offices which might otherwise be equated with the king's unique deputy are found divided among several individuals (...) coronation in Upper Nubia was not a singular event binding across the realm, but a series of interdependent events each conferring localized authority[54] (...) the [coronation journey] initially passed through Memphis, Napata, and Kawa, before its contraction [after the fall of the Double Kingdom] to the Dongola-Napata Reach. (Pope 2014: 276 f.)

[53] His earliest Egyptian monument is from Year 2: Memphis, Serapeum (Vercoutter 1960: 65 ff.; cf. Jurman 2009: 122 f.). Here I cannot enter the ongoing discussion over Michael Bányai's (2013) suggestion that the sequence Shabaqo-Shebitqo should be reversed. For a recent contribution to the discussion, see Broekman (2015).

[54] On the issue Pope refers throughout his book to Török (1992; 1997a).

The coronation journey was interpreted by me as a theological commemoration and confirmation of the federal origins of the Kingdom of Kush. I suggested that the Kushite myth of the origins of the state reflected an actual form of governance that I classified with the 'ambulatory kingships' of the ancient world (Cf. Török 1992; 1995a: 65 ff.; 1997a: 230 ff.). By contrast, Pope (2014: 276) points out that another model, namely the 'segmentary state', which was first introduced by David Edwards (1996; 1998; 1999; 2004) into the Nubiological discussion,[55] bears

> in its emphasis upon national administrative absence, 'reflexive communication', and especially the political functions of the king's ritual circuit, (...) a striking similarity to the 'ambulatory kingship' [for segmentary states] (...) 'are (...) essentially federal in nature'. (Pope 2014: 291, quotation from Fallers (1973: 82))

Considering the political history of the Butana region south of the core of the Double Kingdom, Pope demonstrated the improbability of the theory according to which the city of Meroe was the ancestral seat of the Twenty-Fifth Dynasty. He also argued against the theory that the Butana region would have been annexed right at the Dynasty's inception. Contesting the evidence of a now lost bronze statuette identified by me as Taharqo (Török 1997b: 29, 32, 260, Pls 210-211; Pope 2014: 23 ff.) and revising the find material from Meroe City, which I dated to the Twenty-Fifth Dynasty period, Pope (2014: 276) suggests that

> the earliest evidence of royal construction in the region, the earliest textual evidence to Meroe, and the earliest evidence of royal filiation among those interred at the site all appear during the late 7th century BC[.]

Indeed, the first Kushite king whose name appears in inscriptions from Meroe City (Török 1997b: 26, Figs 120, 123, Pls 117, 118; Pope 2014: 21 ff.), viz., on ritual and votive objects associated with the renewal of royal power on New Year's Day (Török 1997b: 25 ff.), is Senkamanisken, second successor of the last ruler of the Double Kingdom. But trial excavations have uncovered at the city of Meroe building remains carbon-dated to as early as 900-750 BC (Grzymski 2005: 57; 2010; cf. Bradley 1984). Though the early settlement remained unexcavated, its later history suggests that it was the centre of a polity, which owed its importance and wealth to the control of a caravan route leading to the interior of Africa. Its annexation to the Kingdom of Kush by the immediate successors of the Twenty-Fifth Dynasty was inspired by

> the experience of Kushite expansion into Egypt [which] influenced the strategy and structure of Kushite governance in Upper Nubia (Pope 2014: 194, cf. 279)

and it was systematically prepared by contacts between the kingdom and the Meroe region in the Twenty-Fifth Dynasty period, including intermarriages. As a conclusion to my sketchy overview, let me briefly mention one or two examples.

The iconography of Abalo, the mother of Taharqo, suggests that she descended not from the El Kurru dynasty but from a princely/elite family of the Meroe region. Evidence of this is presented by a significant piece of the royal costume, the tasselled cord, which derives from the lasso of a southern hunter/warrior god (Török 1990: 151 ff.; cf. Török 2002: 150 ff.). This special insignia appears on the royal costume first[56] in representations of Taharqo and Abalo in the reliefs of Kawa Temple T.[57] Southern family connections of the dynasty are indicated moreover by the representation of Taharqo's lesser queens who are depicted wearing a special 'African' plumed headdress.[58] Its variants would reappear in representations of the queens of Atlanersa and Aspelta in the later seventh century BC.[59]

[55] For the 'segmentary state', see Southall (1956; 1999).
[56] Provided that there were no earlier, now lost, representations of this insignia.
[57] Macadam (1955: Pls XVb (king), XXI/a (king and queen)), cf. Török (2002: 112 f.).
[58] Macadam (1955: Pl. LXIV/e, f). For the headdress, see Lohwasser (2001: 42 f., 53, 222 ff.).
[59] For representations of Aspelta's queens on the walls of the Aspelta Shrines in the Amun temples of Kawa and Sanam, see Lohwasser (2001: 222 ff.).

The annexation of the Butana Steppe could not occur, however, before the annexation of the medial region between the Fourth Cataract and the confluence of the Nile and the Atbara. The annexation of the region can be dated to the reign of Taharqo, as indicated by an Amun temple excavated recently at Dangeil south of the Fifth Cataract, where fragments of colossal granite royal cult statues of Taharqo, Senkamanisken and Aspelta were recovered (Anderson and Ahmed 2008; 2009; 2014). They are comparable to the statuary from the cachettes discovered in the great Amun temple at Napata (Dunham 1970) and in the Amun temple at Dokki Gel (Kerma) (Bonnet and Valbelle 2004). This attests to the political/governmental/administrative significance of the ancient site at modern Dangeil.

Abbreviations

Berlin.	Staatliche Museen zu Berlin–Preußischer Kulturbesitz, Ägyptisches Museum und Papyrussammlung, Berlin.
FHN	I. Eide et al 1994.
FHN	II. Eide et al 1996.
FHN	III. Eide et al 1998.
FHN IV.	Eide et al 2000.
URK IV.	Sethe 1933.

References

Adams, W. Y. (1977). *Nubia: Corridor to Africa.* London: Princeton University Press.

Adams, W. Y. (1984). The First Colonial Empire: Egypt in Nubia 3200–1200 B.C. *Comparative Studies in Society and History. An International Quarterly* 26: 36-71.

Adams, W. Y. (1992). The Nubian archaeological campaigns of 1959–1969: Myths and realities, success and failures. In: C. Bonnet (ed.) *Études Nubiennes. Conférence de Genève. Actes du VIIe Congrès International d'Études Nubiennes 3-8 septembre 1990. I. Communications Principales*: 23-27. Genève.

Anderson, J. R. and Ahmed, S. M. (2008). The Kushite Kiosk of Dangeil and Other Recent Discoveries. *Sudan & Nubia* 12: 40-47.

Anderson, J. R. and Ahmed, S. M. (2009). What Are These Doing Here Above the Fifth Cataract?!! Napatan Royal Statues at Dangeil. *Sudan & Nubia* 13: 78-86.

Anderson, J. R. and Ahmed, S. M. (2014). Early Kushite royal statues at Dangeil, Sudan. In: J. R. Anderson and D. A. Welsby (eds) *The Fourth Cataract and Beyond. Proceedings of the 12th International Conference for Nubian Studies* (British Museum Publications on Egypt and Sudan 1): 613-619. Leuven: Peeters.

Arkell, A. J. (1955). *A History of the Sudan. From the Earliest Times to 1821.* 2nd ed. 1961. London: Athlone Press.

Aston, D. A. and Taylor, J. H. (1990). The family of Takeloth III and the 'Theban' Twenty-third Dynasty. In: A. Leahy, *Libya and Egypt c. 1300-750 BC*. London: School of Oriental and African Studies: 131-154.

Ayad, M. F. (2009). God's Wife, God's Servant. The God's Wife of Amun (*c.* 740-525 BC). London: Routledge.

Bányai, M. (2013). Ein Vorschlag zur Chronologie der 25. Dynastie in Ägypten. *Journal of Egyptian History* 6: 46-129.

Beckerath, J. von (1984). *Handbuch der ägyptischen Königsnamen. MÄS 20.* München: Deutscher Kunstverlag.

Blöbaum, A. I. (2006). *'Denn ich bin ein König, der die Maat liebt'. Herrscherlegitimation im spätzeitlichen Ägypten. Eine vergleichende Untersuchung der Phraseologie in den offiziellen Königsinschriften vom Beginn der 25. Dynastie bis zum Ende der makedonischen Herrschaft* (Aegyptiaca Monasteriensia 4). Aachen: Shaker.

Bonhême, M.-A. (1987). *Les Noms Royaux dans l'Égypte de la Troisième Période Intermediaire.* Cairo: Institut Français d'Archéologie Orientale du Caire.

Bonnet, C. (2004a). *Le Temple Principal de la Ville De Kerma et son Quartier Religieux. Avec la Collaboration de D. Valbelle, Contribution de B. Privati.* Paris: Errance.

Bonnet, C. (2004b). Un Ensemble Religieux Nubien Devant une Forteresse Égyptienne du Début de la XVIIIe Dynastie. Mission Archéologique Suisse à Doukki Gel – Kerma (Soudan). *Revue d'Histoire de l'Art et d'Archéologie* 57: 95-108.

Bonnet, C and Valbelle, D. (2004). Kerma, Dokki Gel. In: D. A. Welsby and J. R. Anderson (eds) *Ancient Treasures. An Exhibition of Recent Discoveries from the Sudan National Museum*: 109-112. London: The British Museum Press.
Bradley, R. J. (1984). Meroitic Chronology. *Meroitica* 7: 195-211.
Broekman, G. P. F. (2015). The Order of Succession between Shabaka and Shabataka: A Different View on the Chronology of the Twenty-fifth Dynasty. *Göttinger Miszellen* 245: 17-31.
Bryan, B. R. (2000). The eighteenth dynasty before the Amarna Period (*c.* 1550–1352 BC). In: I. Shaw, ed, *The Oxford History of Egypt*: 218-271. Oxford: Oxford University Press.
Budge, E. A. W. (1928). *A History of Ethiopia Nubia & Abyssinia.* London: Methuen & Company.
Budka, J. (2014). Egyptian impact on pot-breaking ceremonies at El-Kurru? A re-examination. In: J. R. Anderson and D. A. Welsby (eds) *The Fourth Cataract and Beyond. Proceedings of the 12th International Conference for Nubian Studies* (British Museum Publications on Egypt and Sudan 1): 641-654. Leuven: Peeters.
Burstein, S. M. (2000). A New Kushite Historiography: Three Recent Contributions to Nubian Studies. *Symbolae Osloenses. Norwegian Journal of Greek and Latin* 75: 190-197.
Burstein, S. M. (2003). Three Milestones in the Historiography of Ancient Nubia. Review Article. *Symbolae Osloenses. Norwegian Journal of Greek and Latin* 78: 137-142.
Caminos, R. A. (1958). *The Chronicle of Prince Osorkon.* Rome: Pontificium Institum Biblicum.
Chapman, S. E. and Dunham, D. (1952). *Decorated Chapels of the Meroitic Pyramids at Meroë and Barkal.* (The Royal Cemeteries of Kush vol. 3). Boston: The Museum of Fine Arts.
Cumming, B. (1982). *Egyptian Historical Records of the Later Eighteenth Dynasty I.* Warminster: Aris & Phillips.
Darnell, J. C. (1986). Irem and the Ghost of Kerma. *Göttinger Miszellen. Beiträge zur ägyptologischen Diskussion* 94: 17-23.
Desanges, J. (1978). *Recherches sur l'Activité des Mediterranéens aux Confins de l'Afrique.* Rome: Ecole Française.
Dijk, J. van (2000). The Amarna Period and the Later New Kingdom. In: I. Shaw, *The Oxford History of Egypt*: 272-313. Oxford: Oxford University Press.
Dodson, A. 2012. *Afterglow of Empire: Egypt from the Fall of the New Kingdom to the Saite Renaissance.* Cairo: American University in Cairo Press.
Drioton, E. and Vandier, J. (1936). *Les Peuples de l'Orient Méditerranéen II. L'Égypte.* Paris: Les Presses Universitaires de France.
Dunham, D. (1950). *El Kurru.* (The Royal Cemeteries of Kush vol. 1). Cambridge: Harvard University Press.
Dunham, D. (1955). *Nuri.* (The Royal Cemeteries of Kush vol. 2). Boston: The Museum of Fine Arts.
Dunham, D. (1957). *Royal Tombs at Meroë and Barkal.* (The Royal Cemeteries of Kush vol. 4). Boston: The Museum of Fine Arts.
Dunham, D. (ed.), (1963). *The West and South Cemeteries at Meroë. Excavated by the Late George Andrew Reisner.* (The Royal Cemeteries of Kush vol. 5). Boston: The Museum of Fine Arts.
Dunham, D. (1970). *The Barkal Temples. Excavated by George Andrew Reisner.* Boston: The Museum of Fine Arts.
Dunham, D. and Macadam M. F. L. (1949). Names and Relationships of the Royal Family of Napata. *The Journal of Egyptian Archaeology* 35: 139-149.
Edwards, D. N. (1996). *The Archaeology of the Meroitic State. New Perspectives on Its Social and Political Organisation* (Cambridge Monographs in African Archaeology 38). Oxford: Archaeopress.
Edwards, D. N. (1998). Meroe and the Sudanic Kingdoms. *Journal of African History* 39: 175-193.
Edwards, D. N. (1999). Meroe in the Savannah – Meroe as a Sudanic Kingdom? In: S. Wenig (ed.) *Studien zum antiken Sudan. Akten der 7. Internationalen Tagung für meroitistische Forschungen vom 14. bis 19. September 1992 in Gosen/bei Berlin* (Meroitica 15): 312-320. Wiesbaden: Harrassowitz.
Edwards, D. N. (2004). *The Nubian Past. An Archaeology of the Sudan.* London-New York: Routledge.
Eide, T., Hägg, T. and Pierce R. H. (1979). Greek, Latin, and Coptic Sources for Nubian History (I). *Sudan Text Bulletin* 1: 3-12.
Eide, T., Hägg, T. and Pierce R. H. (1980). Greek, Latin, and Coptic Sources for Nubian History (II). *Sudan Text Bulletin* 2: 2-15.
Eide, T., Hägg, T. and Pierce R. H. (1984). Greek, Latin, and Coptic Sources for Nubian History (III). *Sudan Text Bulletin* 6: 1-25.

Eide, T., Hägg T., Pierce, R. H. and Török, L. (1994). *Fontes Historiae Nubiorum. Textual Sources for the History of the Middle Nile Region Between the Eighth Century BC and the Sixth Century AD* I. *From the Eighth to the Mid-Fifth Century BC.* Bergen: University of Bergen, Department of Classics.

Eide, T., Hägg T., Pierce, R. H. and Török, L. (1996). *Fontes Historiae Nubiorum. Textual Sources for the History of the Middle Nile Region Between the Eighth Century BC and the Sixth Century AD* II. *From the Mid-Fifth to the First Century BC.* Bergen: University of Bergen, Department of Classics.

Eide, T., Hägg T., Pierce, R. H. and Török, L. (1998). *Fontes Historiae Nubiorum. Textual Sources for the History of the Middle Nile Region Between the Eighth Century BC and the Sixth Century AD* III. *From the First to the Sixth Century AD.* Bergen: University of Bergen, Department of Classics.

Eide, T., Hägg T., Pierce, R. H. and Török, L. (2000). *Fontes Historiae Nubiorum. Textual Sources for the History of the Middle Nile Region Between the Eighth Century BC and the Sixth Century AD* IV. *Corrigenda and Indices.* Bergen: University of Bergen, Department of Classics.

Emberling, G. and Dann, R. J. (2013). New Excavations at El-Kurru: Beyond the Napatan Royal Cemetery. *Sudan & Nubia* 17: 42-60.

Emberling, G., Dann, R. J., Mohamed-Ali, A. S., Therkildsen, R., Duffy, S. M., Yellin, J. W., Antis S. and Karberg T. (2015). In a Royal Cemetery of Kush: Archaeological Investigations at El-Kurru, Northern Sudan 2014–5. *Sudan & Nubia* 19: 54-70.

Emery, W. B. (1965). *Egypt in Nubia.* London: Hutchinson.

Exell, K. and Naunton, C. (2007). Administration. In: T. Wilkinson (ed.) *The Egyptian World*: 91-104. London: Routledge.

Fallers, L. (1973). Political sociology and the anthropological study of African polities. In: R. Bendix and C. M. Brand (eds) *State and Society: A Reader in Comparative Political Sociology*: 73-86. Berkeley: University of California Press.

Frandsen, J. P. (1979). Egyptian imperialism. In: M. T. Larsen (ed.) *Power and Propaganda: A Symposium on Ancient Empires*: 167-190. Copenhagen: Akademisk Forlag.

Gardiner A. H. (1935). Piankhi's Instruction to His Army. *Journal of Egyptian Archaeology* 21: 219-223.

Gardiner, A. H. (1961). *Egypt of the Pharaohs: An Introduction.* Oxford: Oxford University Press.

Gasse, A. and Rondot V. (2003). The Egyptian Conquest and Administration of Nubia during the New Kingdom: The Testimony of the Sehel Rock-Inscriptions. *Sudan & Nubia* 7: 40-46.

Goedicke, H. (1988). Yam – More. *Göttinger Miszellen* 101: 35-42.

Gozzoli, R. B. (2009). *The Writing of History in Ancient Egypt during the First Millennium BC (ca. 1070-180 BC). Trends and Perspectives.* (Golden House Publications Egyptology 5). London: Golden House.

Graefe, E. (1971). Untersuchungen zur Wortfamilie *bj3*. PhD dissertation, University of Cologne.

Griffith, F. L. (1922). Oxford Excavations in Nubia–continued. *University of Liverpool Annals of Archaeology and Anthropology* IX: 67-124.

Grimal, N.-C. (1981). *La Stèle Triomphale de Pi('ankh)y au Musée du Caire JE 48862 et 47086–47089.* Cairo: Institut Français d'Archéologie Orientale.

Grzymski, K. A. (2005). Meroe, Capital of Kush: Old Problems and New Discoveries. *Sudan & Nubia* 9: 47-58.

Grzymski, K. A. (2010). La fondation de Méroé-Ville: Nouvelles données. In: M. Baud, A. Sackho-Autissier and S. Labbé-Toutée (eds) *Méroé. Un Empire sur le Nil*: 65-66. Milan: Officina Libraria.

Habachi, L. (1979). Königssohn von Kusch. *Lexikon der Ägyptologie* III: 630-640.

Hakem, A. M. (1988). *Meroitic Architecture. A Background of An African Civilization.* Khartoum University Press.

Hägg, T. (2004). Forty years in and out of the Novel. In: L. B. Mortensen and T. Eie (eds) *Tomas Hägg: Parthenope. Selected Studies in Ancient Greek Fiction (1969–2004)*: 9-28. Copenhagen: Museum Tusculanum Press.

Hermann, A. (1938). *Die ägyptische Königsnovelle.* (Leipziger Ägyptologische Studien 10). Glückstadt: Augustin.

Hintze, F. (1978). The Kingdom of Kush: The Meroitic Period. In: S. Hochfield and E. Riefstahl (eds) *Africa in Antiquity. The Arts of Ancient Nubia and the Sudan* I. *The Essays*: 89-105. Brooklyn: Brooklyn Museum.

Hintze, F. and Hintze U. (1966). *Alte Kulturen im Sudan.* München: Callwey 1966 (English edition 1968, *Civilizations of the Old Sudan.* Amsterdam: Grüner.)

Hofmann, B. (2004). *Die Königsnovelle. Strukturanalyse am Einzelwerk.* (Ägypten und Altes Testaments 62). Wiesbaden: Harrassowitz.

Horvath, R. J. (1972). A Definition of Colonialism. *Current Anthropology* 13(1): 1-7.
James, P. J., Thorpe, I. J. Kokkinos, N., Morkot, N, and Frankish, J. (1991). *Centuries of Darkness. A Challenge to the Conventional Chronology of Old World Archaeology*. London: J. Cape.
Jansen-Winkeln, K. (1992). Das Ende des Neuen Reiches. *Zeitschrift für Ägyptische Sprache und Altertumskunde*, 119: 22-37.
Jansen-Winkeln, K. (1993). Die ägyptische 'Königsnovelle' als Texttyp. *Wiener Zeitschrift für die Kunde des Morgenlandes* 83: 101-116.
Jansen-Winkeln, K. (1995). Die Plünderung der Königsgräber des Neuen Reiches. *Zeitschrift für Ägyptische Sprache und Altertumskunde* 122: 62-78.
Jansen-Winkeln, K. (2003). Alara and Taharka: zur Geschichte des nubischen Königshauses. *Orientalia*, 72: 141-158.
Jansen-Winkeln, K. (2007). *Inschriften der Spätzeit. Teil* II. *Die 22.-24. Dynastie*. Wiesbaden: Harrassowitz.
Jansen-Winkeln, K. (2009). *Inschriften der Spätzeit. Teil* III. *Die 25. Dynastie*. Wiesbaden: Harrassowitz.
Jurman, C. (2009). From the Libyan dynasties to the Kushites in Memphis. Historical problems and cultural issues. In G. P. F. Broekman, R. J. Demarée and O. E. Kaper (eds) *The Libyan Period in Egypt. Historical and Cultural Studies into the 21st-24th Dynasties. Proceedings of a Conference at Leiden University, 25–27 October 2007*: 113-138. Leuven: Nederlands Instituut voor het Nabije Oosten.
Kahn, D. (2006). Tefnakht's 'Letter of Submission' to Piankhy. *Beiträge zur Sudanforschung* 9: 45-61.
Kahn, D. (2009). The transition from Libyan to Nubian Rule in Egypt: Revisiting the reign of Tefnakht. In: G. P. F. Broekman, R. J. Demarée and O. E. Kaper (eds) *The Libyan Period in Egypt. Historical and Cultural Studies into the 21st-24th Dynasties. Proceedings of a Conference at Leiden University, 25–27 October 2007*: 139-148. Leuven: Nederlands Instituut voor het Nabije Oosten.
Kemp, B. J. (1978). Imperialism and empire in New Kingdom Egypt (*c.* 1575–1087 B.C.). In: P. D. A. Garnsey and C. R. Whittaker (eds) *Imperialism in the Ancient World*: 7-57. Cambridge: Cambridge University Press.
Kemp, B. J. (1983). Old Kingdom, Middle Kingdom and Second Intermediate Period *c.* 2686–1552 BC. In: B. G. Trigger, B. J. Kemp, D. O'Connor and A. B. Lloyd, *Ancient Egypt. A Social History*: 71-182. Cambridge: Cambridge University Press.
Kemp, B. J. (1997). Why Empires Rise. Review Feature, Askut in Nubia. *Cambridge Archaeological Journal* 7: 125-131.
Kendall, T. (1982). *Kush, Lost Kingdom of the Nile: A Loan Exhibition from the Museum of Fine Arts, Boston, Sept. 1981 - Aug. 1984*. Brockton Art Museum.
Kendall, T. (1999a). The Origin of the Napatan State: El Kurru and the evidence for the Royal Ancestors. In: S. Wenig (ed.) *Studien zum antiken Sudan. Akten der 7. Internationalen Tagung für meroitistische Forschungen vom 14. bis 19. September 1992 in Gosen/bei Berlin* (Meroitica 15): 3-117. Wiesbaden: Harrassowitz.
Kendall, T. (1999b). A response to László Török's 'Long Chronology' of El Kurru. In: S. Wenig (ed.) *Studien zum antiken Sudan. Akten der 7. Internationalen Tagung für meroitistische Forschungen vom 14. bis 19. September 1992 in Gosen/bei Berlin* (Meroitica 15): 164-176. Wiesbaden: Harrassowitz.
Kendall, T. (2002). Napatan Temples: A Case Study from Gebel Barkal. Unpublished paper circulated at the Tenth International Conference of Nubian Studies, Rome, September 9-14, 2002.
Kendall, T. (2007). Egypt and Nubia. In T. Wilkinson, (ed.). *The Egyptian World*: 401-416. London: Routledge.
Kendall, T. (2014). Reused relief blocks of Piankhy from B 900: Toward a decipherment of the Osiris Cult at Jebel Barkal. In: J. R. Anderson and D. A. Welsby (eds) *The Fourth Cataract and Beyond. Proceedings of the 12th International Conference for Nubian Studies (British Museum Publications on Egypt and Sudan* 1): 663-686. Leuven: Peeters.
Kessler, D. (1981) Zu den Feldzügen des Tefnachte, Namlot und Pije in Mittelägypten. *Studien zur Altägyptischen Kultur* 9: 227-251.
Kitchen, K. A. (1995). *The Third Intermediate Period in Egypt (1100-650 BC)*. Warminster: Aris & Phillips.
Klug, A. (2002). *Königliche Stelen in der Zeit von Ahmose bis Amenophis III* (Monumenta Aegyptiaca VIII). Turnhout: Brepols.
Leahy, A. (1990). Abydos in the Libyan Period. In: A. Leahy (ed.)1990. *Libya and Egypt c. 1300-750 BC*: 155-200. London: School of Oriental and African Studies.
Leclant, J. (1963). Kashta, Pharaon, en Égypte. *Zeitschrift für ägyptische Sprache und Altertumskunde* 90: 74-81.

Liverani, I. (2004). Hillat el-Arab. In: D. A. Welsby and J. R. Anderson (eds) *Ancient Treasures. An Exhibition of Recent Discoveries from the Sudan National Museum*: 138-147. London: The British Museum Press.

Lohwasser, A. (2001). *Die königlichen Frauen im antiken Reich von Kusch. 25. Dynastie bis zur Zeit des Nastasen* (Meroitica 19). Wiesbaden: Harrassowitz.

Lohwasser, A. (2012). *Aspekte der napatanischen Gesellschaft. Archäologisches Inventar und funeräre Praxis im Friedhof von Sanam - Perspektiven einer kulturhistorischen Interpretation* (Contributions to the Archaeology of Egypt, Nubia and the Levant I). Wien: Der Österreichischen Akademie der Wissenschaften.

Loprieno, A. (1996). The 'King's Novel'. In: A. Loprieno (ed.) *Ancient Egyptian Literature. History and Forms*: 277-295. Leiden: Brill.

Macadam, M. F. L. (1955). *Temples of Kawa II. History and Archaeology of the Site*. Oxford: Griffith Institute.

Mahfouz, El-S. (2005). Les Directeurs des Déserts Aurifères d'Amon. *Revue d'Égyptologie* 56: 55-78.

Manuelian, P. der (1999). George Andrew Reisner. In: K. A. Bard (ed.) *Encyclopedia of the Archaeology of Ancient Egypt*: 661-662. London: Routledge.

Meyer, E. (1928). *Gottesstaat Militärherrschaft und Ständewesen in Ägypten.* (Sitzungsberichte der Preussischen Akademie der Wissenschaften, phil-hist. Klasse 28). Berlin: Verlag der Akademie der Wissenschaften.

Morkot, R. G. (1991). Nubia in the New Kingdom: the Limits of Egyptian Control. In: W. V. Davies, *Egypt and Africa: Nubia from Prehistory to Islam*: 294-301. London: British Museum Press.

Morkot, R. G. (1995). The Economy of Nubia in the New Kingdom. *Actes de la VIIIe Conférence Internationale des Études Nubiennes I. Communications Principales. Cahier de Recherches de l'Institut de Papyrologie et d'Égyptologie de Lille* 17: 175-189.

Morkot, R. G. (2000). *The Black Pharaohs. Egypt's Nubian Rulers.* London: Stacey Publ.

Morkot, R. G. (2001). Egypt and Nubia. In: S. E. Alcock, T. N. D'Altroy, K. D. Morrison and C. M. Sinopoli (eds) *Empires. Perspectives from Archaeology and History*: 227-251. Cambridge: Cambridge University Press.

Morkot, R. G. (2003). On the priestly origin of the Napatan kings: The adaptation, demise and resurrection of ideas in writing Nubian history. In: D. O'Connor and A. Reid (eds) *Ancient Egypt in Africa*: 151-168. London: Routledge.

Müller, I. (2013). *Die Verwaltung Nubiens im Neuen Reich* (Meroitica 18). Wiesbaden: Harrassowitz.

Naunton, C. (2000). The Priests and Officials at Thebes During the Twenty-fifth Dynasty in Egypt. Unpublished PhD dissertation, University of Birmingham.

Naunton, C. (2004). Tebe durante la XXV dinastia. In: S. Einaudi F. Tiradritti (eds) *L'Enigma di Harwa: Alla Scoperta di un Capolavoro del Rinascimento Egizio*: 77-102. Milano: Anthelios.

Naunton, C. (2010). Libyans and Nubians. In: A. B. Lloyd (ed.) *A Companion to Ancient Egypt*: 120-139. New York: Wiley-Blackwell.

O'Connor, D. (1987). The Location of Irem. *Journal of Egyptian Archaeology* 73: 99-136.

O'Connor, D. (1993). *Ancient Nubia: Egypt's Rival in Africa.* Philadelphia: University of Pennsylvania.

Payraudeau, F. (2009). Takeloth III: Considerations on old and new documents. In: G. P. F. Broekman, R. J. Demarée, and O. E. Kaper (eds) *The Libyan Period in Egypt. Historical and Cultural Studies into the 21st-24th Dynasties. Proceedings of a Conference at Leiden University, 25-7 October 2007*: 291-302. Leuven: Nederlands Instituut voor het Nabije Oosten.

Pope, J. (2014). *The Double Kingdom under Taharqo. Studies in the History of Kush and Egypt, c. 690-664 BC* (Culture and History of the Ancient Near East 69). Leiden: Brill.

Priese, K-H. (1970). Der Beginn der kuschitischen Herrschaft in Ägypten. *Zeitschrift für ägyptische Sprache und Altertumskunde* 98: 16-32.

Priese, K-H. (1974). *rm* und *ꜥ3m*, das Land Irame. Ein Beitrag zur Topographie des Sudan im Altertum. *Altorientalische Forschungen* 1: 7-41.

Priese, K-H. (1978). The Kingdom of Kush. The Napatan Period. In: S. Hochfield and E. Riefstahl (eds) *Africa in Antiquity. The Arts of Ancient Nubia and the Sudan* I: 74-88. *The Essays*. Brooklyn: Brooklyn Museum.

Redford, D. B. (1992). *Egypt, Canaan, and Israel in Ancient Times.* Princeton: Princeton University Press.

Redford, D. B. (2004). *From Slave to Pharaoh. The Black Experience of Ancient Egypt.* Baltimore: Johns Hopkins University Press.

Reisner, G. A. (1910). *Archaeological Survey of Nubia, Report for 1907-1908, vol. 1.* Cairo: National Printing Department.

Reisner, G. A. (1919). Outline of the Ancient History of the Sudan IV. The First Kingdom of Ethiopia. *Sudan Notes and Records* 2: 35-67; 237-254.
Reisner, G. A. (1920a). Recent Discoveries in Ethiopia. *Harvard Theological Review* 13: 23-44.
Reisner, G. A. (1920b). The Viceroys of Ethiopia. *Journal of Egyptian Archaeology* 6: 28-55, 73-88.
Reisner, G. A. (1923). The Pyramids of Meroe and the Candaces of Ethiopia. *Bulletin of the Museum of Fine Art* 21 (124): 12-27.
Reisner, G. A. (1931). Inscribed Monuments from Gebel Barkal. *Zeitschrift für ägyptische Sprache und Altertumskunde* 66: 76-100.
Ritner, R. K. (2009). *The Libyan Anarchy: Inscriptions from Egypt's Third Intermediate Period.* Atlanta: Society of Biblical Literature.
Römer, M. (1994). *Gottes- und Priesterherrschaft in Ägypten am Ende des Neuen Reiches. Ein religionsgeschichtliches Phänomen und seine sozialen Grundlagen.* Wiesbaden: Harrassowitz.
Russmann, E. R. (1974). *The Representation of the King in the XXVth Dynasty.* Bruxelles: Fondation Egyptologique Reine Elisabeth.
Säve-Söderbergh, T. (1941). Ägypten und Nubien. Ein Beitrag zur Geschichte altägyptischer Aussenpolitik. PhD dissertation, University of Lund.
Säve-Söderbergh, T. *et al.* (1989). *Middle Nubian Sites. The Scandinavian Joint Expedition to Sudanese Nubia* 4. Partille: Paul Åström.
Säve-Söderbergh, T. (1991). Teh-khet. The cultural and sociopolitical structure of a Nubian Princedom in Thutmoside times. In W. V. Davies (ed.) *Egypt and Africa: Nubia from Prehistory to Islam*: 186-194. London: British Museum Press.
Säve-Söderbergh, T. and L. Troy (1991). *New Kingdom Pharaonic Sites. The Finds and the Sites* (The Scandinavian Joint Expedition to Sudanese Nubia Publications 5:2, 5:3). Partille: Esselte Studium.
Sethe, K. (1933). *Urkunden der 18. Dynastie IV.* 2nd edn. Leipzig: J. C. Hinrichs.
Shaw, I. (ed.) (2000). *The Oxford History of Egypt.* Oxford: Oxford University Press.
Smith, S. T. (1995). *Askut in Nubia. The Economics and Ideology of Egyptian Imperialism in the Second Millennium BC.* London: Kegan Paul International.
Smith, S. T. (1997). Ancient Egyptian Imperialism: Ideological Vision or Economic Expliotation? *Cambridge Archaeological Journal* 7: 301-307.
Smith, S. T. (2003). *Wretched Kush. Ethnic Identities and Boundaries in Egypt's Nubian Empire.* London-New York: Routledge.
Southall, A. (1956). *Alur Society: A Study in Processes and Types of Domination.* Cambridge: W. Heffer & Sons.
Southall, A. (1999). Segmentary state and the ritual phase in political economy. In: S. K. McIntosh (ed.) *Beyond Chiefdoms: Pathways to Complexity in Africa:* 31-38. Cambridge: Cambridge University Press.
Spencer, N. (2012). Insights into Life in Occupied Kush during the New Kingdom: New Research at Amara West. *Der antike Sudan. Mitteilungen der Sudanarchäologischen Gesellschaft zu Berlin e.V.* 23: 21-28.
Spencer, N., Stevens, A. and Binder, M. (2014). *Amara West. Living in Egyptian Nubia.* London: The Trustees of the British Museum.
Spencer, N., Woodward, J. and Macklin, M. (2012). Reassessing the Abandonment of Amara West: The Impact of a Changing Nile? *Sudan & Nubia* 16: 37-43.
Török, L. (1977). Inquiries into the Administration of Meroitic Nubia I-II. *Orientalia*, 46: 34-50.
Török, L. (1984). Economy in the Empire of Kush: A Review of the Written Evidence. *Zeitschrift für ägyptische Sprache und Altertumskunde* 111: 45-69.
Török, L. (1986). *Der meroitische Staat* I. *Untersuchungen und Urkunden zur Geschichte des Sudan im Altertum* (Meroitica 9). Berlin: Akademie-Verlag.
Török, L. (1987). The historical background. Meroe north and south. In: T. Hägg (ed.) *Nubian Culture Past and Present. Kungl. Vitterhets Historie och Antikvitets Akademiens Konferenser* 17: 139-229. Stockholm: Almquist & Wiksell.
Török, L. (1988a). Geschichte Meroes. Ein Beitrag über die Quellenlage und den Forschungsstand. In: W. Haase (ed.) *Aufstieg und Niedergang der Römischen Welt* II: 107-341. 10.1. Berlin: De Gruyter.
Török, L. (1988b). *Late Antique Nubia. History and Archaeology of the Southern Neighbour of Egypt in the 4th-6th c. A.D.* With a Preface by Sir Laurence Kirwan. Budapest: Archaeological Institute of the Hungarian Acad. of Science.

Török, L. (1989). Kush and the External World. *Meroitica* 10: 49-215; 365-379.
Török, L. (1990). The Costume of the Ruler in Meroe. Remarks on Its Origins and Significance. *Archéologie du Nil Moyen* 4: 151-202.
Török, L. (1992). Ambulatory kingship and settlement history. A study on the contribution of archaeology to Meroitic history. In: C. Bonnet (ed.) *Études Nubiennes. Conférence de Genève. Actes du VIIe Congrès International d'Études Nubiennes 3-8 septembre 1990. I. Communications Principals*: 111-126. Genève.
Török, L. (1995a). *The Birth of An Ancient African Kingdom. Kush and Her Myth of the State in the First Millennium BC* (Cahier de Recherches de l'Institut de Papyrologie et d'Égyptologie de Lille, Suppl. 4). Lille.
Török, L. (1995b). Kush: An African State in the First Millennium BC. *Proceedings of the British Academy* 87: 1-38.
Török, L. (1997a). *The Kingdom of Kush. Handbook of the Napatan-Meroitic Civilization* (Handbuch der Orientalistik Erste Abteilung. Der Nahe und Mittlere Osten 31). Leiden: Brill.
Török, L. (1997b). *Meroe City: An Ancient African Capital. John Garstang's Excavations in the Sudan.* With contributions by I. Hofmann and I. Nagy I-II (Egypt Exploration Society Occasional Publications 12). London: Egypt Exploration Society.
Török, L. (1999). The origin of the Napatan State: the long chronology of the El Kurru cemetery. In: S. Wenig, *Studien zum antiken Sudan. Akten der 7. Internationalen Tagung für meroitistische Forschungen vom 14. bis 19. September 1992 in Gosen/bei Berlin* (Meroitica 15): 149-159. Wiesbaden: Harrassowitz.
Török, L. (2002). *The Image of the Ordered World in Ancient Nubian Art. The Construction of the Kushite Mind (800 BC -300 AD)* (Probleme der Ägyptologie 18). Leiden: Brill.
Török, L. (2009). *Between Two Worlds. The Frontier Region between Ancient Nubia and Egypt 3700 BC - AD 500* (Probleme der Ägyptologie 29). Leiden: Brill.
Török, L. (2011). A periphery on the periphery of the Ancient World. The discovery of Nubia in the nineteenth century. In: G. Klaniczay, M. Werner and O. Gecser (eds) *Multiple Antiquities - Multiple Modernities. Ancient Histories in Nineteenth-Century European Cultures*: 365-380. Frankfurt: Campus Verlag.
Trigger, B. G. (1976). *Nubia under the Pharaohs.* London: Westview Press.
Trigger, B. G. (1978). Nubian, Negro, Black, Nilotic? In: S. Hochfield and E. Riefstahl (eds) *Africa in Antiquity. The Arts of Ancient Nubia and the Sudan* I. *The Essays*: 27-35. Brooklyn: Brooklyn Museum.
Trigger, B. G. (1994). Paradigms in Sudan Archaeology. *The International Journal of African Historical Studies* 27: 323-345.
Vercoutter, J. (1960). The Napatan Kings and Apis Worship (Serapeum Burials of the Napatan Period). *Kush. Journal of the Sudan Antiquities Service* 8: 62-76.
Vercoutter, J. (1995). The UNESCO 'Campaign of Nubia' in the Sudan. Success or Failure? *Discussions in Egyptology* 33: 133-140.
Vincentelli, I. (2006). *Hillat El-Arab. The Joint Sudanese-Italian Expedition in the Napatan Region, Sudan* (Sudan Archaeological Research Society Publication Number 15). Oxford: Archaeopress.
Vinogradov, A. K. (1999). '[...] Their Brother, the Chieftain, the son of Rea, Alara [...]?. *Cahier de Recherches de l'Institut de Papyrologie et d'Égyptologie de Lille* 20: 81-94.
Vinogradov, A. K. (2003–2008). Did the Name of Kashta Mean 'the Kushite'? Some Material for the Book of the Kings of Kush. *Kush. Journal of the Sudan Antiquities Service* 19: 219-239.
Welsby, D. A. and Anderson, J. R. (eds) (2004). *Ancient Treasures. An Exhibition of Recent Discoveries from the Sudan National Museum.* London: British Museum Press.
Williams, B. B. (1990). *Twenty-fifth Dynasty and Napatan Remains at Qustul: Cemeteries W and V. The University of Chicago Oriental Institute Nubian Expedition* VII. Chicago: Oriental Institute of the University of Chicago.
Williams, B. B. (1992). *New Kingdom Remains from Cemeteries R, V, S, and W at Qustul and Cemetery K at Adindan.* With a contribution by W.J. Murnane. *The University of Chicago Oriental Institute Nubian Expedition* VI. Chicago: Oriental Institute of the University of Chicago.
Yoyotte, J. (1661). Les Vierges Consacrées d'Amon Thébain. *Comptes Rendus des Séances de l'Académie des Inscriptions et Belles-Lettres* 105 (1): 43-52.
Zibelius, K. (1972). *Afrikanische Orts- und Völkernamen in hierogliphischen und hieratischen Texten.* Wiesbaden: Harrassowitz.
Zibelius-Chen, K. (1988). *Die ägyptische Expansion nach Nubien. Eine Darlegung der Grundfaktoren.* Wiesbaden: Ludwig Reichert.

Zibelius-Chen, K. (1996). Das nachkoloniale Nubien: Politische Fragen der Entstehung des kuschitischen Reiches. In: R. Gundlach, M. Kropp and A. Leibundgut (eds) *Der Sudan in Vergangenheit und Gegenwart (Sudan Past and Present)*: 195-217. Frankfurt am Main: P. Lang.

Zibelius-Chen, K. (1997). Theorie und Realität im Königtum der 25. Dynastie. In: R. Gundlach and C. Raedler (eds) *Selbstverständnis und Realität: Akten des Symposiums zur ägyptischen Königsideologie in Mainz 15.-17. 6. 1995* (Ägypten und Altes Testament 36.1): 81-95. Wiesbaden: Harrassowitz.

Zibelius-Chen, K. (2011). *'Nubisches' Sprachmaterial in hieroglyphischen und hieratischen Texten. Personennamen, Appellativa, Phrasen vom Neuen Reich bis in die napatanische und meroitische Zeit* (Meroitica 25). Wiesbaden: Harrassowitz.

Potsherds on the grave.
On burial traditions in the Renk area, South Sudan

Else Johansen Kleppe
University of Bergen

Introduction

The fieldwork was carried out in the Upper Nile province in the northernmost part of The Republic of South Sudan and this presentation concerns the excavations at Debbat El Eheima and Debbat Bangdit, located on either side of the White Nile near Renk (Figure 1). When I started my work, very little was known about the culture history of this geographic area; the boundary set was around 1700 (Hinkel 1979). My aim was to gain insight into the antiquity of archaeological sites in the area and to get an idea of the socio-culture manifested through material culture remains from the so-called *debbas*. I knew of such sites through archaeological literature and through pottery finds in the National Museum (now the National Corporation for Antiquities and Museums) in Khartoum. Very little was known about the archaeology of this geographical area when I started my work there. The observations of O. G. S. Crawford are of particular importance. His writings inspired me to look into such settlement traces located near the banks of the White Nile in the Renk area (Crawford 1948: 11; 1951: 159-160). The publications from Jebel Moya (Addison 1949a, b) also nourished my curiosity about possible relations with the White Nile sites located in the Upper Nile area. The term *debba* refers to a low mound in flat country (Crawford 1951: 2) and many of these locations are archaeological sites. The low mounds are parts of natural ridges running parallel with the rivers and the highest part is often formed through additional accumulation of material culture remains as a result of ancient habitation. Such places have been preferred for settlement since they were fairly safe from flooding even during years of heavy rains.

The latest calibrations of the 14 C14 dates obtained from the two sites at Debbat El Eheima (UN 24) and Debbat Bangdit (UN 25) show wider ranges (Figure 2) than those from an earlier calibration published (Kleppe 2005: 48-49). These details are of little relevance in the present context as only two dates from Debbat Bangdit relate to documentation of graves. These are included in the discourse related to the documentation presented below. The question about shared cultural features from the two archaeological sites indicating cultural continuity despite the time gap is brought up below.

Household waste, building material and other traces from huts, in- and outdoor fireplaces and graves are typical findings at the sites where excavations have taken place. My focus here is on possible interpretations of a special feature related to graves, i.e., the concentrations of potsherds covering graves. My argument is that they do not just represent practical, functional acts, but also rituals associated with burials and in many cases probably also later mourning ceremonies. The latter could take place even on more than one occasion, and support for such interpretations are sought in the contextual archaeological data from my excavations, in archaeological literature, and in ethnographic and ethnoarchaeological documentation. Nine graves were identified, two at Debbat El Eheima and seven at Debbat Bangdit, but only one grave was totally excavated since only trenches were excavated. It ought to be mentioned that the fieldwork at Debbat Bangdit in 1983 was interrupted by the outbreak of the civil war, and this meant that the original plan set up for my project could not be accomplished. Several papers have been published over the years, and some supplement the present study (Kleppe 1982a; 1982b; 1986a; 1986b; 1989). Ethnoarchaeology and ethnographic observations were included in my fieldwork whenever possible and relevant.

The recent history of the sites visited was recorded, and it ought to be mentioned that Debbat El Eheima was uninhabited when Shilluk from Kaka and Geigar settled there, probably sometime between 1953 and

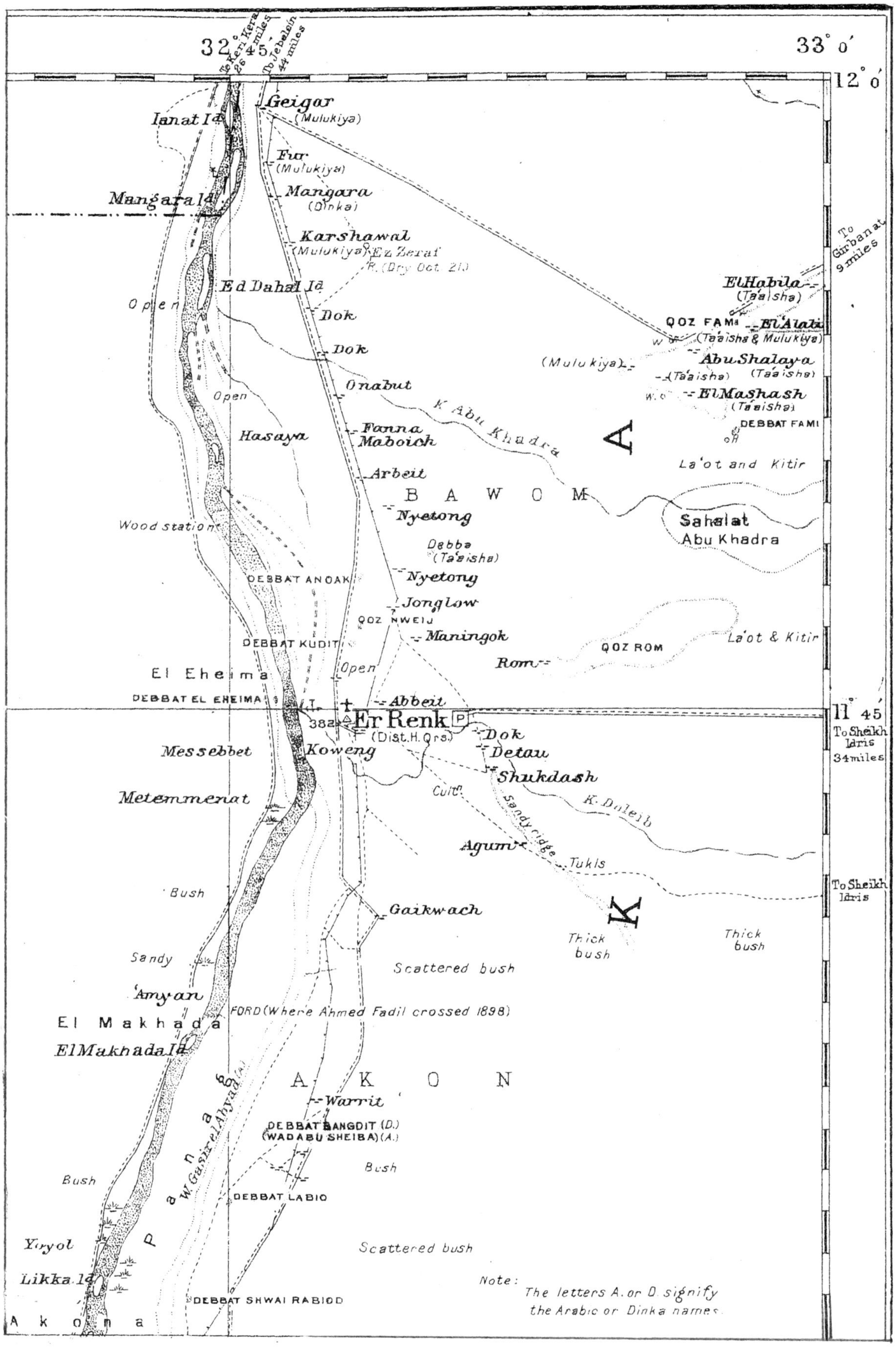

Figure 1. Location of the archaeological sites Debbat El Eheima and Debbat Bangdit.
The archaeological sites of Debbat El Eheima and Debbat Bangdit are located in the northernmost part of South Sudan, which became independent from Sudan in 2011. From map sheet, Er Renk Sheet by the Sudan Survey Department 1936.

Lab. no.	Site and location	Dated material	Size (g) of dated sample	Year BP	$\delta^{13}C$ ‰	Cal. AD/BC	Comments
T-5032	UN 24; sq 9 st 16	Shells	20	3140±80	1.7	1611–1215 BC	
T-5342	UN 24; sq 11 st 9	Shells (1)	21.7	2720±80	0.2	1107–775 BC	
T-4811	UN 24; sq 11 st 17	Shells	34	3300±60	0.8	1738–1447 BC	
T-5344	UN 24; sq 11 st 18	Shells (1)	21.5	3510±50	1.6	1961–1692 BC	
T-5341	UN 24; sq 12 st 5	Shells (1)	21	2470±40	0.4	768–430 BC	
T-4562	UN 24; sq 12 st 7	Charcoal*	4.6	2760±70	-25.4	1107–802 BC	*Small pieces
T-5343	UN 24; sq 12 st 12	Shells (1)	22.2	3120±40	0.8	1496–1278 BC	
T-5063	UN 25; sq 1 st 11	Shells	10.4	1200±80	0.5	AD 670–983	
T-5065	UN 25; sq 1 st 16	Charcoal	1.4	1600±140	-26.1	AD 93–671	
T-5340	UN 25; sq 1 st 16	Shells	3.8	1200±150	1.3	AD 568–1155	
T-5064	UN 25; sq 1 st 17	Shells	17.1	1250±70	0.5	AD 652–951	
T-5066	UN 25; sq 2 st 5	Charcoal	3.8	340±110	-26.1	AD 1399–1878	91.9% probability
T-5067	UN 25; sq 4 st 14	Charcoal	1.1	1100±80	-26.1	AD 695–1149	
T-5068	UN 25; sq 5 st 17	Charcoal	0.7	1340±130	-26.1	AD 428–970	

The shells are from freshwater. The radiocarbon dates are provided with one standard deviation and calibrated by OxCal v4.2 (Bronk Ramsey 2013) based on IntCal13 atmospheric curve (Reimer *et al.* 2013).

Figure 2. C14 dates from Debbat El Eheima (UN 24) and Debbat Bangdit (UN 25), South Sudan.

1957, I was told by people living there. These people cleared the land of the high ground. Eheima is the name of a small insect living in the grass. The Shilluk who settled there called the place Bodho, a name that refers to an expert in spear making named Ayik Bodho. This name is not in use as the village name any longer. Bangdit is the Dinka name of the site, while the Arabic name of this village is Wad Abu Sheiba (cf. Figure 1), but this name was no longer remembered by the villagers when I did fieldwork there. The present settlement was established in 1952, when Abyalang Dinka came to the place.

The excavation of grave remains from the two sites was never questioned during the fieldworks. I do, however, find it relevant to include a brief discourse, including a note, before I present the archaeological documentation.

On excavating human remains

It was never questioned that our archaeological excavations could interfere with former burials. As only trenches were excavated it was less obvious that remains of graves were identified in the archaeological material. Ethic and emic aspects of excavating human remains were very clear to me, but I did not problematize the issue then.[1] Besides, this was not really a part of the archaeological discourse until the so-called Vermillion Accord on Human Remains was adopted by the World Archaeological Congress at its first inter-congress in 1989 (McKeown 2013: 53). The issue had, however, already been put on the agenda at the 1st World Archaeological Congress held in Southampton in 1986 (cf. Hubert 1989). The grave remains revealed at Debbat El Eheima and Debbat Bangdit have not been brought into this discourse.

[1] The handling of human remains from archaeological sites was considered to be unproblematic when the aim was to gain new culture historical insight through studies of human remains. Emic and ethical considerations were hardly ever brought into the discourse when my archaeological excavations took place in the Upper Nile between 1977 and 1983. Only one complete grave of an infant was excavated in connection with my Upper Nile fieldwork. When this grave was found I sent my team away for their break and carried out the excavation and documentation on my own. Nobody questioned this in 1983. The altered concerns meant changes in attitudes towards the local community, not least in ethnohistorical settings like the ones I have worked in. Within the latest generation major changes have taken place, as is expressed in national legislation relating to archaeological excavations, curation issues and issues concerning reburial of human remains. Such issues have in many countries become politically more significant, not least due to the involvement of local people, and their concern for their own traditions and history. The fact that more professional archaeologists have local roots does in many cases function as an extra control of how we interfere with material remains documenting ethnic history. It is part of the duty of the professional archaeologist to explain to the public why there is value in studying such remains and also to let them see that reburial can take place if wanted. With the revision that took place in the Sudan it was made a part of the agreement in the excavation licence that modern cemeteries were not to be excavated (Márquez-Grant and Fibiger 2011: 518). My plea is that archaeological research combined with ethnohistory is put on this agenda.

Grave material from Debbat El Eheima and Debbat Bangdit

The grave remains had a uniform appearance and they were all covered with a layer of potsherds of varying size and thickness. A downcutting through the cultural deposits is an ordinary act when digging a grave, but this was only identified in one case, at Debbat Bangdit (Figure 3). The stratigraphy was complicated, and as a safety measure the archaeological recording was done within 1x1 m^2 units (squares) and in 10 cm layers (strata).

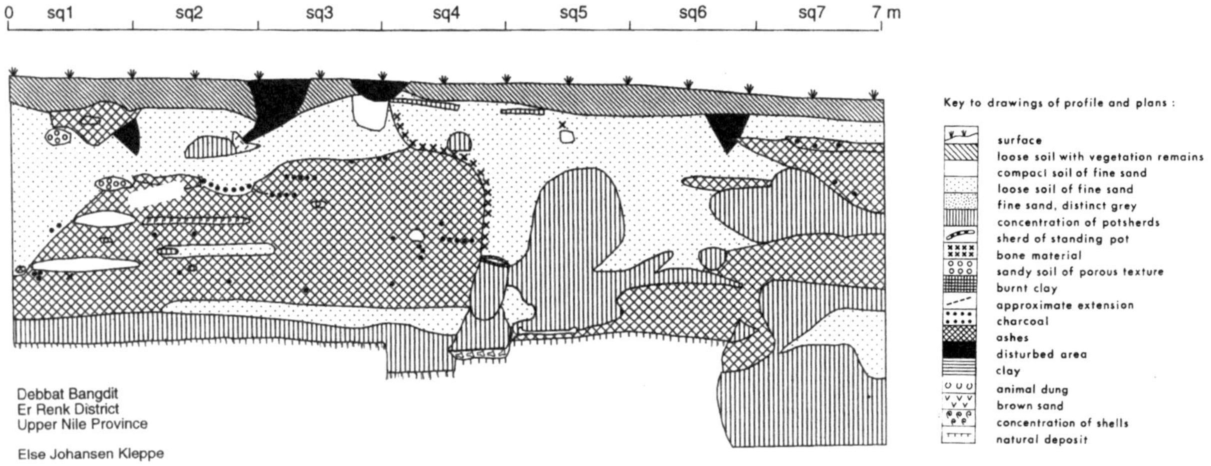

Figure 3. Debbat Bangdit. Section drawn along the S-side of the NE-SW oriented excavation trench.

Most of the archaeological material found was potsherds, but potsherd fragments were also recorded. A potsherd fragment is defined according to one of three criteria (Hulthén 1974: 29): 1) Potsherd of 1 cm^2 or smaller; 2) Potsherd of 2 cm^2 or smaller and with one intact, original surface; 3) Potsherd without traces of an intact, original surface. Many potsherd fragments were recorded at Debbat Bangdit, but very few such fragments were present at Debbat El Eheima. This indicates sociocultural differences, perhaps related to ritual acts, a discourse I return to.

Graves were primarily identified through the presence of human remains variably located immediately below a potsherd cover. The human remains, all from inhumations, were examined by the physical anthropologist Berit J. Sellevold (Sellevold, n.d.). In addition, two dentists, one an expert in forensics, examined teeth remains from three of the graves from Debbat Bangdit (Bjorvatn, Bang and Kleppe 1988). In the following examples, typical grave remains from the two sites are presented.

Debbat El Eheima (UN 24). Parts of two graves were identified and both extended beyond the excavation trench. Their locations were in:

squares 1-2 strata 3-9
squares 5-7 strata 4-10

Grave 1: squares 1-2 strata 3-9. The biggest concentration of potsherds from this site was associated with this grave: nearly 4,900 potsherds were recorded in squares 1-2 strata 3-9. The potsherd concentration covered a distinct area extending E-W in square 1 stratum 7. The shape of the potsherd cover was somewhat irregular, and it was sloping inward towards its deepest extension. It is of special interest to note that of the 739 potsherds registered from square 1 strata 3-4, most sherds found there were from two or three water jars, chamotte-tempered porous and rather thick ware (Figure 4). Human skeletal remains were primarily found in square 1 stratum 8, but also in adjacent strata. Some potsherds located in square 1 stratum 9 might mark the SW extension of the grave. Some bones and shells were found underneath a big rimsherd. A ceramic pot tilting at an angle of *c.* 45º was documented in square 1 from the middle of stratum 8 downwards (Figure 5); it was left *in situ* as it extended further than the excavation, which went down to 110 cm below the surface.

In total, 11 red ceramic beads were associated with this grave, two in square 1 strata 7 and 8, three in square 2 strata 3-4, three in square 2 stratum 6 and three in square 2 stratum 7. Some iron objects were also found[2]: one arrow, one part of a ring (two pieces fitted together), two pieces of an unknown function and two pieces of iron slag. In total, 65 lithic objects were documented within the area of the grave remains. I interpret these as random in relation to the other findings in the grave. The head of the deceased had been placed in the eastern part of the grave judging from the presence of a few human teeth in square 2. The human skeletal remains were very fragmented; they have been identified as being of an adolescent, 16-17 years of age, but the sex could not be determined (Sellevold, n.d.).

Grave 2: squares 5-7 strata 4-10. The upper part of the potsherd concentration covering the part of the grave excavated was located in squares 6-7 stratum 4 and in square 5 stratum 5 (Figure 6). It continued downwards and just below it, in square 6 stratum 9, human remains were revealed under big potsherds of water jars. These formed the lower part of the potsherd concentration. Square 6 was excavated down to a depth of 1 m below the surface, i.e. including stratum 10. All except three of the 355 potsherds located in square 7 stratum 10 were from the same pot (Figure 4).

St sq	12	11	10	9	8	7	6	5	4	3	2	1
1	257	270	538	747	218	379	411	578	751	640	832	1507
2	186	286	108	626	307	166	379	433	262	138	102	60
3	171	47	208	92	214	124	160	284	234	240	678	739
4	130	103	175	297	139	138	112	402	277	240	"	"
5	87	53	83	166	303	102	186	347	330	232	503	472
6	155	52	147	182	361	234	213	70	379	281	325	228
7	147	290	131	124	170	91	279	271		227	460	229
8	64	95	167	95	71	53	140	149		237	409	223
9	61	142	"	97	130	191	174	186		284	370	237
10	60	129	77	74	50	355	83	172		225		89
11	78	73	115	66	192	38						96
12	52	53	68	95	53	9						
13	57	87	75	36	100	52						
14	37	88	73	35	156							
15	15	68	65	37	42							
16	6	51	42	27	55							
17	12	35	33	10	64							
18	11	19	13	12	23							
19			7									

" 2 strata registered together.

Figure 4. Debbat El Eheima (UN 24). Spatial distribution of potsherds from excavation. Potsherds with incised and impressed decorations.

[2] A C14 date (T-4562) cal 1107-802 BC (Figure 2) from square 12 stratum 7 may also date a 3.3 cm-long iron arrow. This indicates an early use of iron in this part of Africa.

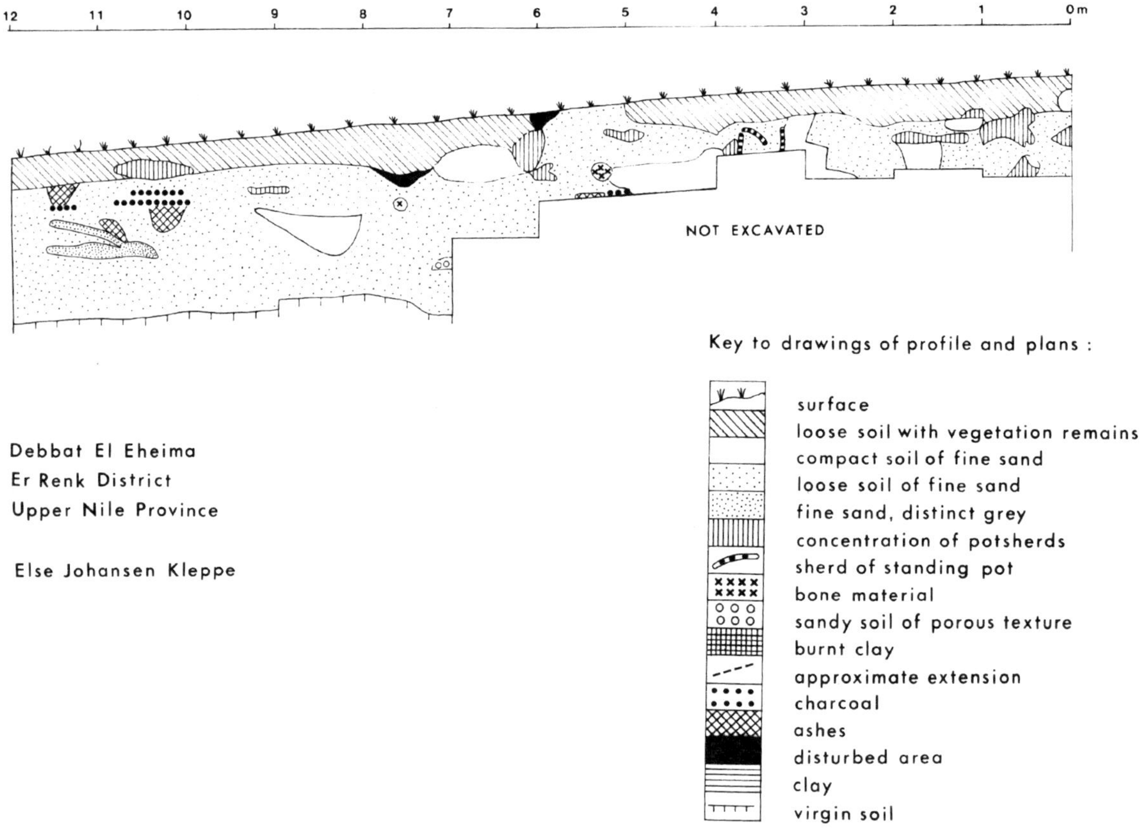

Figure 5. Debbat El Eheima (UN 24). Section drawn along the N side of the ENE-WSW-oriented excavation trench.

In total, five iron objects were found within this unit: one rod, one part of a ring, one arrow, one part of a knife and one unidentified fragment; in addition, 62 lithic objects were found. A fragment of a ceramic bracelet was located in square 6 stratum 5; two shell pendants, both with pierced holes for hanging, were found: one, located in square 5 stratum 6, was rounded and fragmented, the other one, in square 6 stratum 10, was a complete square-shaped pendant; and three pieces of ostrich eggshell, located in square 7 strata 4 and 10 and square 6 stratum 6, showed no traces of secondary working. The SW limit of the grave seems to have been marked by some potsherds stuck to the bottom of the grave. Details on the placement of the deceased cannot be ascertained due to the very fragmented state of the human bone remains. The human skeletal remains were primarily located in squares 6-7 stratum 9; they were identified as being of an adolescent, around 14-18 years of age, but the sex could not be determined (Sellevold, n.d.).

The human skeletal remains from the two graves are of adolescents nearly of the same age and in their late teens; the sex could not be determined. The orientation of the two graves was not clear as the skeletal remains were very fragmented. Small iron objects were found in association with both graves (cf. Kleppe 1986a: 112, Fig. 2): four objects associated with grave 1 and five objects with grave 2. Very few personal adornments were present: 11 small red ceramic beads in grave 1 were found scattered, and two shell pendants were associated with grave 2 and located in squares 5 and 6, strata 6 and 10, respectively. A fragment of a ceramic bracelet was found in square 6 stratum 5. The C14 dates only provide an outer frame for the age of the archaeological deposits excavated at Debbat El Eheima.

Debbat Bangdit (UN 25). The remains of seven graves were identified at this site, and human remains were found in association with all grave remains except those located in square 1. In total, 737 beads were recorded at this site, and most of them were associated with burial remains. One of the graves was totally excavated, i.e. an infant grave. The grave remains excavated had the following locations (cf. Figure 3):

square 1 strata 4-5
square 2 strata 5-9 and part of square 3 strata 6-8
square 2 strata 12-19, parts of square 1 strata 14-17 and of square 3 strata 12-17
squares 4-5 strata 3-18
square 7 strata 16-17, squares 6-7 strata 18-19 and square 5 strata 18-19
squares 4-5 strata 19-21 and part of square 6 strata 19-21
squares 6-7 strata 7-11

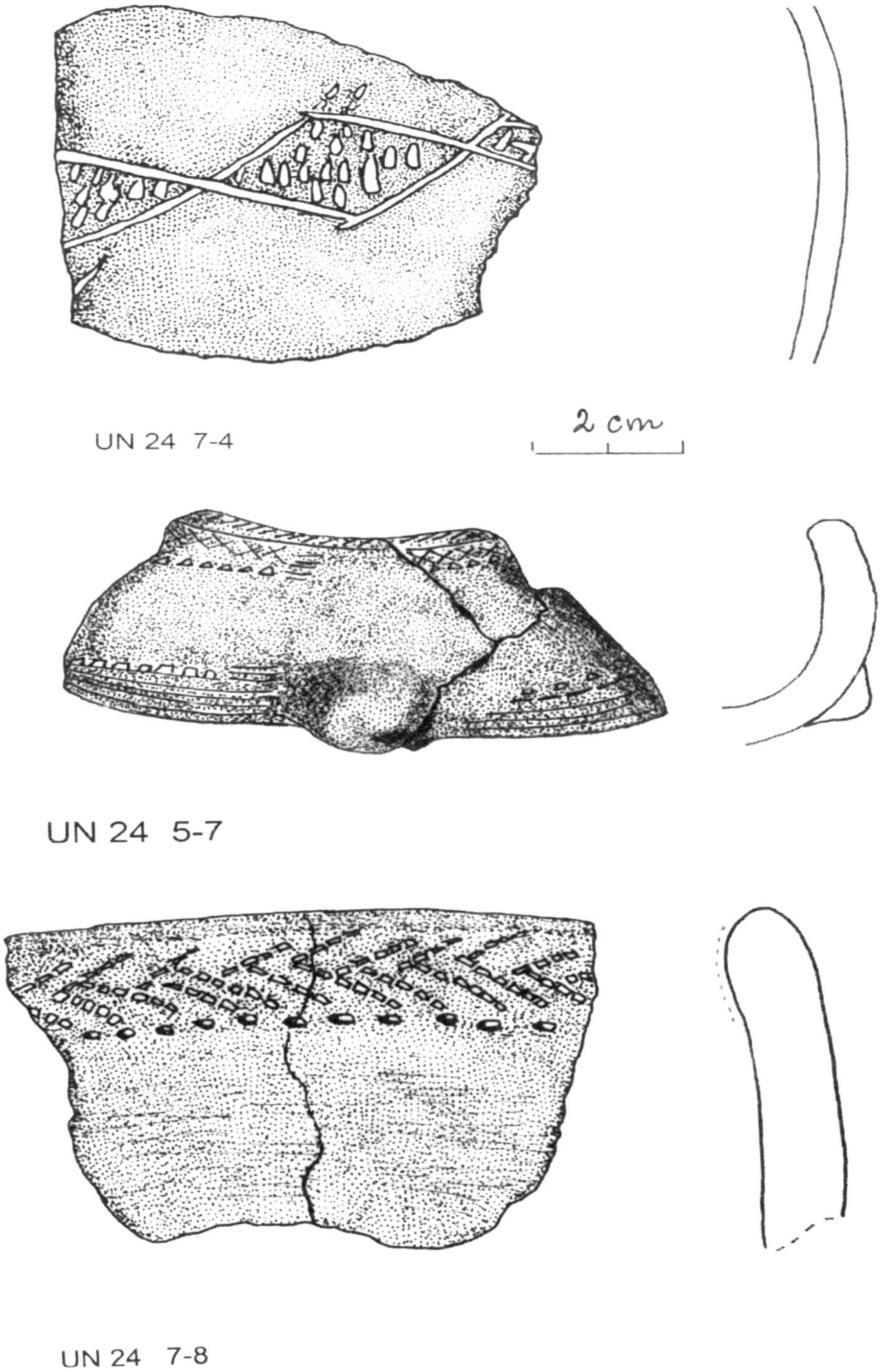

Figure 6. Debbat El Eheima (UN 24). Potsherds from grave 2: a) black sidesherd with burnished surface, of jar of eggshell-like ware (square 7 stratum 4); b) very dark grey burnished rimsherd of bowl of sand- and chamotte-tempered ware; note knob (square 5 stratum 7); c) very dark greyish brown burnished rimsherd of chamotte-tempered plate, decoration on inside (square 7 stratum 8). (Colour refers to Munsell 1975.)

Grave 3: square 1 strata 4-5. A small concentration of potsherds was documented in stratum 4 and it expanded into the NE corner of stratum 5. It is interpreted as being part of a cover over a grave; only a small part was located within the excavation trench towards the NE. No human skeletal remains were present within this unit, but my interpretation is that the potsherd concentration represents the remains of a grave.

Grave 4: square 2 strata 5-9 and part of square 3 strata 6-8. This is the uppermost of two graves recorded in square 2. The potsherd cover over the grave was *c.* 30 cm thick and its horizontal extension was nearly double the size in stratum 8. It also extended into square 3 strata 6-8 and one complete pot was documented standing in the SE part of square 2; its location was between 69 and 81 cm below the surface, i.e. just above the level where the human skeletal remains were documented. A total of 49 beads were associated with this grave (cf. Figure 7): 28 red ceramic beads, 18 disc-shaped ostrich eggshell beads, and one white, one pale green and one pale blue glass bead. There was a clear concentration of beads in square 2 strata 8-9: one shell used as a pottery making tool was found at the NE outskirts of the potsherd concentration in square 2 stratum 6. A human skull was located at the N outskirts in strata 7-8, while all other human skeletal remains from this grave were located in square 2 stratum 9 and oriented SE-NW. A C14 date obtained from a charcoal sample collected in square 2 stratum 5 was dated and its age was cal AD 1399-1878 (91.9% probability (cf. Figure 2)).

The human remains were of a child aged 4-5 years; the sex could not be determined (Sellevold, n.d.). An additional dental analysis was carried out by Kjell Bjorvatn and Gisle Bang, who suggested an age of 3-4 years (Bjorvatn, Bang and Kleppe 1988: 141). With reference to findings from Classic Kerma, it has been argued that the most reliable criterion for estimating the age of a non-adult is dental maturation (Murail *et al.*, 2004: 269). On the basis of the analyses I conclude that the child buried was around 4 years old by the time of death.

Grave 5: square 2 strata 12-19, part of square 1 strata 14-17 and of square 3 strata 12-17. This was the only grave totally excavated. A very thick potsherd cover was documented in strata 12-17, and a part of it was located in the NE corner of square 3 strata 12-17. It had a distinct upper boundary in stratum 12; one complete ceramic bowl was lying on its side at the outskirts of the potsherd cover towards the S in square 2 strata 13-14. Its location was between 1.16 and 1.31 m below the surface. The potsherd cover increased horizontally and extended downwards to stratum 18; at this level it had a very restricted, oblong shape *c.* 60x30 cm, approximately E-W oriented and 10-12 cm thick (Figures 3 and 8), and one big standing pot was located on top of the potsherd cover. The complete pot was located between 1.53 and 1.79 m below the surface, i.e. in square 2 strata 16-17. A small and complete skeleton was revealed within the excavation trench in square 2 stratum 19. The deceased infant had been placed on its right side, in an E-W direction, with the head towards W facing S, and resting on the right side. Just below the skull some small pieces of red ceramic material were found, and immediately N of the grave one rust-coloured irregular object was found. In the soil surrounding the skeletal remains, six undecorated, weathered sidesherds, with maximum dimensions of 1.0-2.3 cm, were found; one piece of iron slag, with a maximum dimension of 2 cm, was found in square 2 stratum 19, along with one piece of ochre and one shell of *Aspatharia*. The latter was located in the NW part of the grave. Many beads were documented close to the buried infant: nine ostrich eggshell beads were located by the ankles and might have been put on a string worn on one ankle, but this could not be confirmed. A long string looped double around the neck composed of 493 disc-shaped ostrich eggshell beads, three pale green glass beads and four red ceramic beads was documented (Figures 7 and 8).

A white striped coating was observed and documented below the small skeleton, i.e. at the very top of stratum 20 (Figure 9). This was the level where natural deposits were reached. I interpret the coating as traces of a reed mat, most likely used as a shroud for the deceased. The reference material is a documentation by J. Vandier (1952: 114-5, Figure 76, bottom illustration), who has depicted impressions of a reed mat from the archaeological site at Merimde in Egypt.

St sq	1	2	3	4	5	6	7
1							
2							
3						1D	
4		1R 1W					1W
5	1R						
6		2R					
7		3D 3R					
8	2R	12D 11R 1W 1G 1B					
9		3D 12R					
10		1D 2R					2D
11	1D 3R	3D 2R					
12	1R	2D 1R				1D	
13						1D	
14		1D 1R			2D		1BB
15					1D		
16					10D		
17					4D	3D	
18		1R		1D	4D	7D 5R 13GF	1GF
19		502D 4R 3G			11D	41D 1R	
20						1D	
21				43D			
22							
23							
24							
25							
26							
27							

Distribution of bead types
D disc-shaped ostrich eggshell beads
R red ceramic beads
G pale green glass beads
W white glass beads
B pale blue glass beads
BB bone bead
GF glass beads with fire traces

Total numbers of beads revealed: 737

Figure 7. Debbat Bangdit (UN 25). Spatial distribution of beads. Total: 737 beads from excavation

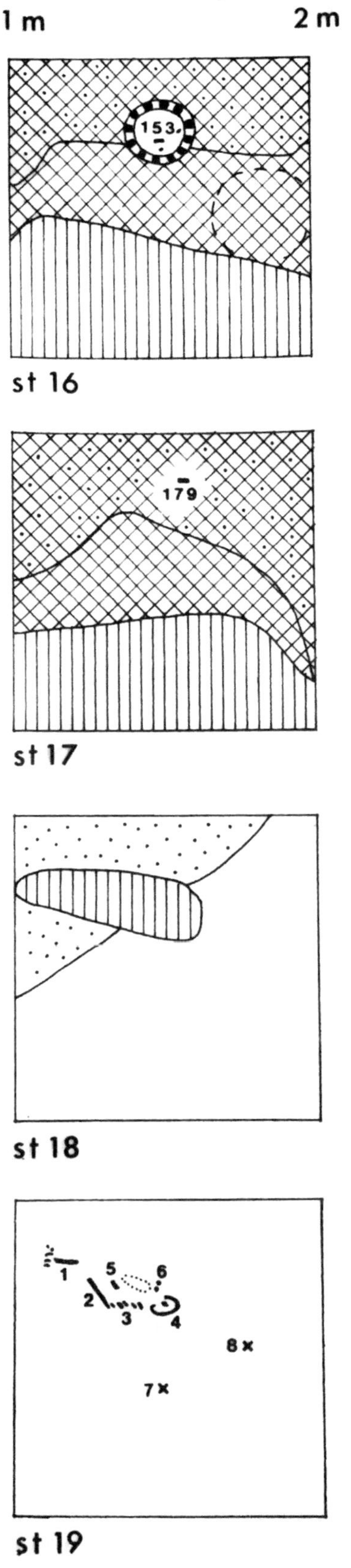

Figure 8. Debbat Bangdit (UN 25). Grave 5. Documentation of infant grave in square 2 strata 16-19. The potsherd cover extends into square 1 strata 14-17 and square 3 strata 12-17. Nos. 1-6 mark the location of skeletal remains. Objects associated with the burial: nine beads in an anklet (left of no. 1), 500 beads in a double-looped necklace (location shown by dotted line in between nos. 5 and 6), one piece of red ochre (no. 7) and one shell of Aspatharia (no. 8).

Figure 9. Debbat Bangdit (UN 25). Grave 5. White striped coating documented in the bottom of infant grave in stratum 19. Interpreted as impressions from a reed mat, an underlay or shroud for the deceased.

Sellevold concluded that the human remains were of a newborn to 6-month-old child whose sex could not be determined (Sellevold n.d.). The dental analysis suggested an age at death of less than 6 months (Bjorvatn, Bang and Kleppe 1988: 142).

Grave 6: squares 4-5 strata 3-18. This was the only grave that at least on one side was marked by a clear downcutting, and a small potsherd concentration in square 4 stratum 3 linked up with it (Figure 3). The upper part of the downcutting was located on the borderline between squares 3 and 4; the downcutting narrowed and from a depth of *c.* 70 cm it was cut more or less straight down to a point where it linked up with the rim and the side of a big standing but tilting water jar located between 1.30 and 1.80 m below the surface in the W part of square 4 strata 14-17. The water jar was left *in situ*. A small concentration of potsherds was documented just below the bottom of the water jar, and W of it another extensive potsherd concentration was documented; its W side might indicate traces of the W side of the downcutting, but its presumed upper part could not be identified. One complete pot was located near the S wall in square 4 stratum 5. Another complete pot was located in square 4 stratum 14. Two big, almost complete pots were located in square 5 strata 15-17. Their location might mark the W side of the grave.

The potsherd cover associated with this grave was documented in square 5 strata 7-15. It ought to be mentioned that there were smaller disturbed areas in square 4 strata 10-11 and in square 5 stratum 9. An orientation of the deceased could not be identified. Human skeletal remains intermingled with animal bones were located in squares 4-5 strata 16-17, resting on another potsherd concentration in a small part of square 4 and square 5 stratum 18. My interpretation is that the potsherd concentration separated this grave from the one partly documented in squares 5-7 stratum 18 and square 7 strata 16-17 (grave 7). A C14 date was obtained in square 4 stratum 14 and its age was cal AD 695-1149.

Areas rich in ashes were documented in square 4 strata 10-13, and in square 4 stratum 14 ash-rich soils were present all over, and part of one object of animal bone was found in this unit. It showed surface traces of fire after it was broken, its section was almost rectangular and the intact end had an edge shaped from the two broad, opposing sides; the present length is 6.2 cm. The other objects located within the area documented as a part of this grave were: 17 ostrich eggshell beads in square 5 strata 14-17; two round iron nail heads, both with a maximum dimension of 1.0 cm, in square 5 strata 4 and 5; one oblong iron piece with an oval section, with a maximum dimension of 3.5 cm and thickness of 1.4 cm, in square 4 stratum 9; one iron point with one barb (two pieces have been fitted together), 4.1 cm in length, in square

5 stratum 16. This iron point was found inside the complete ceramic pot located towards the W; two pieces of iron slag, with a maximum dimension of *c.* 3.0 cm, were located in square 5 stratum 9; and one piece of red burnt clay (R 5 5/6 according to Munsell) with a maximum dimension of 4.3 cm was found in square 5 stratum 9. There was plenty of lithic material within the area excavated of this grave.

Neither cranial fragments nor teeth were present. The human bone remains were of a female and the age at death was estimated to be 19-25 years (Sellevold n.d.).

Grave 7: square 7 strata 16-17, squares 6-7 strata 18-19 and square 5 strata 18-19. The archaeological remains associated with this grave were partly located below grave 6 in squares 4-5 strata 3-18 and partly in squares 6-7 strata 17-18 (cf. Figure 3). The potsherd cover separating the two graves seems to serve two purposes: it is part of the bottom layer of grave 6 and at the same time part of the cover of this one. The bases of two standing pots were located in square 5 stratum 18: one towards the E at 1.81 m, and one towards the W at 1.76 m below the surface. A total of 19 beads were located within the defined area for this grave unit (Figure 7). Parts of a human cranium were located in the W end of the grave on the borderline between squares 6 and 7 strata 17-18; other human remains were found in squares 5-7 in stratum 18. Associated with these human remains and inside the W-most pot, two pieces (fitted together) of a 4.1 cm-long arrow were found. A C14 date cal AD 428-970 was obtained from material located in square 5 stratum 17 (Figure 2).

The human remains were oriented E-W. This grave was partly cut down into natural deposits in its NE corner. A white striped coating was documented immediately below the human bones in both squares 6 and 7 stratum 17. A similar structure was identified in connection with the infant grave. It is interpreted as traces of a reed mat. Natural deposits were reached in parts of stratum 18 and in other parts another potsherd concentration appeared (this may indicate a separate grave located below[3]).

The skeletal remains were of a young male and Sellevold estimated the age at death to be 25-35 years (Sellevold n.d.). The dental analysis suggested the age at death to be *c.* 30 years (Bjorvatn, Bang and Kleppe 1988: 141-2).

Grave 8: squares 4-5 strata 19-21 and part of square 6 strata 19-21. The grave remains were indicated by a SE-NW-oriented potsherd concentration associated with the clear downcutting documented in the section drawn. The remains of this grave unit also link up with the two big standing pots; one is documented in the section (Figure 3). In total, 96 beads were associated with this grave; all except one, a red ceramic bead, were ostrich eggshell beads (cf. Figure 7). The human skeletal remains rested on natural deposits. Part of this grave was cut down into natural deposits in square 5 stratum 21. The human skeletal remains from this unit were left *in situ* and consequently not included in Sellevold's report.

Grave 9: squares 6-7 strata 7-11. Two concentrations of potsherds were documented in square 6 stratum 7 and the one located in the middle of the square was rich in ashes. A small concentration of potsherds was documented in square 7 strata 7-10 and it expanded into square 6 in strata 8-10. Only two ostrich eggshell beads were associated with this grave, both found in square 7 stratum 10; one goat bone with a hole indicating its use as a pendant was located in square 6 stratum 7 (identified by A. Gautier, personal communication); one bone harpoon, 10.6 cm long, was located in square 7 stratum 8. Some human skeletal remains were located in the SW corner in square 6 stratum 11 and in the adjacent part of square 7 stratum 11. The human remains rested on a potsherd concentration. Sellevold estimated the age at death to be 6-10 years; the sex could not be determined (Sellevold n.d.).

Remains of human skeletons were identified in five of the seven grave units identified. No further conclusions can be drawn on the basis of documentation from grave 3 and grave 8. Orientation was evident in grave 4 and grave 5. The human skeletal remains in grave 4 were oriented SE-NW and the skull

[3] The excavation work was stopped at short notice due to the starting political unrest.

was located towards the N; and the complete human skeleton in grave 5 was oriented E-W and the skull was located towards the W, facing S and resting on the right side. Both are children's graves in which three were identified. The sex could not be determined in any of the cases. Grave 4 was of a 4-year-old child, grave 5 of an infant, probably around half a year old, and grave 9 of a 6-10-year-old child. A female aged 19-25 years was identified in grave 6 and a male aged around 30 years in grave 7. Grave 6 and grave 7 seemed to be closely linked judging from the way they are constructed. It leads one to wonder whether they had been wife and husband. Grave 6 and most likely also grave 7 are associated with the only clear downcutting documented (cf. Figure 3).

Some objects found in association with the graves are of interest. Both in grave 4 and grave 5 a shell of *Aspatharia* with wear traces after use as a pottery-making tool were found. The infant grave (grave 5) also contained one iron slag and one piece of ochre. Only one personal adornment was documented in grave 9, i.e. one pendant of a goat bone. Beads abound (Figure 7) and particularly outstanding were the findings associated with the deceased infant in grave 5, where some 500 beads, most of them in a necklace and a few in a chain around an ankle, were documented. Beads, mainly ostrich eggshell beads (18 pieces) and red ceramic beads (25 pieces), were found in grave 4. Grave 6 included 22 ostrich eggshell beads. The beads associated with grave 7 and grave 8 amounted to 103 ostrich eggshell beads of which 43 were clearly from grave 8; one red ceramic bead was also from this grave. Most of the beads clearly associated with grave 7 were small transparent glass beads with traces of fire. In addition, seven ostrich eggshell beads and five red ceramic beads were clearly linked with this grave. Two C14 dates were directly related to the grave remains. From grave 7, a C14 date of cal AD 428-970 was obtained from material located in square 5 stratum 17. From grave 6, a C14 date of cal AD 695-1149 was obtained in square 4 stratum 14.

The concentrations of potsherds covering the various grave remains documented are a unique feature and reference material has been searched for; it is, however, meagre. I have searched ethnographic, ethnohistorical and archaeological literature in order to find answers to these questions. It is important that certain features are shared when selecting information for comparative purposes. Similarity in ecological adaptation and subsistence economy is most relevant; ethnic affiliation is on a different level of precision. Shared broad traditions such as adaptation are relevant for comparison (see also Odner (2000: 29-39). The Shilluk and one of the Dinka subgroups, both with river-bound adaptation, match these conditions and their villages abound on the high grounds running parallel with the river. These places are preferred for habitation nowadays as well as in the past. Similarities at this level are considered important. No direct ethnic match has been attempted, as this is considered premature. Much more detailed research is needed before such conclusions might be reached. I now turn to ethnographic and ethnohistorical documentation that might be relevant for further interpretations of the archaeological material documenting graves and ritual residues resulting from burial rituals.

Ethnographic and other archaeological documentation of burial practices

An ethnographic and ethnohistorical account is presented in detail in order to document how complex such ritual residues might be. The presence of perishable material that has marked the location of a grave is confirmed in an ethnographic recording by Diedrich Westermann (1912: 112-3) and in a photo taken by the linguist A. N. Tucker (Seligman and Seligman 1932: 104-5; photo in between these pages). In connection with his fieldwork, Tucker noticed a Shilluk grave marked by a fence, probably of dry sorghum stakes (Figure 10). Further details on grave digging and burial practice among the Shilluk have been published by Westermann (1912: 112), who has reported that the gravediggers would measure the deceased by binding corn stalks together and this measure would be transferred to 'the place (size) of the grave'. He also stated explicitly that nothing is buried with a corpse, 'but later a hole is made near and objects placed in it'. The wife or a female relative of a dead man 'throws away the hearth stones lying there. A drum is beaten, and the people begin to weep ... [and when the weeping] stops, the people dance mourning -dances. Then the people assembled go around in a procession dancing. Now the burial of the man is finished. A fence is made around the grave; the people wash themselves in the river, and then go back into the village. ... The eating -tools of the dead man are burnt, and the people rub the ashes on their

Figure 10. Shilluk homestead with grave in foreground
(Photo: A. N. Tucker, reproduction from Seligman and Seligman 1932: between 104-105).

forehead ... people now scatter and stay away for four days. After that time beer is made, the beer for rubbing mud on the back of the dead man." In a note, Westermann has explained the expression "beer for rubbing mud on the back": it means beer "for besmearing the grave with mud and smoothing the surface'.'

'After one month has passed, the people talk about the mourning festival. Dura [sorghum] for beer is collected from all the people [and beer is made] ... in the afternoon the drum is beaten. An ox is speared, goats are killed. Then the people go to sleep. The next morning the mourning begins... [cows are killed]. ... . Cooking pots are carried out, and a hole is dug for them (and for the other household things of the dead man) near the place where the head of the dead man lies. And two pots, and a gourd, and a small pot for beer, a mat for covering food, and two dishes, all these things are broken and thrown into the hole' (Westermann 1912: 113).

Westermann (1912: XXXVI) stated explicitly that the ritual he described was that performed for a grown-up man, who was buried just in front of his hut, and the grave site was marked with the horns of an ox killed for the burial feast. He also stated that women and children are buried in the bush. The latter information does not correspond with an eyewitness account of the burial of an old Shilluk woman published by P. J. Angerer, who had witnessed burial ceremonies that had lasted three days, starting on the day when the deceased was put into the grave. In this connection, certain objects were needed: an adze, a spear, a hoe, beads and a piece of cloth, all brought by relatives. A niche grave was dug and two big water jars filled with water and a slaughtered hen wrapped in a straw mat used for covering food were placed close to the grave site (Angerer 1923: 27). The body of the deceased was washed, shaved and wrapped in a clean dress (*lawo*) while this took place. When the gravedigging was finished the corpse was taken out of the hut by four women, and more women joined with cowbells in their hands and the procession went several times around the hut of the deceased before the women stopped at the grave site and became calm. A drum was also beaten. Simultaneously with this procession, men and older boys performed a warlike dance moving towards the grave site where they stopped after a rather wild dance pretending to throw their spears while they were hiding behind their shields (Angerer 1923: 29). At the same time as women and men respectively performed these rituals, the gravediggers split the clean *lawo* into two; one part was stretched out at the bottom of the grave as a bottom sheet, and the corpse was then put in position in the niche and the hen wrapped in the mat was placed in the grave. Finally, the second part of the *lawo* was placed as a cover over the deceased (Angerer 1923: 43). The water jars were emptied into the grave and the water mixed with soil was used as a plastering material to seal off the niche. More wailing by women and dancing by men took place while the grave was filled with soil, and finally a thorn fence was built around the grave (Angerer 1923: 45).

The information obtained from Westermann and Angerer is supported by Wilhelm Hofmayr (1925). Hofmayr mentioned explicitly that the Shilluk always bury their dead within the village and near the family homestead. A grave normally disappeared after a new rainy season, and graves of ordinary people would not be given further attention (Hofmayr 1925: 303). There are two forms of Shilluk graves, an ordinary one and a better one. The ordinary one is constructed of a *c.* 1.2 m deep shaft, while the length and width are measured and adjusted to the size of the deceased (Hofmayr 1925: 300). The 'better one' has another niche on its side, and the deceased is buried there in order not to be exposed directly to the soil. Local beer is invariably poured over a grave after the death dance has been performed and this is always done in the morning between 10 a.m. and 1 p.m. The death dance is for male mourners only and it is their farewell greeting (Hofmayr 1925: 499-500). The hut of a deceased is deserted for three or four days (Hofmayr 1925: 301) and at this stage it is also painted with vertical hand-wide, white stripes, an expression of sorrow (Hofmayr 1925: 399-400). When this period of time has passed the hut is cleaned and people start to use it again; it is only old men who were allowed to be gravediggers (Hofmayr 1925: 300-1). Elsewhere it is mentioned that wives, young people, men who have just had sexual intercourse, twins and men whose wives are pregnant are forbidden to dig graves (Hofmayr 1925: 222). The hair is cut off, no beads worn, and a cow's rope is worn around the neck during the time between burial and the death dance; during this period of time no dancing or other feasting is allowed (1925: 302). The practice of wearing a rope around the neck as a sign of mourning is also confirmed in a source from Kodok (Demsey 1956: 95). There it is also mentioned that no beads are worn and heads are shaved during this period of time. Unfortunately little detailed information has been found about the use of pottery in the ceremonies documented in the written ethnographic sources.

The practice documented in the literature has been confirmed by Shilluk informants in connection with my fieldworks and I consider it to be of primary importance for the further interpretation of the archaeological record. Practices of the other Nilotic group, the Dinka, living in the Renk area nowadays should be brought into the discourse. My search in the literature has not added to the insight presented above; besides, this ethnic group is fairly recent in the Renk area. The Dinka in question belong to the subgroup named Northern or Padang Dinka and these people came from the Bor area, south of Malakal, about 200 years ago according to Ibrahim Bedri (1948: 40). The northernmost section is the Abyalang – also spelled Abialang – Dinka (Sanderson and Sanderson 1981: 241). Other sections of Northern Dinka are the Paloic(h)/Paloc and the Dongjol/Dunjol Dinka. Charles Oyo, a Bor Dinka himself, has told me about mourning rituals taking place after one month, after three months or perhaps after one year amongst his people (see also Kleppe (1999: 69-71 and 136-8)). The meagre information on Northern Dinka practices does at least confirm shared Nilotic traditions on a general level when it comes to mourning ceremonies.

It has been difficult to trace reference material in the archaeological literature. The only example I have found is from one of the many graves excavated at Jebel Moya (Addison 1949b, Plate 29: 1-4). Addison has provided the following information (1949a: 52): 'Occasionally the body was covered, or partially covered, by the pieces of a large broken pot... but in such cases the fragments of a complete pot were never found. In one or two instances... only the head was covered as though to protect it from direct contact with the soil. The practice of strewing potsherds over the body was, however, rare, and is recorded only in a few graves.' The example referred to from Jebel Moya is grave 100/1222 (Addison 1949a: 86, Figure 58). This example from Jebel Moya is the only reference material I have come across. The dates at Jebel Moya have been reassessed recently by M. Brass and J.-L. Schwenniger (2013), who have argued that the first conclusive evidence of burial activity there is from no earlier than the first century BC.

The ethnographic and archaeological documentations show some similarities, and most importantly all burials documented are inhumations. The archaeological record shows that relatively few objects, except for pots, were involved in the rituals associated with death and burial and possible later ceremonies. Some indications of social position may be identified through specific objects, a point dealt with in the following.

Discourse

Potsherds on graves definitely served a practical, functional purpose, i.e. to cover a grave at the time of burial, but at the same time it is also interpreted as a manifestation of ritual acts performed. Pots have been broken over the graves. Some potsherd covers on the graves were massive, and the most extensive were those documented in squares 5 and 7 at Debbat Bangdit (Figure 3). A total of 33,965 potsherds were registered in the excavations at Debbat El Eheima, and 30,229 at Debbat Bangdit. Of the broken pottery associated with one grave located in squares 1-2 strata 3-9 at Debbat El Eheima, 739 potsherds found in square 1 strata 3-4 were of two or perhaps three water jars. Most likely ceramic jars, pots and plates were broken over the grave at the time when an actual burial took place. There were very few potsherd fragments at Debbat El Eheima, but 7,641 at Debbat Bangdit. The explanation for this may simply be that some ceramic wares produce more sherd fragments than others when pots are broken. So it may reflect a chronological difference. Potsherd fragments may be a general by-product when, for instance, water jars are deliberately broken because such pots are made of porous ware, most often tempered with chamotte. One or a few complete, often standing water pots or other types of storage pots are often associated with a potsherd cover over a grave. These are also interpreted as part of a ritual residue, but their function has remained unknown so far.

It is important to underline that particularly among Shilluk, who are the potters of the area, nowadays special pots together with other objects are considered personal belongings and they are never inherited, but destroyed when the owner dies. The idea behind the breaking of pots has been explained by Nigel Barley with reference to practice in Africa: '[P]ottery is more than something you cook with. It is something to think with, bringing together biological, technological and social change in a single metaphor. The irreversibility of a broken vessel offers a way of speaking of the irreversibility of human time, the change from living to dead. The ritual smashing of pottery creates a clean break between the two' (Barley 1995: 152) This view definitely applies to my work in the Renk area.

Ritual acts performed might differ depending on the status of a deceased, and different age groups might be subject to different rituals. The age groups represented in the archaeological record are infants and children, adolescents and younger adults. Some archaeological observations related to the burials of infants, children and adolescents are of interest. A shell of *Aspatharia* was found both in grave 4, a grave of an infant, and grave 5, a grave of a child. The iron objects, mostly fragments associated with graves, are of special interest. Such objects were associated with grave 1, grave 2 and grave 6, all graves of adolescents; the sex was not determined. It is important to bear in mind that most of the iron objects were in a very poor state of preservation (cf. Figure 6).

The ethnographic examples show complex rituals that are difficult to interpret unambiguously from archaeological documentation. Some ritual acts may mark different stages of mourning. Such ceremonies can take place sometime after a burial, for instance a month later and even on later occasions depending on the status of a deceased. The practice of covering graves with potsherds seems to be a shared cultural feature in the Renk area. The potsherd covers are the only clear markers of locations of graves documented in the excavations; it is, however, reasonable to add that most likely there had existed other, probably perished demarcations of graves. The potsherd covers function as grave covers, but they are also ritual residues and probably the results of ritual acts interpreted as demarcations of two different spheres: that of the dead and that of the living.

Towards a conclusion

Graves have generally been located close to the homestead of the deceased; the status of the deceased would probably determine their location. The size of a grave seems to vary according to the age, or rather perhaps the height, of a deceased. The use of potsherd covers on graves seems to have been a practice for at least 3000 years in the Renk area. Potsherd accumulations as ritual residues are complex to interpret. Variations in rituals performed depending on the social status and role of the individual buried may be part of the explanation. Later mourning rituals might have increased the complexity and such acts may be hard to document through archaeological excavations.

Acknowledgement

I thank R. H. Pierce for including me in the archaeological reconnaissance tour to the Malakal area in 1976 and for always being interested in and ready to discuss my archaeological research in the Upper Nile province.

References

Addison, F. (1949a and b). *Jebel Moya 1-2*. London: Oxford University Press.

Angerer, P. J. (1923). Ein Begräbnis bei den Schilluk. *Stern der Neger* 3-4: 27-29 and 5-6: 43-45.

Barley, N. (1995). *Dancing on the Grave. Encounters with Death*. London: John Murray.

Bedri, I. (1948). More Notes on the Padang Dinka. *Sudan Notes and Records* 29 (1): 40-57.

Bjorvatn, K., Bang, G. and Kleppe, E. J. (1988). Tenner og tannfragmenter forteller historie. Analyser fra tre gravfunn i Den hvite Nildal, Sør-Sudan. *Den norske tannlegeforenings tidende* 98(4): 140-147.

Brass, M. and Schwenniger, J.-L. (2013). Jebel Moya (Sudan): New Dates from a Mortuary Complex at the Southern Meroitic Frontier. *Azania* 48 (4): 455-472.

Bronk Ramsey, C., Scott, M. and van der Plicht, H. (2013). Calibrationfor archaeological and environmental terrestrial samples in the time range 26?50 ka cal BP. *Radiocarbon* 55 (4): 2021-2027.

Crawford, O. G. S. (1948). People Without a History. *Antiquity* 22: 8-12.

Crawford, O. G. S. (1951). *The Fung Kingdom of Sennar with a Geographical Account of the Middle Nile Region*. Gloucester: John Bellows.

Demsey, J. (1956). *Mission on the Nile*. New York: Philosophical Library.

Hinkel, F. W. (1979). *The Archaeological Map of the Sudan. A Guide to its Use and Explanation of its Principles*. Berlin: Akademie Verlag.

Hofmayr, W. (1925). Die Schilluk. Geschichte, Religion und Leben eines Niloten-Stammes. *Anthropos* 2 (5): 1-521 and following illustrations.

Hubert, J. (1989). A proper place for the dead: A critical review of the 'reburial' issue. In: R. Layton (ed.) *Conflict in the Archaeology of Living Traditions*. (One World Archaeology 8): 131-166. London: Routledge.

Hulthén, B. (1974). On Documentation of Pottery. *Acta Archaeological Lundensia* Series in 8° minore 3.

Kleppe, E. J. (1982a). The debbas on the White Nile, Southern Sudan. In: J. Mack and P. Robertshaw (eds) Culture History in the Southern Sudan. Nairobi: The British Institute in Eastern Africa. *Memoir* 8: 59-70.

Kleppe, E. J. (1982b). Habitation mounds in Shilluk land. In: P. van Moorsel (ed.) *New Discoveries in Nubia. Proceedings of the Colloquium on Nubian Studies. The Hague 1979*: 57-66. Leiden: Nederlands Instituut voor het Nabije Oosten.

Kleppe, E. J. (1986a). The past lives on in the present. Debbat El Eheima revisited. The prehistory of Southern Sudan. Approaches made before 1950. In: M. Krause (ed.) *Nubische Studien. Tagungsakten der 5. Internationalen Konferenz der International Society for Nubian Studies, Heidelberg 22.-25. September 1982: 109-112* and 113-120. Mainz am Rhein: Zabern.

Kleppe, E. J. (1986b). Religion expressed through bead use: an ethnoarchaeological study of Shilluk, Southern Sudan. In: G. Steinsland (ed.) *Words and Objects*: 78-90. Oslo: Universitetsforlaget.

Kleppe, E. J. (1989). Divine kingdoms in northern Africa: Material manifestations of social institutions. In: I. Hodder (ed.) *The Meanings of Things. Material Culture and Symbolic Expressions:* 195-201. London: Allen and Unwin.
Kleppe, E. J. (1999). Material and Verbal Manifestations of Socio-cultural Institutions in an African Kingship. The Shilluk of Southern Sudan. Unpublished PhD dissertation, University of Bergen.
Kleppe, E. J. (2005). Etnohistorie og arkeologisk kildemateriale fra Upper Nile, Sør-Sudan. *Årbok for Bergen Museum 2004*: 43-52.
McKeown, C. T. (2013). *In the Smaller Scope of Conscience: The Struggle for National Repatriation Legislation 1986–1990*. Tuscon: University of Arizona Press.
Márquez-Grant, N. and Fibiger, L. (2011). *The Routledge Handbook of Archaeological Human Remains and Legislation. An International Guide to Laws and Practice in the Excavation and Treatment of Archaeological Human Remains*. London: Routledge.
[Munsell] (1975). *Munsell Soil Color Charts*. Baltimore: Munsell Color.
Murail, P., Maureille, B., Peresinotto, D. and Geus, F. (2004). An Infant Cemetery of the Classic Kerma Period (1750–1500 BC, Island of Sai, Sudan). *Antiquity* 78: 267-77.
Odner, K. (2000). *Tradition and Transmission. Bantu, Indo-European and Circumpolar Great Traditions* (Bergen Studies in Social Anthropology 54).
Reimer, P. J. *et al.* (2013). IntCal13 and Marine13 Radiocarbon Age Calibration Curves 0–50,000 Years cal BP. *Radiocarbon* 55: 1869-1887.
Sanderson, L. P. and Sanderson, N. (1981). *Education, Religion and Politics in Southern Sudan 1899–1964*. London: Ithaca Press.
Seligman, C. G. and Seligman, B. Z. (1932). *Pagan Tribes of the Nilotic Sudan*. London: Routledge and Kegan.
Sellevold, B. J. (n.d.). Skeletal Remains from Debbat El Eheima and Debbat Bangdit (Unpublished report).
Vandier, J. (1952). *Manuel D'Archéologie Égyptienne* 1, 1. Paris: A. and J. Picard.
Westermann, D. (1912). *The Shilluk People. Their Language and Folklore*. Westport (CT): Negro Universities Press.

Reconstructing a codex with the Coptic Encomia on Apa Victor

Alexandros Tsakos
University of Bergen

This paper is a modest contribution to the volume commemorating the fruits of the long academic career of Richard Holton Pierce, on the occasion of his 80th birthday (24 October 2015). Its author has the privilege of presenting a treasure from Pierce's archive and aims therefore not only to make this discovery known, but also to promote the importance of working with scientific archives.

Introduction

Among those that were gathered in a seminar room at the University of Bergen on 26th October 2015, I was surely the one who had had the chance to cross paths with Pierce most recently. When I came to Bergen in 2008, Pierce was a name of major importance to my studies since he is one of the editors of *Fontes Historiae Nubiorum*, a collection of sources on Nubian history, which has been used by most Nubiologists or others who occasionally write about Nubia, and which still remains the main point of reference for anyone studying the sources of the Nubian past (Eide *et al.* 1994; 1996; 1998; 2000). But I did not get to know Pierce before 2011, when an effort began to assemble all the archival material on Sudan that was kept at the University of Bergen or in the hands of the researchers who have marked the more than half a century of collaboration between Bergen and Sudan. I approached him because I wished to digitize the photographs that he took while working in the field in Lower Nubia, Sudan, as one of the archaeologists of the Oriental Institute Nubian Expedition, active at Serra East and Dorginarti (he and his wife Wenche Pierce excavated the latter site). It soon became obvious that there would be much more to discover in the material that Pierce has assembled in his long academic career.

Pierce's archive

I have had the opportunity to work with Pierce's archive systematically since summer 2014, because I was granted permission by the Department of Archaeology, History, Cultural Studies and Religion to use for archival work the time in my postdoctoral project allocated for duties other than teaching.

It is impossible to estimate the actual volume of Pierce's archive. One needs to pick out a category of special interest, and work one's way through everything that Pierce has bought, copied and noted. My interest in the literacy of the Christian Nubian society, and my responsibility for teaching Coptic at the UiB, made me focus for a while on the collection of material on Coptic language and literature that Pierce has assembled.

This material consists of several printed books and more than 100 folders of printed articles, of personal notes, of ingenious diagrams and, last but not least, of annotated handwritten copies of original Coptic manuscripts. Pierce used this material for his teaching of Coptic language to students of linguistics who needed to study a non-Indo-European language, for his own interest in lexicographical and phonological topics, for the sake of his own studies of the civilizations of the Nile from prehistory to modern times, and for contributing to the research of his students at master, doctoral or postdoctoral level.

In the paragraphs that follow, I will present a discovery that I made while working more closely with his archive on Coptic literature and particularly the corpus of texts about a specific Coptic martyr who was initially planned to be the case study of the doctoral dissertation of Professor Saphinaz Naguib.[1]

[1] I would like to thank Professor Saphinaz Naguib for her comments on my paper.

Apa Victor's Encomium

In the late 1970s, Naguib proposed to Pierce a topic on the Coptic martyr Apa Victor the General, the son of the Roman governor Romanos, who miraculously survived death three times before being martyred during the persecution under Diocletian (Van Esbroeck 1991: 2303-2308). In the end, Naguib changed her thesis topic (Naguib 1990), though she later returned to Apa Victor in a postdoctoral project, producing three very insightful articles about this Coptic martyr (Naguib 1993; 1994; 1997).

Pierce had already done his homework in preparation for their collaboration, though. Not only had he copied the completely preserved Martyrdom and Encomium on Apa Victor in Egypt, namely from the British Museum codex Or. 7022 first edited by Budge (1914: xxiii-xlv, 1-101, 253-355), but he had then proceeded to copy all the other testimonies of the two Encomia on Apa Victor, namely 92 leaves bound in the miscellanies from Paris, BnF Copte 129^{15} and 129^{16}, edited by Bouriant (1893), two leaves from Vienna edited by Till (1935: 45-55), and two leaves from Moscow and one from Berlin, edited by von Lemm (1911).

Von Lemm had already realized that the Berlin and Moscow fragments were part of the same codex, the largest portion of which was bound together with other works in the volumes BnF Copte 129^{15} and 129^{16} (the identification was repeated by Elanskaya (1994: 75-76)). Pierce went a step further: through copying all the fragments, he realized that the first leaf from Moscow precedes directly the first leaf from Vienna. In his folders the two copies are placed together and there is clear proof that there was nothing accidental about this reconstruction:

Figure 1:

1. The individual pages are numbered according to their pagination in the original codex, thus the last page of the first Moscow folio is marked as nr. 18 (ιн) and the first page of the Vienna folio is marked as nr. 19 (ιθ). Despite the paleographic differences between the hands of the 'Austrian' and the 'Russian' fragments,[2] there is no reason to separate codicologically the fragments identified to date.
2. In Pierce's folders, there is a quote from an article by Orlandi (1972) where it is stated that 'le fait le plus important est que les manuscrits ont été tous démembrés et vendus aux voyageurs par petits groups de feuillets (pour chaque codex): il n'y a qu'un seul codex, que je sache, qui soit arrivé presque entier à Paris'. This quote is followed by note nr. 11, which Pierce also copies: 'C'était un 'synaxaire' comprenant des textes sur S. Victor; cf. l'édition de U. Bouriant, MMAFC 8 (1893): 147-242; et O. von Lemm, ZÄS 48 (1911): 81-86'.
3. Nevertheless, there are also two important codicological details, already illustrated by von Lemm in the table he compiled to show the original placement of the individual fragments, namely that the scribe(s) started a new quire-numbering after quire 5 and he must have missed numbering two pages between pages 18 and 110. There is unfortunately very little preserved between these two places to spot the mistake, but Pierce made an attempt to amend this, namely by showing how the codex would have been made up if the individual folia had been arranged in quires – based on the folia numbers from Paris as listed by von Lemm – and by repeating pages 79-80 exactly where the scribes also decided to restart the quire numbering. Furthermore, Pierce's reconstruction was based on the codicological assumption that the codex consisted of quaternions (groups of four leaves), as can be seen in Figure 1c. Although this type of binding was quite probable, the system proposed fails to create the 18 quires that the entire codex was expected to contain (5 plus 13); it thence became impossible to predict the exact codicological distribution of the preserved folia. I think that this was what stopped Pierce from publishing his discovery.

[2] This was first pointed out to me by Alin Suciu, whom I thank for fruitful discussions concerning paleographic and codicological issues tackled in this paper.

Figure 1

In any case, he was the first person to observe that the first Viennese fragment followed the first one from Moscow in the original codex, which should most probably be identified as one of the dismembered codices from the library of the White Monastery of Apa Shenute in Egypt.

Approximately a decade after the work conducted by Pierce, Jürgen Horn published his doctoral dissertation on Apa Victor, son of Romanos (Horn 1988). On pages 46-49, he listed the attestations of the Encomium, and noted (idem: 47, note 2): 'Die Zusammengehörigkeit der von Till edierten Wiener Blätter mit der von Bouriant herausgegebenen Pariser Hs. wurde vom Herausgeber nicht erkannt. Ich werde an anderer Stelle darauf ausführlich eingehen.'

To the best of my knowledge, Horn has never completed this work, but he may have managed to solve the codicological puzzle. Someone might find the answer in his archive in the future.

Further insights into the manuscript and literary tradition around Apa Victor, son of Romanos, could also be expected to appear by working with the archive of Saphinaz Naguib.

Epilogue

Preserving and studying the archives assembled by past generations of university professors and researchers seems to have become part of the strategic investments of many universities around the world. Quite often, the digitization of the material assembled during the careers of the distinguished figures of our academic milieus is considered a sufficient means of preserving the knowledge that these archives represent. Without diminishing the value of the digitization process and its output, it should nevertheless be added that an archive is more than the digital copies that constitute it. It is also a repository of the knowledge that passed from one generation to the next, a witness of what informed the university education of a given generation. It is thus heritage, a repository of memory; and memory is primarily the result of a lived reality. It occurs, for example, around monuments, and in Greek – another language that Pierce served diligently – memory (μνήμη) and monument (μνημείο) have common etymological roots. Thus, memory lies first and foremost with tangible manifestations, and for an archive this means the masses of papers that constitute it. If it is not wanted that this memory should fade away, it should therefore be preserved as a set of physical objects. Now, it is true that objects need space, and since space costs, obtaining space for archiving is among the most difficult challenges that the universities interested in preserving their intellectual heritage are facing. One needs to argue for the necessity of preserving the physical dimension of an archive. In my opinion, this can be achieved by understanding the archives as potential centres of learning and research. So, my experience from working with the archive of Richard Holton Pierce is that his academic labour could and should be used as a focal point, a real space, around which all those who wish to refer to the knowledge represented by the material he has assembled in his long career can gather to study, discuss, write, teach and learn. Pierce's archive can become in Bergen the central element of a centre for the study of Egypt, Nubia, the Red Sea and the Nile Valley, in a diachronic sense – the only sense in which Pierce understood what Egyptology is about.

References

Bouriant, U. (1893). L'Éloge de l'Apa Victor, Fils de Romanos. *Mémoires de la Mission Archéologique Française au Caire*, 8: 145-266.

Budge, E. A. W. (1914). *Coptic Martyrdoms etc. in the Dialect of Upper Egypt*. London: British Museum.

Eide, T., Hägg, T., Pierce R. H. and Török L. (eds) (1994; 1996; 1998; 2000). *Fontes Historiae Nubiorum: Textual Sources for the History of the Middle Nile Region between the Eighth Century B.C. and the Sixth Century A.D.* Volumes 1-4. Bergen: John Grieg AS.

Elanskaya, A.I. (1994). *The Literary Coptic Manuscripts in the A.S. Pushkin State Fine Arts Museum in Moscow.* Leiden: Brill.

Horn, J. (1988). Untersuchungen zu Frömmigkeit und Literatur des Christlichen Ägypten: Das Martyrium des Viktor, Sohnes des Romanos. PhD Dissertation, University of Göttingen.

Lemm, O. von. (1911). Zu einem Enkomium auf den hl. Viktor. *Zeitschrift für Ägyptische Sprache und Altertumskunde* 48: 81-86.
Naguib, S. (1990). *Le Clergé Féminin d'Amon Thébain à la 21ème Dynastie* (Orientalia Lovaniensia Analecta 38). Leuven: Peeters.
Naguib, S. (1993). Martyr and apostate: Victor, Son of Romanos and Diocletian. A case of intertextuality in Coptic religious memory. *Temenos. Studies in Comparative Religion*, 29: 101-113. Åbo: The Donner Institute for Research in Religious and Cultural History.
Naguib, S. (1994). The martyr as witness. Coptic and Copto-Arabic Hagiographies as Mediators of Religious Memory. *Numen. International Review for the History of Religions* 41: 223-254.
Naguib, S. (1997). The Era of Martyrs. Texts and Contexts of Religious Memory. In: N. van Doorn-Harder and K. Vogt (eds) *Between Desert and City: The Coptic Orthodox Church Today* (Institute for Comparative Research in Human Culture, Serie B: Skrifter XCVII): 121-141. Oslo: Novus.
Orlandi, T. (1972). Un Projet Milanais Concernant les Manuscrits Coptes du Monastère Blanc. *Le Muséon* 85: 403-413.
Till, W. (1935). *Koptische Heiligen- und Märtyrlegenden* (Orientalia Christiana Analecta 102). Rome: Pontificium Institutum Orientalium Studiorum.
Van Esbroeck, M. (1991). Victor Stratelates, Saint. In: Atiya, A.S. (ed.) *Coptic Encyclopedia* 7: 2303a-2308a. New York: Macmillan.

Bridging Gaps: Archaeological sources and resources in museums

Saphinaz-Amal Naguib
University of Oslo

Introduction

Museums and archaeology share a common engagement to find, recover, safeguard, study and explicate the material world.[1] This brief open-ended essay is about the methods and scopes of museums regarding their use of archaeology as a source and a resource in exhibitions about Ancient Egypt and Nubia, and how archaeological finds and research in different academic fields may serve to generate, expand and sustain museums' activities. Bridging the gaps between disciplines and laying the grounds for free-choice learning and for the elaboration and dissemination of knowledge is, in my view, a first step. The second step has to do with a self-reflective turn we have been witnessing during the last decade or so in European museums holding archaeological material from non-Western countries. This new turn has to do with an increased awareness of the sustainability of such endeavours. Establishing a politics of trust between museums, cultural and research institutions and local populations is the next step.

Objects of knowledge and free-choice learning

During the late 1980s, a number of museums around the world, for various reasons, had to reassess their museological projects and practices. According to Dominique Poulot (2005; cf. Naguib 2004; 2013), the shift from what he describes as the 'depot museum' to the 'exhibition museum' has transformed the institution of the museum both in its conception and in its management. Permanent exhibitions have a shorter lifespan and are regularly reorganized; they often travel, are thematically oriented and make use of various participatory approaches. Aesthetics, the production of experiences, design, the originality of the display and performance are central elements. From the perspective of a didactic, taxonomic and descriptive museology, the trend is now to use polyphonic narrative and a museology of intersecting gazes. Multimedia has been a major instrument in bringing this approach to fruition and new potentials are appearing all the time (Naguib 2004: 58f.). The polyphonic narrative in exhibitions about ancient cultures juxtaposes different perspectives and connects research with education, entertainment and dissemination. It directs attention to the many lives and changing meanings an artefact has had, to its relation to other objects, to sites, to people, to cultural practices and to geopolitical contexts. Thus, biographic narratives about archaeological objects may include presentations of excavations, comparisons between modern archaeological methods and those of the past, and also dealing with difficult matters such as forgery, illicit excavations, and the plundering and destruction of cultural heritage (Naguib forthcoming).

These new approaches to archaeological material in museums offer the flexibility needed for free-choice learning, which, according to John Falk and Lynn Dierking (2000), forms the basis of lifelong, self-motivated learning. The idea behind free-choice learning is that anyone – young and old – can decide what, where, when and how she or he wants to learn. Museums play an important role in making learning attractive through their exhibitions and outreach programmes. Both museums and archaeology have the materiality of things as their focal point. Their task is to not only protect the unique but also to reclaim the humble, often fragmentary things such as potsherds, ostraca, statuettes, scraps of papyri, pieces of coffins, linen wrappings or beads, and make them into 'objects of knowledge'. Materiality encompasses,

[1] According to the ICOM Statutes, adopted by the 22nd General Assembly in Vienna, 24.08.2007: 'A museum is a non-profit, permanent institution in the service of society and its development, open to the public, which acquires, conserves, researches, communicates and exhibits the tangible and intangible heritage of humanity and its environment for the purposes of education, study and enjoyment' (retrieved 23.4.2016).

then, the material properties of things, their shape, type, age and style as well as their relations to people and to what things convey about the more intangible aspects of culture. Several exhibitions about ancient Egypt combine the biographies and materiality of things with multidisciplinarity. In planning and organizing exhibitions about ancient Egypt and Nubia, museums draw upon the knowledge of scholars and experts in different disciplines and fields within these. Instead of setting an ancient civilization like the Egyptian one in a 'time out of time' mode and what Anna Wieczorkiewicz (2005) has described as 'fairy tales', 'ghost' and 'detective and adventurer' stories, exhibitions rely on different approaches and combine an aesthetic-historical frame of representation with education and entertainment. In addition, exhibitions have become more self-reflective and probe accounts about excavations, local politics, environment and scholars. The catalogues and other publications produced include various in-depth studies in addition to pictures of objects with shorter texts describing the different artefacts with details about materials, size, date, provenance and translations of texts if the pieces are inscribed. Among the more recent exhibitions adopting this approach are *Ancient Egypt transformed: The Middle Kingdom*[2] at the Metropolitan Museum, New York (Oppenheim *et al.*: 2015) and *Faith after the Pharaohs*[3] at the British Museum (Fluck, Helmecke and O'Connell 2015). Another one is the exhibition *Taharqa - The Black Pharaoh*[4] at the Ny Carlsberg Glyptotek in Copenhagen, which was supplemented by publications about the historical background of the collection and central figures such as Carl Jacobsen, Valdemar Schmidt, Flinders Petrie and John Garstang, who had been so committed to building it up (Bagh 2011; 2015; Jørgensen 2015). In these kinds of exhibitions, the artefacts exhibited do not 'speak for themselves' as art objects in a timeless decontextualized environment. Instead, they are set in a mixture of their own contemporaneity and of the different regimes of historicity they have witnessed. They are presented with the learning and enjoyment wishes of varied audiences in mind. Online exhibitions complete the in-house exhibitions and continue to offer the public the possibility of learning more about the work of archaeologists and other experts even after the exhibitions have been taken down. Thanks to the new media, the visitor has the illusion of being in direct dialogue with objects of the past and realizes that scientific interpretations are not absolute but prone to continuous reassessments. Different questions are asked; new answers are provided.

The self-reflective turn and *disjecta membra*

One of the major problems that museums holding collections from ancient Egypt and Nubia have had to deal with is the thorny question of the *disjecta membra*. For centuries, monuments, archaeological finds and artefacts of all sorts and sizes have been taken away from their original contexts and dispersed around the world in different museums and collections. Some, like the Rosetta Stone or the painted bust of Nefertiti, have become iconic pieces of their museum's collections. Others, like Egyptian obelisks, have become landmarks in various capitals. Most, however, are either exhibited in museums' galleries or kept in museums' storerooms or in private collections, or have simply disappeared.

Parallel to the multidisciplinary and free learning approaches we witness that self-reflection has become an added element in both permanent and temporary exhibitions about ancient cultures, ancient Egypt and Nubia included. The self-reflective approach brings to the fore the ways in which both archaeology and the institution of the museum have evolved. It entails a somewhat critical look at oneself by reviewing and explicating the circumstances in which certain actions and events took place. In the context of museums, it means interrogating their own histories of collecting and excavating. It involves mapping the trajectories of objects in time and space in order to reconstruct the various networks that brought them to the museum and to review their status in the museum's collection. Taking the example of the Vorderasiatisches Museum im Pergamonmuseum, Berlin, Markus Hilgert and France Desmarais argue that archaeological museums, especially in western Europe, are today facing

[2] http://www.metmuseum.org/exhibitions/listings/2015/ancient-egypt-transformed (12.10.2015-24.1.2016).
[3] http://www.britishmuseum.org/whats_on/exhibitions/faith_after_the_pharaohs.aspx (29.10.2015-7.2.2016).
[4] http://www.glyptoteket.com/whats-on/calendar/taharqa-the-black-pharaoh (10.4-28.6.2015).

> complex challenges related to the political and cultural crises in the countries from which the objects in their collections originate. The future of archaeological museums as public spaces of education, transcultural encounters and multi-perspective discourse, as well as their social and political significance, will hinge on their willingness and ability to meet these challenges, take on their individual historical burdens and make the appropriate ethical choices... (Hilgert and Desmarais 2015: 22).

For Hilgert and Desmarais, museums must take responsibility for their past. They have to account for and document the history and provenance of the objects in their care, and make this information broadly available to both the countries of origin and internationally.

The exhibition *In the Light of Amarna. 100 Years of the Find of Nefertiti*[5] was an example of the self-reflective turn in museums and of bringing together pieces that originally belonged to the same site. To mark the anniversary of the discovery of one of the most renowned 'bones of contention' in archaeology, namely the bust of Nefertiti on 6th December 1912, the Egyptian Museum and Papyrus Collection at the Neues Museum in Berlin inaugurated this special exhibition (Seyfried 2012). It comprised about 400 objects and several had never been shown publicly before. Fifty of these were loans from other museums in Germany and internationally such as the Metropolitan Museum of Art, the British Museum and the Petrie Museum of Egyptian Archaeology. The exhibition did not just focus on religion and art during the Amarna period but offered a comprehensive overview of daily life in Akhetaton, as Tell el-Amarna was called at the time. Further, it also placed the discovery of the bust of Nefertiti within the context of Borchardt's excavations in 1912 and examined the history of the depiction of the bust of Nefertiti both as an archaeological object and as a widely marketed ideal of beauty. It was clear that the organizers hoped the exhibition would be a blockbuster. The exhibition and several articles in the catalogue of the exhibition examined the way in which foreign powers, here the British, French and German, worked in colonial settings and how they negotiated the division of labour between them. The texts produced for the exhibition explicated the conditions in which the excavations, sponsored by the businessman James Simon (1851-1932) and the Deutsche Orient-Gesellschaft, were initiated. They also touched upon the claims of repatriation that were launched by the Egyptian government in 1924. However, these details on the geopolitical conditions and economic facts were presented from the German point of view and mainly as disputes between the French and German authorities. The catalogue is silent about the Egyptian national socio-political and cultural situation at the time. Ironically, the colonial period in Egypt is also known as its cosmopolitan era. During the nineteenth century and until WWII, Egypt was a popular destination for Europeans. The quest for rare and exotic experiences and picturesque sites was not the only reason. Politics, economy and the establishment of new markets and job opportunities were other important factors in this attraction. This coincided with the policy of modernization introduced by the Egyptian rulers at the time. They welcomed foreign capital and recruited European scholars, businesspersons, urban planners, engineers, architects and skilled workers for their various projects (Naguib 2001; 2002; 2008). Among the foreign investors were institutions and individuals such as the Deutsche Orient-Gesellschaft and James Simon, and Denmark's Ny Carlsberg Foundation and Carl Jacobsen, who sponsored excavations in different locations in Egypt and Nubia (Bagh 2011; 2015; Jørgensen 2015). As Donald Malcom Reid rightly points out, archaeology in Egypt and Nubia had become the terrain of conflicting interests among Western imperialist powers. Decisions about Egyptian excavations and the politics of division of finds known as *partage à parties égales* were taken without involving Egyptian scholars and specialists in the field. The division of power between Britain and France was reinforced by the *entente cordiale* of 1904. France continued to dominate the cultural life in Egypt and controlled the concessions of archaeological excavations to foreign missions as well as the protection and documentation of the country's antiquities. The most prestigious institutions they created are the Service des Antiquités de l'Egypte, today the Ministry of State for Antiquities (MSA), and the Egyptian Museum in Cairo. Both institutions were under French leadership from 1858 until the revolution of 1952. Their main function has been to fight the looting of antiquities, the administration of

[5] http://imlichtvonamarna.de/ (December 7th 2012 - April 13th 2013).

concessions for excavation, the documentation and registration of monuments, and the preservation and conservation of the ancient Egyptian and Nubian cultural heritage (Reid 2002; 2015).

The second challenge Western archaeological museums face according to Hilgert and Desmarais relates to the manner in which exhibitions are conceived and how they shape 'surrogate cultures' by putting together groups of objects from various archaeological settings (Hilgert and Desmarais 2015: 23). Thus, it also concerns the controversial question of *disjecta membra* and by extension the legitimacy and ethical dimensions attached to cultural property. The world of museums is divided on the question of repatriation of cultural property and the different factions on these issues all have persuasive arguments for their cause. Defending the rights of the British Museum on the issue of the Elgin Marbles, Neil MacGregor, then director of the museum, declared:

> All great works of art are surely the common inheritance of humanity ... it is essential that there are places where the great creations of all civilizations can be seen together, and where the visitor can focus on what unites rather than what divides us. (MacGregor 2004).

John Henry Merryman (1986; 2009) proposed two dimensions to the discussions regarding policies about cultural property. One approach is 'nation-oriented' and the other is 'object-oriented'. The nation-oriented approach is tied to cultural nationalism. Accordingly, objects *belong* within the physical boundaries of the nations within which they are found or within which they are historically associated: the Elgin Marbles belong to Greece, Italian Renaissance paintings belong to Italy. (Merryman 2009: 187)

The object-oriented approach is more cosmopolitan and underscores three conceptually interdependent factors. These are *preservation* and the safeguard of various forms of material culture, *truth* in imparting knowledge and information about the object, and *access* for both scholars and the public. In *Who Owns Antiquity? Museums and the Battle over Our Ancient Heritage* (2008), James Cuno challenges the nationalistic positions and claims by countries like Italy, Greece, Egypt, Turkey and China that the acquisition of undocumented antiquities by museums encourages the looting of archaeological sites and that the ancient artefacts are the property of the state. He writes that 'antiquities are the cultural property of all humankind', they are the 'evidence of the world's ancient past and not that of a particular modern nation... antiquity knows no borders' (Cuno 2008: 127). He reiterates these arguments later in *Whose Culture? The Promise of Museums and the Debate over Antiquities* (2009), and in *Museums Matter: In Praise of the Encyclopedic Museum* (2011), and stresses the role of museums in conveying knowledge about 'our common past' and 'our common heritage' and how this knowledge can lead us to respect for, and understanding of, different cultures today. He argues that '[i]t is the promise of the encyclopedic museum to counter the nationalization of culture and its claim on antiquity' (Cuno 2009: 28), and that '[b]y displaying the sheer variety of art from varied visual cultures, the encyclopedic museums encourage a cosmopolitan view of the world' (Cuno 2011: 62). The cosmopolitan perception of, and practice in, antiquities has slowly been making its way in museums and archaeology (Meskell 2009). It draws upon Anthony Appiah Kvame's statement that from a cosmopolitan standpoint the universal always takes precedence over the local or national culture (Appiah 2006). Such an approach takes into account the various regimes of historicity that antiquities convey and how these intertwine in intricate ways. In practice, it implies that cultural artefacts and antiquities that have been taken more or less legally out of their countries of origin during colonial times are today transnational and, hence, belong to world culture and to humanity's common heritage. The road to viable solutions for these complex matters is still long and tortuous and it will surely take many years for the different parties to come to terms.

Developing politics of trust and the road to cosmopolitan practices

As mentioned above, multidisciplinarity and free-choice learning are the first steps in developing archaeology as a source and a resource for museums. Self-reflection in museums holding ancient Egyptian and Nubian archaeological collections is an important second step. Until now, these have been short-term measures used mainly in the planning and organization of temporary exhibitions. In order to develop long-term methods and a politics of trust among the many institutions, audiences and stakeholders supporting them, museums need to elaborate and put into practice varied sustainable projects that engage with both national authorities and local communities.

Sustainability is an ongoing process of social and cultural learning. Jon Hawkes maintained that culture constitutes the 'fourth pillar' of sustainable development besides the economic, social and environmental ones (Hawkes 2001). Adding the cultural dimension to sustainability acknowledges the significance of more intangible elements of culture pertaining to notions of identity, education, different bodies of knowledge and ways of enduring in times of change. Archaeological site museums and interpretation centres on the sites may play an important role in this matter in the future. Efforts in this sense are being implemented by different excavation projects, such as, for instance, the Amarna project.[6] Such projects have to be carefully planned and monitored. Writing about archaeological site museums in Turkey, Nevra Ertürk lists some of the main challenges such museums may encounter. Among the most important are the insufficient number of staff, inadequate facilities and poor display techniques, ongoing excavations, abandonment after the excavation seasons are over, inaccessibility and a lack of communication between the tourist and cultural sectors (Ertürk 2006: 343-344). The looting and acts of vandalism that have taken place in recent years in a number of locations in Egypt and the Middle East, especially in Irak and Syria, are significant reminders that it is crucial to elaborate and apply durable, cosmopolitan, practical solutions. Archaeological site museums and interpretation centres, which may be organized as branches of other, more established national and international museums, the so-called universal/encyclopaedic museums, require viable and effective management in order to achieve appropriate on-site preservation, documentation, research, training and exhibition. The main advantage of such practices in archaeological sites and museums is that the finds recovered from the excavations remain in their geographic and cultural contexts. They will not add to the countless ancient Egyptian *disjecta membra* in the already overfilled storerooms of other museums. Instead, they will be displayed in exhibitions on site and may be sent out on loan for special exhibitions abroad. Such projects and plans imply elaborating and putting into practice a cosmopolitan vision of museums and archaeology. To be realistic and sustainable, the projects must be well funded and must benefit the locality in which they are initiated. This demands the instigation of plans to raise public awareness and education among the local populations and encouraging their active involvement through workable long-term collaborative programmes.

Concluding thoughts

In their use of archaeology as a source and resource, museums in Western countries holding ancient Egyptian and Nubian artefacts emphasize the materiality and affective presence of the objects displayed. They apply an aesthetic framework in exhibitions, and experiment with different formats for visitor participation and free-choice learning. Exhibitions are more self-reflective; online, virtual exhibitions are available on the Internet and make the collections more accessible to varied audiences. These approaches bring the faraway past nearer to the present and render it more comprehensible. However, these same museums and Egyptian authorities still need to address and settle the many controversies regarding questions of cultural property and the restitution of antiquities. Demands for repatriation of cultural property have prompted novel perceptions of ownership pertaining to the realm of museums, especially among universal/encyclopaedic museums. Rather than boasting about their collections and presenting themselves as temples of knowledge, they now underscore their role as the custodians of a universal and diverse cultural heritage and of the world's memory. They stand now as cosmopolitan institutions that promote the dissemination of knowledge and respect for all cultures whether these have disappeared long ago or are still alive. More than 30 years ago, John H. Merryman (1986) argued that a way of resolving restitution claims might involve instigating a cosmopolitan approach to antiquities – what he called 'cultural internationalism'. This step entails instituting cultural agreements between the different parties in terms of long-term loans or joint stewardship as a form of 'sharing' culture (Lyons 2014: 262). Marc-André Renold goes even further in this direction. Taking the Rosetta Stone as an example, he suggests

[6] http://www.amarnaproject.com/

that a way of resolving disputes about ownership of antiquities and other cultural artefacts that have been taken away from the nation of origin would be to think in terms of cultural co-ownership (Renold 2015). The attitude of Egyptian authorities seems to have become more receptive to such ideas and open to negotiation. An article published in the aftermath of the 'Arab Spring' in the Egyptian newspaper *Al-Ahram Weekly* reflects this. The article takes up the case of the bust of Nefertiti and describes the Neues Museum in Berlin as Nefertiti's foster home. Here, the tone has changed from accusations of theft and claims of restitution of stolen art to the acceptance of facts and the acknowledgement of the care the bust of the queen and other Egyptian antiquities are receiving in that museum.[7]

Acknowledgements

This article was completed during my stay as a member of the research group *After Discourse: Things, Archaeology, and Heritage in the 21st Century*, at the Centre for Advanced Study (CAS), at the Norwegian Academy of Science and Letters in Oslo during the academic year 2016-2017. It is part of the wider project *Object Matters: Archaeology and Heritage in the 21st Century*, http://objectmatters.ruinmemories.org/. An earlier draft was presented at the 2014 conference of ICOM's International Committee of Egyptology (CIPEG), held at the Ny Carlsberg Glyptotek in Copenhagen. I am grateful to the participants for their useful comments.

References

Appiah, K. A. (2006). *Cosmopolitanism: Ethics in a World of Strangers*. New York: W.V. Norton.

Bagh, T. (2011). *Finds from W.M.F. Petrie's Excavations in Egypt in the Ny Carlsberg Glyptotek* (Meddelelser fra Ny Carlsberg Glyptotek, Ny serie nr. 13). Copenhagen: Ny Carlsberg Glyptotek.

Bagh, T. (2015). *Finds from J. Garstang's Excavations in Meroe and F.Ll. Griffith's in Kawa, Sudan in the Ny Carlsberg Glyptotek* (Meddelelser fra Ny Carlsberg Glyptotek, Ny serie nr. 17). Copenhagen: Ny Carlsberg Glyptotek.

Cuno, J. (2008). *Who Owns Antiquity? Museums and the Battle over Our Ancient Heritage*. Princeton: Princeton University Press.

Cuno, J. (ed.) (2009). *Whose Culture? The Promise of Museums and the Debate over Antiquities*. Princeton: Princeton University Press.

Cuno, J. (2011). *Museums Matter : In Praise of the Encyclopedic Museum*. Chicago: University of Chicago Press.

Ertürk, N. (2006). A Management Model for Archaeological Site Museums in Turkey. *Museum Management and Curatorship* 21: 336-348.

Falk, J. and Dierking, L. (2000). *Learning from Museums: Visitor Experiences and the Making of Meaning*. Lanham: AltaMira Press.

Fluck, C., Helmecke, G. and O'Connell, E. R. (eds) (2015). *Egypt: Faith after the Pharaohs*. London: British Museum Press.

Hawkes, J. (2001). *The Fourth Pillar of Sustainability: Culture's Essential Role in Public Planning*. Victorian Cultural Development Network. Common Ground P/L: Melbourne; http://www.culturaldevelopment.net.au/community/Downloads/HawkesJon(2001)TheFourthPillarOfSustainability.pdf (retrieved 15.3.2016).

Hilgert, M. and Desmarais, F. (2015). From Collecting to Protecting. The Role of the Archaeological Museum in Safeguarding Heritage. *ICOM News* 68 (3-4): 22-23.

Jørgensen, M. (2015). *Begyndelsen til det hele. Historien om brygger Carl Jacobsens ægyptiske samling 1884-1925*. København: Ny Carlsberg Glyptotek.

Lyons, C. L. (2014). Thinking about Antiquities: Museums and Internationalism. *International Journal of Cultural Property* 21 (3): 251- 265.

MacGregor, N. (2004). Oi, Hands Off Our Marbles! *The Sunday Times*, 18 January, section 5: 7.

Merryman, J. H. (1986). Two Ways of Thinking about Cultural Property. *American Journal of International Law* 80 (4): 831-853.

[7] http://weekly.ahram.org.eg/News/4691/47/Nefertiti's-foster-home.aspx (last accessed 25.11.2013).

Merryman, J.H. (2009). The Nation and the Object. In: J. Cuno (ed.) *Whose Culture? The Promise of Museums and the Debate over Antiquities*: 183-203. Princeton: Princeton University Press.
Meskell, L. (ed.) (2009). *Cosmopolitan Archaeologies*. Durham: Duke University Press.
Naguib, S. A. (2001). Modelling a Cosmopolitan Womanhood in Egypt (1850–1950). The Role of Nannies and French Catholic Girl Schools. *Acta Orientalia* 62: 92-106.
Naguib, S. A. (2002). Legal pluralism in the Mediterranean. The case of the mixed courts of Egypt 1875–1949. In: S. Naguib (ed.) The Intangible Heritage of the Mediterranean. Transmission, Adaptation and Innovation; 169-180. Occasional Papers from the Department of Culture Studies nr. 3. Oslo. Unpublished manuscript.
Naguib, S. A. (2004). From Temple to Information Centre. New Perspectives on the Role of Museums in the 21st Century. *Bulletin of the Egyptian Museum* 1: 55-60.
Naguib, S. A. (2008). Heritage in Movement. Rethinking Cultural Borrowings in the Mediterranean. *International Journal of Heritage Studies* 14 (5): 467-480.
Naguib, S. A. (2013). Translating the Ancient Egyptian worldview in museums. In: R. Nyord and K. Ryholt (eds) *Lotus and Laurel – Studies on Egyptian Language and Religion in Honour of Paul John Frandsen*: 233-240. Copenhagen: Museum Tusculanum.
Naguib, S. A. (forthcoming). Exploring Biographies. Ancient Egyptian funerary statuettes at the University Museum of Cultural History in Oslo. In: *CLARA Classical Art and Archaeology*; https://www.journals.uio.no/index.php/CLARA/index
Oppenheim, A., Arnold, Do., Arnold, Di. and Kei, Y. (eds) (2015). *Ancient Egypt Transformed: The Middle Kingdom*. New York : Metropolitan Museum of Art.
Poulot, D. (2005). *Musée et Muséologie*. Paris : La Découverte.
Reid, D. M. (2002). *Whose Pharaohs? Archaeology, Museums, and Egyptian National Identity from Napoleon to World War I*. Cairo: The American University in Cairo Press.
Reid, D. M. (2015). *Contesting Antiquity in Egypt. Archaeologies, Museums & the Struggle for Identities from World War I to Nasser*. Cairo: The American University in Cairo Press.
Renold, M. A. (2015). Cultural Co-ownership: Preventing and Solving Cultural Property Claims. *International Journal of Cultural Property* 22 (2–3): 163-176.
Seyfried, F. (ed.) (2012). *In the Light of Amarna. 100 Years of the Nefertiti Discovery*. Ägyptische Museum und Papyrussammlung. Berlin: Staatliche Museen zu Berlin.
Wieczorkiewicz, A. (2005). Unwrapping mummies and telling their stories: Egyptian mummies in museum rhetoric. In: M. Bouquet and N. Porto, *Science, Magic and Religion. The Ritual Processes of Museum Magic*: 51-71. New York: Berghahn Books.

'Egypt and the recalcitrant Pharaoh.' Origin and function of a biblical motif[1]

Kåre Berge
NLA Høgskolen Bergen

An ethnic charter myth

The so-called Exodus story in the bible (Exodus 1-15) appears as an 'Israelite' ethnic or national charter myth (Toorn 1996: 182, 287, 2001). The term 'charter myth' refers to narratives about a group's ethnic or national past, which serve as a 'charter' for social actions and identity formation in the actual group. As such, the narrative is a practice of ethnic or national identity; it is a retrospective moral pattern of behaviour. The narrative gives the present social structure meaning and moral significance through a narrative reference to the past.

Ethnic identity is a phenomenon that is invented and constructed by creating boundaries that define the difference between Us (the in-group) and Other or Them (the out-group). Ethno-symbolism, i.e., nationality and ethnicity investigated from the perspective of Geisteswissenschaften, contains an emotional element. In the Exodus story, ethnic boundary markers are allotted to the notions of 'Egypt' and 'Pharaoh'. It is the purpose of this paper to assess the literary connections of these two notions in the Exodus narrative and their possible historical and mythical origin.

Biblical 'Egypt'

In the bible, Egypt is the most common 'foreign nation'. It appears more than 680 times, while Assyria appears 151 times and Babylon 262. This is remarkable, since the latter two nations represented more acute historical threats to the two political kingdoms of Israel and Judah than Egypt. In the Book of Isaiah, whose prophet is set in the time of the Iron Age Assyrian hegemony of Syria-Palestine, Egypt occurs 51 times, as compared to Assyria's 44; and in the book of Jeremiah, whose preoccupation is very much with the Babylonian conquest of the two kingdoms, Egypt appears 62 times, as compared to Babylon's 169.

'Egypt' does not carry a single meaning in the texts of the Hebrew bible, but rather is associated with multiple topoi. It is used to warn against searching for military help from Pharaoh, against serving as a place of refuge, in threats of Egyptian attacks against Israel, or in direct oracles of judgment against Egypt. One topos overshadows the others, however. This is the idea of Israelite bondage and rescue from Egypt. We do not know the origin or age of this topos. It dominates in rather late biblical texts in Exodus through to Deuteronomy, in the so-called historical books and in the post-exilic Book of Ezekiel. This topos was known by the literati who created the books of the prophets Hosea (2:14-15; 9:10; 11:1, 5; 12:10, 14) and Amos (2:10; 3:1; 9:7), but there are no details. Even when these prophets are set in the eighth century, we cannot know whether these texts testify to eighth-century knowledge. Amos 4:10 mentions pestilence sent against Egypt, which might correspond to one of the plagues in Egypt (Ex. 9:3), but pestilence is a common topos in biblical and ancient Oriental curses and can hardly count as evidence of the biblical topos of the rescue from Egypt, as witnessed in, for example, Esarhaddon's Accession Treaty (Parpola 1987: 172).

The story of the plagues in Egypt, the recalcitrant Egyptian Pharaoh, the killing of the firstborn of the Egyptians and the Israelites' crossing of the sea occurs in different ways in the bible, but is not widely distributed. It appears in the Book of Exodus as the founding myth of Pesach, in the Book of Psalms in penitential prayers as a reference to God's unfathomable mercy and the Israelites' incomprehensible

[1] During the 1990s, when I was writing a book on the biblical Exodus narrative, I was lucky enough to benefit from Professor Richard Holton Pierce's broad knowledge of, and insight into, Egyptian texts and language, but also the theory of text and language. This is a small expression of gratitude.

rebellion against God (Psalms 78; 105; 106), and in summary references and standard formulas in the Book of Jeremiah (33: 21). As such, the topos appears only in late biblical texts. We do not know why Egypt is the central location for these ideas.

'Traditional' biblical scholarship has looked for an origin of the topos in the Late Bronze Age in the thirteenth century B.C.E. Today, however, a number of influential scholars argue for an origin in the time period from the Late Monarchic through to the Persian period. Some scholars trust the Hosea and Amos texts as evidence from the eighth century (Liverani 2005: 278-79). Finkelstein refers to the Kuntillet 'Ajrud inscriptions (in the north-eastern Sinai) as evidence of Samarian activity in this area, with possible interference with Egypt (Finkelstein 2013: 148-50), but it does not testify to any 'Egypt Exodus story'. Some scholars argue that this motif had its origin in Canaan and that the motif was later transferred to Egypt in biblical memory (Na'aman 2011). This paper only presents evidence of Egyptian activity in Syria-Palestine as possible backgrounds for the motif.

From biblical, Palestinian and Egyptian sources, we have clear evidence of Egyptian activity in this area in the Middle and Late Bronze Ages and Early Iron Age. Egyptian presence in Palestine during the 19th and 20th Dynasties is witnessed, especially in Beth-shean and Megiddo (thirteenth - twelfth century B.C.E.) (Finkelstein 2013: 21). In an inscription from Beth-shean, Sethos I 'had taught the princes of Syria a lesson' in his first year (1290) (Weippert 2010: 156). The so-called Merneptah stele is one of the only known inscriptions mentioning Egyptian activity in Palestine. It is unclear how Egyptian control of 'Canaan/Israel' (Merneptah stele) influenced the highlands. Egyptian influence seems mainly to have concentrated on the Negev desert, the coastal plain and the areas from Megiddo and to the north-east, with only a few references to the Judaean highlands, with occasional evidence of later Egyptian activity. Israel Finkelstein states that the collapse of Egyptian rule in Palestine was followed by a wave of settlement in the highlands (Finkelstein 2013: 22).

In biblical texts, there is the memory of 'King Shishak of Egypt' and his military campaign against Jerusalem (1 Kgs 14:25-26 NRSV):

> In the fifth year of King Rehoboam, King Shishak of Egypt came up against Jerusalem; he took away the treasures of the house of the Lord and the treasures of the king's house; he took everything. He also took away all the shields of gold that Solomon had made; so King Rehoboam made shields of bronze instead, and committed them to the hands of the officers of the guard, who kept the door of the king's house.

This was – if the text reflects historical realities – about 925 B.C.E. Shishak has long been identified as Pharaoh Shoshenq I, whose campaigns are counted on the Bubastite portal at Karnak. It is a much discussed feature of this list that Jerusalem is lacking, while a number of other towns in the highlands north of Jerusalem, the Jezreel Valley, areas in Transjordan and in Western Palestine are counted, for example Beth-shean, Rehob, Gibeon and Megiddo, and also in the Negev. There seems to be no sound reason against the assumption that this Pharaoh attacked areas in 'Israel' (Finkelstein 2013: 76-77).

A lethal Egyptian attack seems to have taken place on the Judaean king Josiah in a battle at Megiddo (ca. 609 B.C.E.), according to biblical evidence (2 Kgs 23:19, 2 Kgs 23:29-30 (NRSV)):

> Now the rest of the acts of Josiah, and all that he did, are they not written in the Book of the Annals of the Kings of Judah? In his days Pharaoh Necho, king of Egypt, went up to the king of Assyria to the river Euphrates. King Josiah went to meet him; but when Pharaoh Necho met him at Megiddo, he killed him. His servants carried him dead in a chariot from Megiddo, brought him to Jerusalem, and buried him in his own tomb. The people of the land took Jehoahaz son of Josiah, anointed him, and made him king in place of his father.

This must have been Necho II. The ostracon Karnak LS 462.4, which is a later historical source, however, mentions a campaign by Psammeticus (I, in his 28th year, 637 B.C.E.) towards Syria, but it does not mention anything about the campaign itself, just that he stayed in Daphne, a fortress in the eastern Nile delta. More substantial is the Ryland papyrus (IX), which mentions a campaign in Syria by King Psammeticus (II, in his 4th year, 591 B.C.E.). This must have been after the decisive defeat of the Egyptian army by Nebuchadnezzar at Carchemish in 605 B.C.E. The Babylonian Chronicle 5 (by Weippert, called Ostracon E) tells that he, though still a crown prince, totally defeated the Egyptians and tore them completely apart: 'not a single person returned to his homeland' (Weippert 2010: 415). It is possible, although not documented, that the Judahite king had to submit to the Egyptian king from 637 or at least in the time span from 616 B.C.E. until the defeat at Carchemish about ten years later. The Babylonian chronicle also informs us about an Egyptian campaign against the Babylonians in Nabopolassar's tenth year (616 B.C.E.) and then again in year 17 (609) (Weippert 2010: 410, 13). It is unclear how the possible Egyptian control of at least the coastal line of Palestine ('Syria') corresponds to the biblical notices about Josiah's apparent control of the highlands north of Jerusalem, all the way to Samaria, which was a part of the Assyrian province of the former kingdom of Israel.

The theme of the Egyptian bondage and rescue from the land has no evident origin in these historical witnesses. It may, however, justify the view that the Egyptian oppression and attacks against the two kingdoms could serve as a 'site of memory' for ideas of a rescue from the Egyptians, as Na'aman suggests (see above), but does not explain the origin of the motif itself.

Notable among Egyptologists dealing with biblical texts on 'Israel in Egypt' are Donald B. Redford and Jan Assmann, both of whom try to explain the motif's origin. Let me give a brief presentation of their respective takes on the theme, which go in different directions, at least at first sight.

Israel in Egypt as an 'Erinnerungsfigur' – Jan Assmann

Jan Assmann does not deal with history but memory (Assmann 1997; 1998; 2003). Moses is a figure of memory, not of history (Assmann 1997: 18). The Exodus story tells us nothing about Ramesses II, Egypt is just a symbolic construction, and the text informs us more about the political theology of the seventh to fifth century B.C.E. than about the Late Bronze Age. As an 'Erinnerungsfigur', a figure of memory, it is a symbolic expression of the so-called 'mosaische Unterscheidung' (Assmann 2002: 248). On the other hand, also according to Assmann, without the Amarna period, there would probably be no Moses as a 'figure of memory'. What Assmann seems to indicate is that the whole idea of 'Moses in Egypt' originates from the Amarna experiences and is developed from this, but there is a long way and a significant change during the tradition that lead on to the Moses story in its current form in the biblical text. In fact, the historical complexity of the Egypt-Israel continuum disappears in the biblical narrative, which becomes a 'konstellativer Mythos' that has the semantic energy of a 'Gegenreligion' witnessed in the Old Testament. Somehow, according to Assmann, this also has connections with the extra-biblical legends developed from the Amarna religion. Assmann's idea of 'Gegenreligion' refers back to Theo Sundermeier's distinction between primary and secondary religion (Assmann 2003: 11), but takes it a step further. This is book religion, the monotheistic distinction between false and true religion, a religion of exclusive truth, and a theology of negation (of other gods), of intolerance. The narrative (not the historical reality) of this negation appears in the form of 'eine Geschichte der Gewalt in einer Serie von Massakern' (Assmann 2003: 36). This, he says, is what appears in the biblical narratives.

According to Assmann, the religious revolution by Amenophis IV is all that is historically interesting, but only insofar as it represents the first 'Gegenreligion' in the world, although in terms that are very different from the Mosaic one. Any historical connection between Amenophis and the memory of Moses is 'science fiction' (Assmann 1998: 48). The connection is only one of memory and tradition. In Assmann's view, this connection is through the combination of the Jews and the Amarna time in Josephus's Contra Apionem, in which Josephus deals with (and refers to) Manetho's picture of Amenophis and the Jews, and in the other extra-biblical narratives of Moses in Egypt, all of which are written in the final centuries B.C.E. and in the early Christian centuries. Again, Assmann holds that there is (probably) no historical connection between Moses and Egypt in the Amarna Age. On the contrary, the first historical meeting between the Jews (as described by Manetho and by Josephus) and the Egyptians was possibly in the sixth century B.C.E., when refugees from Judah went to Egypt (Assmann 1998: 58), although Assmann does not exclude a possible distant connection with the Amarna religion. The point made by Assmann is that the Amarna religion, like the biblical one, appears as a 'Gegenreligion' as described above, in a similar but also very different manner to the Mosaic religion.

Assmann postulates that the Exodus story originates from the theological idea of the divine election of Israel (which, according to scholars today, mostly dates to the seventh century B.C.E.), which connected with 'Canaanite folk legends' and memories of Canaanite Hyksos in Egypt. He does not claim any connection between the Hyksos and the Israelites (Assmann 1998: 68). On the other hand, the idea of a 'Gegenreligion' developed in Egypt after the Amarna period, when the Hyksos became (in Egyptian memory) the stereotypical religious enemy, testified to by Manetho and others: the land of Egypt is in a miserable situation, due to the invisibility of the gods. This results from the land being polluted by leprosy. The strange peoples, in Assmann's reading the representatives of idolatry, have to be expelled from the land. The historical religion of Akhenaton is of no importance in Assmann's concept except for its function in the narrative of the expelled ('[die] Geschichte der Aussätzigen') in the later debate about Moses and Egypt; that is, as a narrative topos (Assmann 1998: 28-29).

So, according to Assmann, what is the connection between Egypt and the biblical Moses-Egypt story? It is through the Amarna traditions, as expressed in different 'Legenden über die 'Aussätzigen' (Assmann 1998: 278) known through texts from the final centuries B.C.E. These traditions have a long history before they appear in the texts known by us (p. 278):

> Die Amarna-Episode geriet innerhalb von höchstens achtzig Jahren in vollständige Vergessenheit. Die Erfahrungen waren aber traumatisch genug, um Legenden schauerlicher religiöser Frevel hervorzubringen, die ... im offiziellen Gedächtnis gewissermassen fliessend wurden und sich mit allen möglichen Erinnerungen und Erfahrungen früher und späterer Zeit anreichern konnten.

Assmann also postulates a historical contact between the Judaeans and Egypt in the wake of the Jerusalem destruction after 600. The main point, however, is the cultural or rather political meaning of the story, which is incompatible with the Amarna religion. Moses the Egyptian becomes a figure of memory, which does not mean that the name refers to a real person and a real event, but more like a symbol or a mental concept, which stands for the cultural separation of biblical, monotheistic 'Gegenreligion' from false, polytheistic religion, figuring the memory of a 'conversion' (Assmann 1998: 24-25), a term that refers more to a 'mentality' than a historical event. In his view, the political theology of the Exodus story is expressed through political terminology, but after the story it is no longer represented as a political order and institution but as a separate order beside the political. Religion becomes 'eine ausdifferenzierte Handlungsphäre'. This is what he also calls an 'Umbuchung' of political terminology, which also means a liberation of the religious space from the power of the state. This is what the Exodus story is about (Assmann 2002: 50-51).

To my mind, there is something in this idea of 'Umbuchung' that corresponds to elements in other biblical texts. In my opinion, the ideology of another biblical book, Deuteronomy, represents the attempt of a Judaean group to establish an informal, that is, religious authority outside the Persian political authority system in the post-exilic Persian province of Yehud. Assmann's postulated links back to the Amarna religion seem highly speculative. However, a possible connection between the biblical Exodus motif and the Egyptian 'Legenden der Aussätzungen' warrants further investigation.

Historically, there are other points of contact between Egypt and the Syrian/Palestine/Israelite area. Sources long before the origin of biblical texts show how ambassadors with Egyptian links travelled through different city states in northern Israel and Syria, and an Egyptian text dated to the time of Ramesses III notes that there was an Egyptian temple in Gaza (Weippert, HTAT text 068, p. 173f.). In Persian and early Hellenistic times, a time frame relevant to major parts of the Hebrew bible, we have texts from the Jewish community at Elephantine, Yeb. What is remarkable about this group is that they celebrated Yahweh (Yaho) in their Yaho temple, but the texts also refer to some other deities (Becking 2011: 411). The independence of Elephantine Jews (in itself probably an anachronistic term) from the Jerusalem community is debated. Letters show the presence of mutual contact (see especially Kratz (2006)). In addition, we know from biblical sources that Jews fled to Egypt during the Babylonian conquest of Jerusalem and the kingdom of Judah (right after 600 B.C.E.) (2 Kgs 25:26, as also mentioned by Assmann). These points of contact hardly explain the centrality of Egypt in biblical texts, but at least they open up the opportunity to see some connections. We do not know whether other diaspora groups had their own Yahweh temples, but Ezra 8:17 may indicate that there was one in Casiphia, possibly a place in Babylonia.

A Persian-time 'Moses?' – Donald B. Redford

Another Egyptologist, Donald Redford, goes in part in the same direction. The Joseph and Moses stories exhibit clear signs of being created in the Persian period (Redford 2011: 299-307). This applies in particular to the biblical names Goshen, Pithom and Ramses. Redford follows Assmann in connecting the literary traditions of '(1) the Osarseph story, derived from an etiology of the Amarna age; (2) the Bocchoris story, a product of the Saite tradition, (3) the Exodus account of Exodus 1-14; and (4) the Egypto-Jewish riposte' (p. 328), which is 'contained in the Judeo-pagan polemic, reflected in Artapanus and Josephus (among others)' (p. 324). Redford states (p. 328):

> All four reflect communal stances assumed by the exigencies of the late fifth and fourth centuries B.C.E. and underpinned by a cycle of mnemo-historic orality, no part of which is extraneous to the whole or occupies a privileged position in tradition history.

Redford first lists a number of features in Artapanus and Josephus, which pretended to have more detailed knowledge of 'Moses in Egypt' than Exodus (see the list on p. 326). Decisive in Redford's argument is the fact that the Exodus account betrays an awareness of the other Egyptian stories. Redford refers to the Egyptian sensitivity toward the abomination of slaughtering sacred animals (Ex. 8:26), the return of the shepherds (Ex. 3:1), the fear of increased enemy forces (Ex. 1:10), the potter's kiln (the ashes in Ex. 9:8-10) and leprosy (Ex. 9:10-11).

As a conclusion, Redford states that the Moses of the Exodus narrative has nothing to do with Egypt, and 'is thoroughly alien to the culture of the Nile land. Furthermore, the story lacks narrative integrity, containing undeveloped folklore that reduces the individual plagues to mythemes outside a syntagmatic structure.' (p. 325)

Like Assmann, Redford seems to presume, however, that the Egypt stories listed above derive some memories and a historical core from the reigns of Amenophis III and Akhenaten (fourteenth century B.C.E.) (p. 309), and from Bocchoris of the 24th Dynasty (ca. 717-711 B.C.E.) (pp. 311-312). The Joseph-Moses stories fall within the general West-Semitic memory and collective consciousness of a movement from the Levantine coast into Egypt in the Middle Bronze Age and their subsequent expulsion, the so-called 'Hyksos phenomenon'. The argument for linking the Exodus story to this tradition is the prophetical claim that Israel participated in an exodus (the prophets Amos, Hosea, Micah and others). While it is correct that a scholarly tradition has dated these texts to the eighth century, there is no clear evidence of such a dating, and the references listed by Redford may come from a much later time.

However, even when Redford does find early historical roots, the main impression of these stories, according to him, anchors them in the Saite period. The point is that the whole Exodus story (together with the Joseph novella in Genesis) breathes the literary ideals and 'the denigration of kingship in popular oral tradition issued in the plot of the weak and/or deceitful king who must be saved by the intercession of a magician/wise man' (p. 283), as reflected in, for example, Herodotus. Redford identifies a story type that arose during the Kushite-Saite period and became common in the Persian and Ptolemaic eras. This type includes 'the crisis that desperately requires solution, the inability of the king to act, the dream or night vision and the magician/wise man who saves the day' (p. 285).

So, how is the Moses-Egypt story of the biblical text linked to Egypt? In Redford's reading, the historical background is the Egyptian emergence from Persian occupation, internal restoration and active foreign policy, especially towards the Levant in the years 414-390 B.C.E. The biblical Exodus story is an 'inversion' of the self-conscious Egyptian apprehension toward the north (p. 322f.):

> [T]he rigors of Persian occupation and the successful rebellion of Sais and Mendes (411-399 B.C.E.) provided the background to the legend of the detrimental nature of northern occupation, the continued threat from the north, and the desirability of expelling the indigestible alien elements.

In this reading, the exodus narrative appears as 'an inverted expulsion myth', so to speak, a myth in which the expulsion is seen from the other side, from those expelled. It is the idea of the 'foreign' groups in Egypt that side with the enemy seeking to return the Persians into Egypt (Ex. 1:8-10). However, it is not easy to follow Redford's logic here. If the folklore talks about the foreign invasion and deliverance, and ideas of how the Egyptians have expelled the occupiers, how do Genesis and Exodus 'perfectly mirror' the reality of these times, as he states? This 'mirroring' seems more relevant to the Joseph story than to the Moses narrative: the Persian occupation in the fifth century was a period, he claims, that enabled the descent of foreign groups into Egypt. It is also possible, according to Redford, to explain a wish among these groups to return, but this does not explain the Moses story. So Redford's extensive presentation of relevant material and reflections does not present us with any specific explanation of the origin of the Exodus story, although his material points in the direction of a Persian (or even later) period of origin.

Egypt, Pharaoh and the monster myth

Let me now move to a more internal biblical interpretation of the different motifs behind the Moses-Egypt story. This helps in seeing how the notions of Egypt and Pharaoh function as narrative mythemes (essential kernels) in the story.

First, it is possible to argue that there are links to biblical wisdom, which on the other hand is international, linked thematically to Egyptian and Mesopotamian wisdom literature. In the bible, this wisdom connects with notions of the Torah in a system of piety that I have called Torah didacticism. Thus, the whole story of the Exodus ends with a notice about a polluted water source turned sweet (Ex. 15:26):

> There the Lord made for them a statute and an ordinance and there he put them to the rest. He said, 'If you will listen carefully to the voice of the Lord your God, and do what is right in his sight, and give heed to his commandments and keep all his statutes, I will not bring upon you any of the diseases that I brought upon the Egyptians; for I am the Lord who heals you'.

In addition, Pharaoh pretends to be wise, attempting to stop the Israelites from growing into a dangerous and large people by throwing the Israelite male infants into the Nile. However, he himself, or at least his army, is killed by water, while the Israelites walk through the parted water on dry ground. Ironically, his own daughter, while bathing at the Nile shore, rescues the Moses baby, the one who causes Pharaoh's army to drown. In biblical terms, this resembles the Tun-Ergehen notions present in many wisdom texts in the bible (Psalm 1). The biblical Psalm 78, the most extensive narrative of the Plague story, begins its presentation by calling it an instruction, a song that imparts wisdom, which tells riddles of the past. The riddle that is told for instruction is exactly about God's rescue of the people through the plagues in Egypt, and the people's failure to be faithful. They deceived him and lied to him.

Second, this wisdom-related Torah piety only explains half of the story. Why this special picture of Pharaoh and all the plagues? There is another link. This is the myth of God's battle with the sea monster. In her 1973 book, God's Battle with the Monster, Mary K. Wakeman documented how this myth underlies the Exodus story (Wakeman 1973). In another article, I have demonstrated the didactical significance of 'water' in the Exodus story (Berge 2014a). In the present paper, I will turn my attention more to the mythic side of the water. This feature, and its relation to the monster myth, has been further investigated by Diana Edelman (Edelman 2012: 162-66).

As stated at the beginning of this paper, the Exodus story is a part of an ethnic charter myth, a myth of identity, in which identity is expressed through the notion of 'othering'. It is clear from the Book of Ezekiel chapters 29 and 32 that the mythic element of the sea monster played a role in the process of 'bordering' and 'othering' in the concept of identity in exilic and post-exilic biblical literature. In this, even Egypt or Pharaoh is described as tannin, the sea monster (Ezek. 29:3 and 32:2), and the idea of salty water becoming sweet, as in the text cited from Ex. 15:25, is a part of the temple visions in Ezek. 48:8 and Zech. 14:8. So there are clear links to this monster myth in biblical literature, although they are more explicit outside of the Exodus story.

Now, Diana Edelman has listed a number of biblical references to the mythic complex of thought concerning the establishment of kingship in heaven and the cosmic order, represented in the Ba'al cycle from Ugarit and the Enuma Elish, among which are Isa. 27:1; 51:9-10; Ps. 66:6; 74:13; 89:6, 8, 10-11; Job 7:12; 9:13 and Ezek. 29:3-6; 32:2-8. The Ba'al 'cycle recounts the successful contest of the storm god to occupy the throne of the gods, dislodging Yam, the god of the sea', she says (p. 163). As the biblical cases noted above show, reflections of this myth appear in ample notions of Yahweh defeating Rahab, Yam (the Sea), Lotan or Tannin. It is not so directly apparent in the Exodus myth, but Edelman demonstrates that there are clear references. In the book of Exodus,

> chaotic forces disrupt the established order and require the king of heaven once more to manifest as a warrior, defeat human or divine enemies, and re-establish order. Yahweh's supremacy and status as the only god in heaven is challenged by a false god, Pharaoh. (p. 163)

In Ex. 14:21-22, Yahweh becomes Israel's sovereign king 'and enters into a formal, binding pact that establishes law, justice and loyalty as the basis of their special relationship' (pp. 165-66).

Following the lead of Edelman, it is possible to say that Pharaoh fits into the role of the sea monster in the monster myth. He seemingly controls the water of the Nile, but it turns out to be the Israelite God Yahweh who controls it, first by turning its water into blood, and secondly by killing Pharaoh's army by water. As in the creation myth of Genesis 1, which also contains remains of the fight against the chaotic water monster, God divides the water and lets the dry ground appear, which opens a path for the Israelites to cross over. Through this battle against Pharaoh, Yahweh manifests himself as the supreme God, 'so that you may know that there is no one like me in the whole land/on the whole earth' (Ex. 9:14), and 'so that my name may be declared in all the earth/all the land' (v. 16), which is clearly a royal epithet. The heavenly king takes his position against the monsters, also called 'all the Gods in Egypt'.

Back to the monster myth, 'The monster is by definition irregular, irrational, erratic, lacking positive intention. God differs from the monster in one respect that is never accepted, and that is that he (who is the law) regulates the exercise of his powers. The reality that is God is by definition intended, and legal' (Wakeman 1973: 138). This is a good picture of Pharaoh and the Israelite God, who 'sets law and judgment' just as he turns bitter or salty water sweet at the end of the Exodus narrative (Ex. 15:26).

Telling origin myths is a way of 'remembering' for the purpose of creating or maintaining identity. This is clear from the Pesach ritual that concludes the Plague narrative. Central to this ritual is the retelling of the myth, the teaching of the myth to the young generation (12:24).

This is also an instance of identity formation through 'othering', a notion I have developed in another article (Berge 2014b). Their sacrificial practice of Pesach is a ritual of separation and demarcation. It is no ritual of atonement. The blood on the doorposts distinguishes the Israelites from the Egyptians. But even the wandering through the split sea divides, and through this separates the Israelites from the non-Israelites.

Liminal Symbolism and the Shaping of Identity

The notion of water is part of a wider set of liminal symbolism in the Exodus story. By 'liminality', I refer to ideas of being 'betwixt and between'; it is a term defined by A. van Gennep (for applications of his model, see below). A number of studies have noted the liminal character of the Exodus story and applied van Gennep's tripartite ritual scheme of rites of passage to the Exodus - Wilderness - Conquest, in different ways. E. Leach mentions briefly the biblical wilderness as a liminal zone in V. Turner's sense (Leach in Leach and Aycock 1983: 41), the symbolism of which he has developed in another publication (Leach in Alter and Kermode 1987: 587ff.). R. Hendel has regarded the escape from Egyptian slavery as the separation phase, the encounter with Yahweh at Sinai as the liminal one and the journey homeward as the reaggregation phase (Hendel 1989: 158-61). He also compares Moses' Midianite sojourn to rites of initiation in other cultures. P. McNutt combines the iron furnace metaphor of Israel's stay in Egypt (the root metaphor of transforming iron from a soft ore to a metal of strength) with the processual structure of rites of passage (McNutt 1990). She finds the Ancestral period (Genesis) to be the previous state, the Egypt/Wilderness period (Exodus - Deuteronomy) to be the transition state and Israel in the Promised Land to be the transformed state. The process of aggregation (rebirth) starts in Exodus 15, but it is the wilderness that symbolizes liminality or marginality par excellence. The final rebirth is the crossing of the Jordan river. Interestingly, McNutt also notes that Pharaoh and the plagues are representatives of the chaos of liminality, but her special focus at this point is on the Midianites/Kenites (in Genesis 37ff. and in Exodus) as marginal figures and mediators in the process of transition.

As for the Pesah ritual (Exodus 12), the folklore studies by S. Niditch indicate that it represents the liminal transition phase of rites of passage (Niditch 1993), whereas W. H. C. Propp suspects there is an initiation rite (rite of passage) behind the Exodus-Wandering-Conquest tradition (Propp 1999). He also makes the point that the typical rite of passage leads the candidate back to his (physical) starting point, which is not the case in the Exodus story, unless one regards the absence from Canaan in Genesis as the story's starting point (p. 35f.; see also pp. 239f.). Specifically, he points to the wandering in the desert as liminal; and the Pesah-Massot as a rite of passage from season to season (the spring), in which the week-long celebration of Massot is presented as a liminal (transitional) period. In addition to that, he also indicates that there is a ritual pattern of male initiation behind the episode in Ex. 4:24-26, and possibly also behind the Pesah (Propp 1993: 513f.). Both scholars use the van Gennep terminology in its more original, concrete meaning as a description of types and phases of a ritual process.

This presentation of different scholars shows that there are a number of ways to apply liminal symbolism to the Exodus narrative. In any case, the Exodus story is a story of initiation, a narrative of institution, or rather of installation or inauguration. This is a story of legitimation and identity formation. The function of a rite of passage is to endow somebody with social prerogatives of rights and duties. Through such rites, and probably also through the relevant stories and myths, one changes the person's or group's reality by altering their vision of their reality; this also includes a change in conduct. All this is what the Exodus myth leads up to, as is clear in the small notice of polluted water turned sweet in Exodus 15:24-26, which terminates the concluding battle hymn about the crossing of the sea.

As a conclusion, the Exodus story/Moses-Egypt story appears as a narrative that integrates a number of motifs from biblical and Canaanite traditions, while also playing on Egyptian folklore or legends in biblical 'post-exilic' time, that is, the late Persian period. Historical material from the Bronze Age would not be found in the story. The lack of consistency indicates a complicated process of origin, but in no case does the text provide historical evidence of an Israelite liberation from the Ramesses period. The notions and motifs coming from different literary and mythical contexts and contributing to the topos of 'Egypt and Pharaoh' create an identity of 'Israel' through bordering and 'othering'.

References

Alter, Robert and Kermode, Frank (eds) (1987). *The Literary Guide to the Bible.* Cambridge (MA): The Belknap Press of Harvard University Press.

Assmann, Jan (1997). *Moses the Egyptian: The Memory of Egypt in Western Monotheism*: 276. Cambridge (MA): Harvard University Press.

Assmann, Jan (1998). *Moses der Ägypter. Entzifferung einer Gedächtnisspur.* Frankfurt: Fischer Taschenbuch Verlag.

Assmann, Jan (2002). *Herrschaft und Heil. Politische Theologie in Altägypten, Israel und Europa.* Frankfurt: Fischer Taschenbuch Verlag.

Assmann, Jan (2003). *Die Mosaische Unterscheidung.* München: Carl Hanser Verlag.

Becking, Bob (2011). Yehudite identity in Elephantine. In: O. Lipschits, G. N. Knoppers and M. Oeming (eds) *Judah and the Judeans in the Achaemenid Period*: 403-20. Winona Lake: Eisenbrauns.

Berge, K. (2014a). Polluted, bitter, and sweet water as a matter of ethnic identity:Formation in Persian Yehud. In Ehud Ben Zvi and Christoph Levin (eds) *Thinking of Water in the Early Second Temple Period* (Beihefte zur Zeitschrift für die alttestamentliche Wissenschaft, 461): 103-22. Berlin/Boston: De Gruyter.

Berge, K. (2014b). Categorical identities: 'Ethnified otherness and sameness' – A tool for understanding boundary negotiotiation in the Pentateuch? In: Ehud Ben Zvi and Diana V. Edelman (eds) *Imagining the Other and Constructing Israelite Identity in the Early Second Temple Period Library of Hebrew Bible* (Old Testament Studies 456): 70-88. London and New York: Bloomsbury.

Edelman, Diana (2012). Exodus and Pesach-Massot as evolving social memory. In: E. Ben Zvi and C. Levin (eds) *Remembering and Forgetting in Early Second Temple* (Forschungen zum Alten Testament): 161-194. Tübingen: Mohr Siebeck.

Finkelstein, Israel (2013). *The Forgotten Kingdom: The Archaeology and History of Northern Israel* (Ancient Near Eastern Monographs). Atlanta: Society of Biblical Literature.

Hendel, R. S. (1989). Sacrifice as a Cultural System: The Ritual Symbolism of Exodus 24,3-8. *Zeitschrift für die Alttestamentliche Wissenschaft* 101: 366-390.

Kratz, R.G. (2006). The Second Temple of Jeb and of Jerusalem. In: O. Lipschits and M. Oeming (eds) *Judah and the Judeans in the Persian Period*: 247-264. Winona Lake: Eisenbrauns.

Leach, Edmund and Aycock, D. Alan (1983). *Structuralist Interpretations of Biblical Myths.* Cambridge: Cambridge University Press.

Liverani, M. (2005). *Israel's History and the History of Israel.* London: Equinox.

McNutt, Paula (1990). The Forging of Israel: Iron Technology, Symbolism, and Tradition in Ancient Society. *Journal for the Study of the Old Testament* (Supplement Series). Sheffield: Almond Press.

Na'aman, Nadav (2011). The Exodus Story: Between Historical Memory and Historiographical Composition. *Journal of Ancient Near Eastern Religions* 11: 39-69.

Niditch, Susan (1993). *Folklore and the Hebrew Bible.* Minneapolis: Fortress Press.

Parpola, Simo (1987). Neo-Assyrian Treaties from the Royal Archives of Niniveh. *Journal of Cuneiform Studies* 39 (2): 161-89.

Propp, W. H. C. (1993). The Bloody Bridegroom (Exodus 4:24–26). *Vetus Testamentum* 43: 495-518.

Propp, W. H. C. (1999). Exodus 1–18: *A New Translation with Introduction and Commentary* (The Anchor Bible 2). New York: Doubleday.

Redford, Donald (2011). Some observations on the traditions surrounding 'Israel in Egypt'. In: O. Lipschits, G.N. Knoppers and M. Oeming (eds) *Judah and the Judeans in the Achaemenid Period: Negotiating Identity in an International Context*: 279-364. Winona Lake: Eisenbrauns.

Toorn, K. van der (1996). *Family Religion in Babylonia, Syria and Israel: Continuity and Change in the Forms of Religious Life* (SHANE 7). Leiden: Brill.

Toorn, K. van der (2001). The Exodus as charter myth. In: J. W. van Henten and A. Houtepen (eds) *Religious Identity and the Invention of Tradition: Papers Read at Noster Conference in Soesterberg*, Januar 4–6. (Studies in Theology and Religion 3): 113. Assen: Royal van Gorcum.

Wakeman, Mary K. (1973). *God's Battle with the Monster: A Study in Biblical Imagery* VIII: 149 s. Leiden: Brill,

Weippert, Manfred (2010). *Historisches Textbuch zum Alten Testament.* (Grundrisse zum Alten Testament. Das Alte Testament Deutch, Ergänzungsreihe 10). Göttingen: Vandenhoeck & Ruprecht.

A 'Sayings Gospel' attested at Nag Hammadi

Einar Thomassen
University of Bergen

Nag Hammadi studies have a long history at the University of Bergen, harking back to the earliest days of the Religion department in the late 1960s. The excitement created at the time by the newly discovered texts, and by the prospects they offered for rewriting the history of early Christianity in the multi-religious context of the ancient world, was a formative factor in the development of religious studies in Bergen and would eventually make our department a significant contributor to international Nag Hammadi research. For this development, the presence of an eminent Egyptologist and Coptologist in our local research environment was decisively important. It is a true pleasure to dedicate this small study to Professor Richard Holton Pierce, who became an invaluable support and mentor during a critical phase of Nag Hammadi studies in Bergen, and remained so over the many years that followed.

It is generally assumed that the gospels of Matthew and Luke incorporate materials from an otherwise unknown common source mainly consisting of sayings attributed to Jesus – the so-called 'Q document'. The notion that written collections of 'words of Jesus' actually existed and circulated in the early phase of Christianity was tangibly confirmed by the discovery of a Coptic version of the full *Gospel of Thomas* in the Nag Hammadi Library. The relationship of *Thomas* to the canonical gospels continues to be hotly debated: was *Thomas* put together on the basis of the canonical texts or does it represent an independent tradition? That debate is not the subject of the present paper. Instead, I wish to direct attention towards another Nag Hammadi text that gives evidence of the existence of collections of sayings and thus provides further material for discussing the use and functions of such collections in early Christianity. That the *Interpretation of Knowledge* makes use of such a collection was pointed out and briefly discussed in my commentary in Funk, Painchaud and Thomassen (2010: 127-29). I believe the matter is of sufficient interest to merit a more extensive discussion.

Interp. Know. is a homily (or possibly a letter; see Emmel [(2003]) that is preserved (in a very damaged state) as the first tractate of Nag Hammadi Codex XI. The text was first edited by Pagels and Turner (1990). A new edition and a more extensive commentary were provided by Plisch (1996). The most recent edition is Funk, Painchaud and Thomassen (2010). In one of its passages, *Interp. Know.* describes the Saviour as 'the teacher of immortality' who brought a 'school of life'. The doctrine taught by this Saviour-Teacher is then presented in the form of a series of quotations. This is the relevant paragraph (taken from my translation in Meyer [2007: 651-62, here 656-57]):

> For [by] speaking to the Church he [became] for it a teacher of immortality. [He] destroyed the arrogant [teacher] who [taught] it to [die. *This* teacher brought] a school of [life]. For [this teacher has] a different (kind of) school. [He] taught us the [living] letters. He took [us] away from the letters of the world, the ones that taught us our death. And his teaching was this: (1) do not call anyone your father upon earth. One is your Father, who is in the heavens. (2) You are the light of the world, my brothers and fellow companions who do the will of the Father. (3) For what is the profit if you (m.sg.) gain the world and forfeit your (m.sg.) soul? For while we were in the darkness we used to call many 'father', because we were ignorant of the true Father. And this is the greatest of all sins .... (*Interp. Know.* 9:17-38)

What interests us here in particular are the three quotations representing the Teacher's instruction. They are all, of course, familiar sayings of Jesus that can also be found in the synoptic gospels. The first of them, 'Do not call anyone your father upon earth. One is your Father, who is in the heavens' (9:28-30) corresponds to Matt 23:9. The form of that saying in our text, albeit not devoid of interest for textual criticism,[1] will not be further discussed here. We shall concentrate instead on the second and third sayings, which exhibit some particularly interesting variations compared to their parallels in the canonical gospels.

I

This is the Coptic text of the second saying (9:30-33), with an attempted reconstruction of the Greek:

> ⲛ̄ⲧ̣ⲱ̣ⲧⲛ̄ ⲡⲉ ⲡⲟⲩⲁⲉⲓⲛ ⲙ̄ⲡⲕⲟⲥⲙⲟⲥ ⲛⲁⲥⲛⲏⲩ ⲁⲩⲱ ⲛⲁϣⲃ̄ⲣ̄ⲕⲟⲓⲛⲱⲛⲟⲥ ⲛⲉϯⲣⲉ ⲙ̄ⲡⲟⲩⲱϣⲉ ⲙ̄[ⲡ]ⲉⲓⲱⲧ
>
> * ὑμεῖς ἐστε τὸ φῶς τοῦ κόσμου, ἀδελφοί μου καὶ συγκοινωνοί μου οἱ ποιοῦντες τὸ θέλημα τοῦ πατρός

The first part of the saying corresponds to Matt 5:14a. The second part has parallels in Matt 12:50 and Luke 8:21, which are both rewritings of Mark 3:35:

Mark 3:35	Matt 12:50	Luke 8:21
ὃς [γὰρ] ἂν ποιήσῃ τὸ θέλημα τοῦ θεοῦ, οὗτος ἀδελφός μου καὶ ἀδελφὴ καὶ μήτηρ ἐστίν.	ὅστις γὰρ ἂν ποιήσῃ τὸ θέλημα τοῦ πατρός μου τοῦ ἐν οὐρανοῖς αὐτός μου ἀδελφὸς καὶ ἀδελφὴ καὶ μήτηρ ἐστίν.	Μήτηρ μου καὶ ἀδελφοί μου οὗτοί εἰσιν οἱ τὸν λόγον τοῦ θεοῦ ἀκούοντες καὶ ποιοῦντες.

It would appear that the saying in *Interp. Know.* contains elements from Luke's version (οἱ ... ποιοῦντες) as well as from Matthew (τὸ θέλημα τοῦ πατρός). It may thus represent a harmonization of the texts of the two canonical gospels. However, before we draw that conclusion, *Interp. Know.*'s text needs to be set alongside several other versions of the saying found in early Christian sources:

Gos. Eb. (in Epiph. *Pan.* 30.14.5)	*Gos. Thom.* 99	*2 Clem.* 9.11	Clem. Alex. *Ecl.* 20.3	*Interp. Know.* 9:31-33
οὗτοί εἰσιν οἱ ἀδελφοί μου καὶ ἡ μήτηρ καὶ ἀδελφαὶ οἱ ποιοῦντες τὰ θελήματα τοῦ πατρός μου	ⲛⲉⲧⲛ̄ⲛⲉⲉⲓⲙⲁ ⲉϯⲣⲉ ⲙ̄ⲡⲟⲩⲱϣ ⲙ̄ⲡⲁⲉⲓⲱⲧ ⲛⲁⲉⲓ ⲛⲉ ⲛⲁⲥⲛⲏⲩ ⲙⲛ̄ ⲧⲁⲙⲁⲁⲩ	καὶ γὰρ εἶπεν ὁ κύριος· ἀδελφοί μου οὗτοί εἰσιν οἱ ποιοῦντες τὸ θέλημα τοῦ πατρός μου	ἀδελφοί μου γάρ, φησὶν ὁ κύριος, καὶ συγκληρονόμοι οἱ ποιοῦντες τὸ θέλημα τοῦ πατρός μου	ⲛⲁⲥⲛⲏⲩ ⲁⲩⲱ ⲛⲁϣⲃ̄ⲣ̄ⲕⲟⲓⲛⲱⲛⲟⲥ ⲛⲉϯⲣⲉ ⲙ̄ⲡⲟⲩⲱϣⲉ ⲙ̄[ⲡ]ⲉⲓⲱⲧ

All these versions display the same combination of Matthean and Lukan phrases as is found in *Interp. Know.* It is further to be observed that the *Gospel of the Ebionites* and the *Gospel of Thomas* both report the saying within the same frame story as the synoptic gospels, that is, as the response of Jesus to the information that his brothers and his mother are 'standing outside'. In *2 Clement*, Clement of Alexandria and *Interp. Know.*, on the other hand, that context is lacking. The mother as well is absent in these versions, so that the saying here appears as a general statement about the 'brothers' of Jesus. The most plausible scenario that will explain the relationship between these texts is to assume that *Gos. Eb.* and *Gos. Thom.*, rather than both harmonizing independently Matthew and Luke, or one of them being dependent on the other, share a common source that had already harmonized the Matthean and the Lukan versions of the story – most probably a gospel harmony of some kind.[2] The same source also provided a version of the saying that

[1] The Coptic text, ⲙ̄ⲛ̄ⲙⲟⲩⲧⲉ̣ ⲛⲏⲧⲛ̄ ⲁⲉⲓⲱⲧ ϩⲓϫⲛ̣̄ ⲡⲕⲁϩ ⲟⲩⲉⲉⲓ ⲡ[ⲉ] ⲡ̣ⲉⲧⲛ̄ⲉⲓⲱⲧ ⲉⲑ̄ⲛ̄ ⲛ̄ⲙ̄ⲡⲏⲩⲉ, presupposes ὑμῖν rather than ὑμῶν and ὁ ἐν τοῖς οὐρανοῖς instead of ὁ οὐράνιος in Matt 23.9a. These variants agree with the form of the text used by Clement of Alexandria (Cosaert 2008: 106) and with the 'Western' textform, but also with the Coptic versions.

[2] I find convincing the most recent discussion of the issue in Luomanen (2012: 206-12). The hypothesis that *Gos. Eb.* and *Gos. Thom.* reflect a

omitted the narrative framework and gave it as a context-free statement about the true brothers of Jesus. The sort of text through which this transmission took place was probably a collection of sayings of Jesus such as is often assumed to have been used by *2 Clement*, which, in addition to the present saying, quotes several sayings of the Lord (both with and without canonical parallels) as coming from a 'gospel'.[3] It is plausible, therefore, that *Interp. Know.* derived the saying from a source of this nature, rather than from the synoptic gospels themselves. (Plisch [1996: 106, n.87] considers this possibility in passing, but does not pursue the issue.) This hypothesis will be confirmed in the course of this paper.

The particular version of the saying found in *Interp. Know.*, however, shows a particular affinity with the one attested by Clement of Alexandria, *Ecl.* 20.3, in which the added word συγκληρονόμοι forms a remarkable parallel to ⲛⲁϣⲃ̄ⲣ̄ⲕⲟⲓⲛⲱⲛⲟⲥ (< *συγκοινωνοί) in *Interp. Know.* Two observations are to be made here. The first is that the word συγκληρονόμοι was not added to the *logion* by Clement himself, as has sometimes been thought (Köster 1957: 79; Mees 1970, 1: 197), but was already a feature of the source he used. This had already been noted by Lightfoot (if I understand him correctly), who in a note to *2 Clem.* 9 quoted the passage in *Ecl.* and remarked: '... the context shows that συγκληρονόμοι is deliberately given as part of the quotation' (Lightfoot 1890, 2: 231, n.15). In fact, Clement gives the quotation in order to support his assertion that, 'The Saviour leads us into the freedom of the Father as sons who are fellow heirs and friends' (συγκληρονόμους υἱούς) (20.2). He would hardly have used the saying from the Lord as a proof text unless it already contained the word συγκληρονόμοι. This assumption is confirmed by the fact that Clement alludes to the same version of the saying in *Quis dives* 9.2 (also cf. Clem. Alex. *Str.* 2.134.1-2): '... and those who fulfil the Father's will He makes not slaves, in the manner of a slave, but sons and brothers and fellow heirs' (οὐχὶ δὲ δούλους ποιῶν ὡς δοῦλος, ἀλλὰ καὶ υἱοὺς καὶ ἀδελφοὺς καὶ συγκληρονόμους τοὺς ἐπιτελοῦντας τὸ θέλημα τοῦ πατρός).

It is further to be noted that Hippolytus of Rome, in his *Benedictions of Isaac, Jacob, and Moses*, three times quotes the formula 'my brothers and fellow heirs' as a saying of the Lord ((1) ἔλεγεν ὁ κύριος· ἀδελφοί μου καὶ συγκληρονόμοι *Ben. Jac.* XVI (ed. Diobouniotis [TU 38.1] 32.11-12; ed. Brière, Mariès, Mercier [Patr. Or. 28.1-2] 74:9-10); (2) ἔφη ὁ κύριος· ἀδελφοί μου καὶ συγκληρονόμοι *ibid.* XXVII (Diobouniotis 42:18-19; Brière, Mariès, Mercier 112:9-10); (3) *Ben. Mos.* 189 Brière, Mariès, Mercier). Hippolytus never gives the rest of the text found in Clement – '... are those who do the will of the Father' – so we cannot know whether he knew the saying in that form, but he does provide evidence that the formula 'my brothers and fellow heirs' circulated as a saying of the Lord. Clement cannot have invented it. Many other instances of ἀδελφοί μου καὶ συγκληρονόνοι are given by Warns (1985: 368-69, n.7522), who also argues that συγκληρονόνοι must have been part of the saying received by Clement. A TLG search also reveals a number of occurrences of this combination. The supplement 'are those who do the will of my Father' is not found, however, nor is the expression quoted as a saying of the Lord in those instances. The combination may easily have arisen independently (as Philo, *Gaium* 87 ἀδελφόν καὶ συγκληρόμον, suggests) and subsequently been introduced into the dominical saying, with good theological meaning.

Interp. Know. uses, of course, the expression 'fellow companions' and not 'fellow heirs'. Since this particular variant is not attested elsewhere, it is most probably to be explained as a secondary variation on συγκληρονόμοι made deliberately, either in the course of transmission of the saying or by the author of *Interp. Know.* himself. The substitution of the one συν-word for the other does not affect the formal identity of the two versions of the saying; the variant συγκοινωνοί presupposes a previous συγκληρονόμοι. Moreover, the prepositional prefix in συγκοινωνοί may be considered semantically redundant and for that reason as well is best explained as the result of modifying another word containing that prefix.

The second observation to be made is that in *Ecl.* 20.3 Clement immediately goes on to quote Matt 23:9a, 'Call no one father to yourselves on earth'. As we saw above, Matt 23.9 is quoted by *Interp. Know.* as well,

tradition independent of, and also used by, the Synoptics (Patterson and others) creates a series of problems, as Luomanen shows.

3 *2 Clem.* 8.5 λέγει γὰρ ὁ κύριος ἐν τῷ εὐαγγελίῳ. Köster 1957: 70-111; Koester 1990: 349-60; Warns 1985: 323-474; Lindemann 1992: 174; Gregory and Tuckett 2005: esp. 277-78 (where they are unnecessarily hesitant about ascribing the saying to a source distinct from Matthew and Luke); Tuckett 2015: esp. 40-41.

immediately before the saying we have been discussing. This can hardly be a coincidence. Clement and the author of *Interp. Know.* appear to have been using a source that not only gave the saying about the Saviour's true family in a form shared by these two writers, but which also quoted the saying about the one true Father in close proximity to the first one. This juxtaposition of the two sayings, together with the fact that both authors emphatically quote them as the words of the Saviour, confirms the assumption that the shared source had the form of a collection of sayings of Jesus.

II

We now turn to the third saying (9:33-35), which reads as follows, with a reconstruction of the Greek:

ⲉⲩ ⲅⲁⲣ ⲡⲉ ⲫⲏⲩ ⲉⲕϣⲁⲛϯϩⲏⲩ ⲙ̄ⲡⲕⲟⲥⲙⲟⲥ ⲛ̄ⲕϯⲁⲥⲓ ⲛ̄ⲧⲉⲕⲯⲩⲭⲏ

* τί γὰρ τὸ ὄφελος, ἐὰν τὸν κόσμον κερδήσῃς, τὴν δὲ ψυχήν σου ζημιωθῇς;

The synoptic gospels, on the other hand, have:

Mark 8:36	Matt 16:26	Luke 9:25
τί γὰρ ὠφελεῖ ἄνθρωπον κερδῆσαι τὸν κόσμον ὅλον καὶ ζημιωθῆναι τὴν ψυχὴν αὐτοῦ;	τί γὰρ ὠφεληθήσεται ἄνθρωπος ἐὰν τὸν κόσμον ὅλον κερδήσῃ τὴν δὲ ψυχὴν αὐτοῦ ζημιωθῇ;	τί γὰρ ὠφελεῖται ἄνθρωπος κερδήσας τὸν κόσμον ὅλον ἑαυτὸν δὲ ἀπολέσας ἢ ζημιωθείς;

The form of the saying in *Interp. Know.* is different from the canonical versions in two major respects. First, it employs the nominal form * τὸ ὄφελος rather than a form of the verb ὠφελεῖν. Second, the conditional clause is phrased in the second person singular, κερδήσῃς, instead of the third person with ἄνθρωπος as the subject. Again, *Interp. Know.*'s version of the saying is not unique. Just as was the case with the previous saying, this one is attested in Clement of Alexandria and (at least partly) in *2 Clement*:

Clem. Alex. *Str.* 6.112.3	*2 Clem.* 6.2	*Interp. Know.* 9:33-35
τί γὰρ ὄφελος, ἐὰν τὸν κόσμον κερδήσῃς, φησί, τὴν δὲ ψυχὴν ἀπολέσῃς;	τί γὰρ τὸ ὄφελος, ἐάν τις τὸν κόσμον ὅλον κερδήσῃ, τὴν δὲ ψυχὴν ζημιωθῇ;	ⲉⲩ ⲅⲁⲣ ⲡⲉ ⲫⲏⲩ ⲉⲕϣⲁⲛϯϩⲏⲩ ⲙ̄ⲡⲕⲟⲥⲙⲟⲥ ⲛ̄ⲕϯⲁⲥⲓ ⲛ̄ⲧⲉⲕⲯⲩⲭⲏ

The versions of *Interp. Know.* and Clement of Alexandria are clearly very close. Clement's use of ἀπολέσῃς rather than ζημιωθῇς is probably not very significant: Clement's ἀπολέσῃς corresponds to the version in Luke 9:25 and may represent an interference from that text (see also, however, Matt 16: 25). ⲛ̄ⲕϯⲁⲥⲓ in *Interp. Know.* 9:34 most probably reflects ζημιωθῇς, ϯⲟⲥⲉ being the regular translation of ζημιοῦσθαι in the Sahidic NT, but the Coptic verb is not impossible as a translation of ἀπολλύναι; cf. Crum's *Dictionary*, 257a. Moreover, there is notable fluctuation between ζημιοῦσθαι and ἀπολλύναι in the transmission of this saying (cf. Warns 1985: 398). The version in *2 Clement* uses a third person expression with τις instead of the second person form of the two other versions, and it also adds ὅλον. These variations may be due to secondary influence from the canonical versions of the saying. Warns (1985: 395-96) argues that in 6.2, the author of *2 Clem.* deliberately changed the text of his source from the second to the third person by using τις. This suggestion is not as fanciful as Tuckett thinks (2015: 180 n.11), since if the three versions have a shared history of transmission at a certain point, the deviation in *2 Clem.* is more easily explained as a modification of the text represented by the other two versions than the other way around (also cf. the discussion in the following section of this paper). Moreover, ὅλον, which appears in *2 Clem.* and *Mart. Vict.* (see next paragraph), but is missing in Clement of Alexandria, *Interp. Know.* and one of the three manuscripts of *2 Clem.*, may also be due to interference from the canonical texts.

To be added to the file is also a clearly related version of the saying found in the Coptic *Martyrdom of Victor* (Budge 1914: 10:21-22): 'If you gain the whole world and forfeit your soul, what is the profit?' (ⲉⲕϣⲁⲛⲧ̄ϯϩⲏⲩ ⲙ̄ⲡⲕⲟⲥⲙⲟⲥ ⲧⲏⲣϥ̄ ⲛ̄ⲅϯⲟⲥⲉ ⲛ̄ⲧⲉⲕⲯⲩⲭⲏ ⲟⲩ ⲡⲉ ⲡϩⲏⲩ). (Slightly varying versions of the saying are found in two other manuscripts of the *Martyrdom*; on this, see Horn [1994].) It is evident that the saying in the particular form attested by these sources circulated independently of the texts of the canonical gospels. Moreover, its occurrence in *2 Clement* suggests that it circulated as part of a collection of sayings of the Lord. This observation with regard to the third of the sayings in *Interp. Know.* corroborates, then, the hypothesis made above with regard to the first two. All three sayings appear to derive from a source of this nature. This source is clearly related to the collection of sayings used by *2 Clement*, though it cannot simply be identical to it, as the variation in the second saying containing the words καὶ συγκληρονόμοι shows. On the other hand, this variant points in the direction of a source shared with Clement of Alexandria, who provides attestation for two of the sayings in the same form as *Interp. Know.*, and also quotes the third one in close proximity to one of them.

III

What conclusions can be drawn from these observations? First of all, and obviously, *Interp. Know.* provides additional evidence of the existence, circulation and use of collections of the sayings of Jesus in early Christianity. This is the genre that is positively attested by the λόγοι 'Ιησοῦ of the Oxyrhynchus fragments and the *Gospel of Thomas*, and whose existence can be inferred from Q as well as from scattered quotations of sayings of Jesus in early Christian literature.

Second, the collection used by *Interp. Know.* was known by Clement of Alexandria as well. It also seems to have circulated more widely in Egypt, as is suggested by the occurrence of one of the sayings in the *Martyrdom of Victor*. This points in the direction of Egypt as a possible place of origin for *Interp. Know.*

Third, the collection shared by *Interp. Know.* and Clement of Alexandria has clear affinities with the one used in *2 Clement*. It was not, however, simply identical to it. The two collections must nevertheless have a shared history of transmission to some extent. It seems that several related collections of this type may have existed, whose interconnections can only occasionally be glimpsed.

Fourth, the form of the sayings is not such as readily to invite the assumption that they originated independently of the canonical gospels. The first saying comes from the special materials of Matthew, whereas the other two belong to the synoptic materials derived from Mark. It is notable that in no. 3, the conditional clause into which Matthew changed Mark's infinitive construction is reproduced. This suggests that the text presupposes Matthew (Cf. Koester 1990: 350; Gregory and Tuckett 2005: 267; Tuckett 2015: 180), though it remains somewhat difficult to account for the two significant differences vis-à-vis Matthew's text, that is, the use of the second person address form rather than the parabolic third person form found in the synoptic texts, and the presence of the nominal expression τὸ ὄφελος instead of the verb ὠφελεῖν. This second difference is apparently to be explained as a consequence of the first: when ἄνθρωπος was replaced by a second person expression, the verbal form had to be changed as well, and the more general, and simpler, expression τί (τὸ) ὄφελος was then selected rather than a directly personal expression such as, for instance, τί σε ὠφελήσει. The motive behind this transformation of the saying from the third to the second person nevertheless remains obscure.

As stated above, the form of saying no. 2, about Jesus' true family, is best explained as having originated as a harmonization of Matthew and Luke. In the version contained in the common source of *Interp. Know.* and Clement of Alexandria, however, the word συγκληρονόνοι was inserted as well. This interpolation may have been influenced by Rom 8:16–17: ... ἐσμὲν τέκνα θεοῦ. εἰ δὲ τέκνα, καὶ κληρονόμοι: κληρονόμοι μὲν θεοῦ, συγκληρονόμοι δὲ Χριστοῦ.

Fifth, why did *Interp. Know.* (or its source) replace συγκληρονόνοι with συγκοινωνοί? The combination of ἀδελφός and συγκοινωνός appears in Rev 1:9, where John presents himself to his readers as their fellow participant in persecution and the kingdom. Fellowship (with the Saviour) in suffering may be implied in the selection of the word συγκοινωνοί in *Interp. Know.* since that particular idea is in fact important in this text (see in particular *Interp. Know.*, p. 5). However, that idea is not explicitly articulated in the present context, and it seems more likely that the notion of companionship has other connotations in this instance. It should be noted that *Interp. Know.* combines the saying with Matt 5: 14. Thus, the idea of being brothers and companions of the Saviour is here associated with that of being 'the light of the world'. The combination of the two ideas is not, to my knowledge, attested elsewhere; it may have been created by the author of *Interp. Know.* himself. At any rate, the combination must reflect an underlying ideological motive. In that respect, it is somewhat surprising that the saying 'You are the light of the world' is rarely quoted or alluded to, either elsewhere in the Nag Hammadi Library or in other gnostic sources. The only instance that readily presents itself is Irenaeus, *Adv. haer.* 1.6.1, which states that the spirituals sent down together with the Saviour as his Church body are 'the salt and the light of the world'.[4] It is not implausible that this characteristic Valentinian idea may in fact lie behind the combination, and that the introduction of the word συγκοινωνοί is to be explained along these lines as well. In this interpretation, the 'fellow companions' are the members of the Valentinian spiritual Church, a κοινωνία that was manifested on earth by the advent of the Saviour, being his body and sharing his transcendent origins (cf. Thomassen 2006: 41-43, 49-50, etc.).

Sixth, it is worthy of note that collections of sayings of Jesus were still being used by Clement of Alexandria, around 200, as well as by less 'orthodox' groups such as the Valentinians. Although collections of this kind seem to have a history that stretches back to before the invention of the narrative gospel, the interest in, and the use of, works of this genre faded out, or were discouraged, during the early centuries, and few traces of them remain. In certain quarters, however, such collections continued to be used, as the *Gospel of Thomas* testifies. The Valentinians may well have been one of the groups that did so. In his *Letter to Flora*, the Valentinian teacher Ptolemy asserts that, 'We shall draw the proofs of what we say from the words of our Saviour; for through these alone are we led without stumbling to the comprehension of that which is' (Epiph. *Pan.* 33.3.8). This statement suggests that the Valentinians took a special interest in the sayings of Jesus (cf. Robinson 1971: 99) – even more, perhaps, than in the narrative gospels as such. They may consequently have continued to use sayings gospels for a longer time than mainstream Christianity. A further indication of such usage is the fact that sayings from the *Gospel of Thomas* are quoted in the *Gospel of Philip*, which itself in some respects continues the genre (Turner 1996: 206-7).

A last observation that can be made is that the sayings found in *Interp. Know.* are generally sapiential in character.[5] They conform, in other words, to the genre of λόγοι σοφῶν as described by Robinson and Koester (1971). In that respect, it should be recalled that *Interp. Know.* portrays Jesus as a teacher – one who sets up a new school and forces the old one to go out of business. It is precisely in his role as a teacher that Jesus pronounces the sayings that have been discussed. The scene is very similar to the one described in the *Gospel of Truth* (19:17-20:14), where Jesus also appears as a schoolteacher, revealing 'the Book of the living'. The Valentinians thus seem not only to have cultivated an interest in the Saviour's sayings, and to have used collections of such sayings, but they also portrayed the Saviour speaking these sayings as a teacher, in accordance with the model of the sage, with which the *Gattung* of sayings collections as such is associated. The Valentinian Jesus, of course, no longer speaks just wisdom, but *gnosis*. More precisely, he speaks *gnosis as* wisdom, and wisdom *as gnosis* – a fact that gives food for further thought regarding the historical relationship between those two phenomena.

[4] It may be observed, however, that Matt 5:16 is quoted in Clem. Alex. *Exc. Theod.* 3.1 and 41.3, and that Matt 5:14-16 has a parallel in *Gos. Thom.* 24.

[5] A partial exception to this form-critical characterization is represented by the second saying, which introduces an element of sectarian self-description into the universalism of the wisdom saying form.

References

Budge, E. A. W. (1914). *Coptic Martyrdoms, etc. in the Dialect of Upper Egypt.* (Coptic Texts 4). London: British Museum. Reprinted New York: AMS Press 1977.

Cosaert, C. P. (2008). *The Texts of the Gospels in Clement of Alexandria* (The New Testament in the Greek Fathers 9). Atlanta: Society of Biblical Literature.

Emmel, S. (2003). Exploring the pathway that leads from Paul to Gnosticism: What is the genre of The Interpretation of Knowledge (NHC XI,1)? In: M. Fassnacht *et al.* (eds) *Die Weisheit - Ursprünge und Rezeption: Festschrift für Karl Löning zum 65. Geburtstag*: 257–276. Münster: Aschendorff.

Funk, W.-P., Painchaud, L. and Thomassen, E. (2010). *L'Interprétation de la Gnose (NH XI,1).* (Bibliothèque Copte de Nag Hammadi, section 'Textes' 34). Québec: Presses de l'Université Laval and Louvain: Peeters.

Gregory, A. F. and Tuckett, C. M. (2005). *2 Clement* and the Writings that later formed the New Testament. In: Gregory, A. F. and Tuckett, C. M. (eds) *The Reception of the New Testament in the Apostolic Fathers*: 251–292. Oxford: Oxford University Press.

Horn, J. (1994). 'Es steht geschrieben: Wenn du die ganze Welt gewönnest ....' Zur Überlieferung eines Herrenwortes in der koptischen Literatur. In W. Beltz (ed.), *Der Gottesspruch in der kopt. Literatur: Hans-Martin Schenke zum 65. Geburtstag* (Hallesche Beiträge zur Orientwissenschaft 15): 46-58. Halle [Saale].

Köster, H. (1957). *Synoptische* Überlieferung *bei den Apostolischen Vätern.* (Texte und Untersuchungen 65). Berlin: Akademie-Verlag.

Koester, H. (1990). *Ancient Christian Gospels: Their History and Development.* London: SCM.

Lightfoot, J. B. (1890). *The Apostolic Fathers. Part 1. S. Clement of Rome.* London: Macmillan. Reprinted Peabody, (MA): Hendrickson 1989.

Lindemann, A. (1992). *Die Clemensbriefe.* (Handbuch zum Neuen Testament, 17: Die Apostolischen Väter I). Tübingen: Mohr Siebeck.

Luomanen, P. (2012). *Recovering Jewish-Christian Sects and Gospels.* (Vigiliae Christianae Supplements 110). Leiden: Brill.

Mees, M. (1970). *Die Zitate aus dem Neuen Testament bei Clemens von Alexandrien.* 2 vols. (Quaderni di 'Vetera Christianorum', 2). Bari: Instituto di Letteratura Cristiana Antica.

Meyer, M. (ed.). (2007). *The Nag Hammadi Scriptures.* New York: HarperOne.

Pagels, E. H. and Turner, J. D. (1990). NHC XI, 1: The interpretation of knowledge. In: C. W. Hedrick (ed.) *Nag Hammadi Codices XI, XII, XIII*: 21–88. (Nag Hammadi and Manichaean Studies, 28). Leiden: Brill.

Plisch, U.-K. (1996). *Die Auslegung der Erkenntnis (Nag Hammadi-Codex XI,1)* (Texte und Untersuchungen 142). Berlin: Akademie Verlag.

Robinson, J. M. and Koester, H. (1971). *Trajectories through Early Christianity.* Philadelphia: Fortress.

Robinson, J. M. (1971). LOGOI SOPHON: On the Gattung of Q. In: Robinson and Koester 1971: 71–113.

Thomassen, E. (2006). *The Spiritual Seed: The Church of the 'Valentinians'* (Nag Hammadi and Manichaean Studies 60). Leiden: Brill.

Tuckett, C. (2015). *2 Clement: Introduction, Text, and Commentary.* (Oxford Apostolic Fathers). Oxford: Oxford University Press.

Turner, M. (1996). *The Gospel According to Philip.* (Nag Hammadi and Manichaean Studies 38). Leiden: Brill.

Warns, R. (1985). Untersuchungen zum 2. Clemens-Brief. Phd dissertation, Philipps-Universität Marburg.

Chaotic mothers and creepy shadows
Metaphors of procreation and vision in *On the Origin of the World* (NHC II, 5)

Ingvild Sælid Gilhus
University of Bergen

On the Origin of the World, tractate number five in Nag Hammadi Codex II, shares its mythological world with the first and fourth tractate in the codex, the *Apocryphon of John* and the *Hypostasis of the Archons*.[1] I had the great pleasure of reading the *Hypostasis of the Archons* with Professor Richard Holton Pierce when I was working on my doctoral dissertation. In the present contribution, offered here in homage to him, I will concentrate on the closely related tractate, *On the Origin of the World*.[2] In the codex it has the title the *Exegesis on the Soul*. Since this is also the title of the sixth tractate in the codex, it has been argued that the scribe made a mistake. The tractate has either got the modern title, *On the Origin of the World*, which is used in this contribution,[3] or been labelled 'the Treatise without a Title' (cf. Jenott 2013: 223, note 10).

Both the *Hypostasis of the Archons* and *On the Origin of the World* start with an initial problem. In the *Hypostasis of the Archons* the problem is the nature of the evil archons or powers of this world; in *On the Origin of the World* it is a specific problem, the delusion that the world originated in Chaos. The introductions to both the two tractates refer to traditional authorities – Paul's letter to the Ephesians in the case of the *Hypostasis of the Archons* and philosophical debates in the wake of the *Theogony* of Hesiod in *On the Origin of the World* (Mansfield 1981: 180).[4] For Hesiod, Chaos was the first step in the cosmology, but he did not claim that Chaos had existed forever (*Theogony* 116). On the contrary, he said that Chaos 'came into existence'. Authors and philosophers after him posed the obvious question, where did it come from? By flagging the ambition to explain the origin of Chaos, the tractate apparently aspires to write itself into the philosophical debate of its time.

On the Origin of the World purports to be about Chaos, and a description of Chaos and its origin is prominent in the introduction, but it is not a main theme in the tractate (Wintermute 1972). Painchaud suggests that the tractate follows a literary convention according to which the introduction does not really introduce the main topic. While this seems to be the case, it must also be added that the interest in the origin of Chaos, which is reflected in its first pages, is closely connected to the tractate's preoccupation with the end, because the end is dependent on the beginning. The ambition in the present contribution is to unravel the metaphorical tangles of Chaos and to discuss the creation models in the first part of the tractate (97: 24-99: 28). But to begin with, a short overview of the content of the tractate is helpful.

Overview

In *On the Origin of the World*, the demonstration of where Chaos comes from is done in a formal way in a philosophical *apodeixis* by referring to common knowledge. The use of this rhetorical technical term signals learnedness and makes the reader expect that he or she will receive new and superior knowledge. While the tractate explicitly speaks against those who believed that Chaos was the real beginning of

[1] An earlier version of the Chaos theme in *Orig.World* is treated in my article, 'Hva er kaos? Om verdens opprinnelse i kodeks II fra Nag Hammadi'. (Gilhus 2008a). The Coptic text of *Orig.World* with a translation is in B. Layton (ed.) *Nag Hammadi Codex II, 2-7 together with* XIII, 2*, Brit. Lib. Or. 4926(1), and P. Oxy. 1, 654, 655. Volume Two. Leiden: Brill 1989.

[2] There are three known witnesses to *Orig.World*. In addition to the complete version in Codex II, there are ten lines from the beginning of the tractate preserved in Nag Hammadi Codex XIII in the Coptic Museum in Cairo, and 30 fragments from a third version in the British Museum (Or. 4926(1)) (Oeyen 1975; Painchaud 1995: 527, 532-70). These three witnesses, plus the fact that someone had bothered to translate the text from Greek to Coptic, indicates that *Orig.World* was a rather popular text.

[3] Hans-Martin Schenke created the title (1959: 246).

[4] In the first case, the users of the tractate obviously did not know what scholars know today, that it is a Deutero-Pauline letter.

everything, it was probably not intended only for them, but for readers who already believed that the supreme god was the ultimate creator and saw Chaos as something secondary. The readers could have been Christians, Jews, Manicheans or Neoplatonists or people who fluctuated between these groups.[5] However, since the specific version of the tractate found at Nag Hammadi was part of a codex, which, together with 12 others, was buried in the area of the original Pachomian monasteries, it is reasonable to suppose that monks owned and read these codices (cf. Lundhaug and Jenott 2015). This means that a tractate like *On the Origin of the World* was read to support the monks' way of life. One of the things that made this tractate relevant for monastic reading was its strong ascetic perspective, a perspective that has been labelled 'generally encratitic' (Dunning 2009: 82).

While the tractate shares its mythological world with the *Hypostasis of the Archons* it has a more sophisticated introduction and a more elaborate intertwining of classical and biblical mythology.[6] The tractate reflects a rich textual world, combining elements from different traditions, such as Classical, Egyptian and Manichean myths, Jewish pseudo-epigraphic writings and Hermetic literature, as well as themes from novels. In short, the tractate reflects highly developed religious, literary and philosophical milieus in Egypt in late antiquity and is an end product of complex editorial and translation processes.[7] The composition of its cosmology is dependent on Platonism with its division between a world of ideas and a world of matter, where the latter is created after the model of the first ideal world. The Genesis narrative is another structuring influence on the tractate.

Similarly to the *Apocryphon of John* and the *Hypostasis of the Archons, On the Origin of the World* can be seen as a myth-producing commentary on the first chapters of Genesis, which is dependent on advanced exegetical traditions. Similarly to the two other tractates, it describes the double origin of human beings, in the transcendent world above and the material world below, and the consequences of this double origin – the inevitability of death and the possibility of salvation.

The main lines in the narrative run as follows: there is a transcendent world, characterized as 'the eternal realm of truth' and 'limitless light', with immortal beings. The transcendent world has always existed, even before Chaos came into being. One of its entities, the female Pistis, creates Sophia, who is the source of Chaos, matter and the arch-begetter Ialdabaoth. He creates androgynous sons and death, who in their turn create heavenly realms of thrones, temples, chariots and virgins.

Sabaoth, one of the sons of Ialdabaoth, loathes his father. Because of this loathing he is, in spite of his lowly origin, placed in the eighth heaven together with Zoe, a messenger from Sophia, who teaches him about spiritual matters. Because of his authority he creates his own dwelling place and a throne upon a chariot ('Cherubim'), archangels, 72 gods who rule over the 72 languages of the peoples and myriads of angels. His firstborn is Israel, while 'another being' is called Jesus Christ. They are on his right; on his left sits the virgin of the holy spirit (who is Pronoia). Sabaoth himself is on the right of Pistis, with Sophia and Ialdabaoth on the left. Right is justice and left is wickedness.

At his side, Ialdabaoth has his forethought, the female Pronoia. She is shown an image of a heavenly man, an emissary (*aggelos*) – Adam of Light, who kindles her sexual desire and makes her gush forth her blood. From the mixture of this blood and fire from the light, Eros appears. He kindles sexual lust in every creature. After him the grape vine, a fig tree and a pomegranate tree sprout up. Justice creates Paradise. To the north of Paradise appear the tree of life, the tree of knowledge of good and evil, and the tree of

[5] Plotin says: 'We begin by posing space, a place, a Chaos; into this container, whether conceived in our imagination as created or pre-existent, we introduce God and proceed to inquire, we say, for example, whence and how He comes to be there... But the difficulty disappears if we eliminate all space before we attempt to conceive God' (*Ennead*. 6.8, in Miller 2001:116).

[6] The tractate is also related to another Nag Hammadi text, *Eugnostos* (in Codex III and V).

[7] The research on *On the Origin of the World* started ca. 1950. During the 1990s, Louis Painchaud brought the understanding of it a large step forward both because of his commentaries and his hypothesis of its composition (1995b). One of the problems he tries to solve is why the tractate gives the impression of being a 'well-planned literary composition' while at the same time being clearly incoherent in several passages (Painchaud 1995b: 218). Painchaud distinguishes between three editorial levels in the text – a primitive text, a first redaction and a second redaction.

oil to anoint kings. Because of Eros and the creative activity of the archons, the earth is filled with plants and animals.

Adam of Light remains stuck in the eighth heaven where he creates an abode with angels, archangels and similar creatures, and is not allowed back into the transcendent world. The archons create the earthly Adam as a trap for the light, and his progeny becomes numerous. Spiritual messengers such as Adam of Light, Eve of Life (the Instructor/the Beast), Hermaphrodites and the Serpent are sent to the fallen world.

When Sophia sees that the archons cursed Adam and Eve, she chased them out of heaven and cast them down to earth as evil spirits. They instruct 'mankind in many kinds of error and magic and potions and worship of idols and spilling of blood and altars and temples and sacrifices and libations to all the spirits of the earth' (123: 8-12), cooperating with fate (*heimarmene*). The phoenix is partly presented as a positive mythological model. In the same way as there are three phoenixes there are three types of men (spiritual, psychic and earthly) and three types of baptism.

The tractate predicts that everything in the material world will be destroyed in the end. The enigmatic immortal race, 'the fourth race' – the race without a king – will then return to its abode in the spiritual world.

The root of Chaos

While the concept of 'Chaos' appears in two other tractates in Codex II – the *Apocryphon of John*[8] and the *Hypostasis of the Archons*[9] – only *On the Origin of the World* goes more deeply into the question about what Chaos is and how it originated (cf. Kaiser 2009: 29).

> Since everyone, the world's gods and human beings, say that nothing existed prior to Chaos, I shall demonstrate that all of them are wrong because they neither know [the origin] of Chaos, nor its root (*noune*). Here is the demonstration (*apodeixis*).
>
> (97: 24-30)

Chaos is in this tractate not only the original gap or void, but a space that includes the cosmos below with heavens, gods, powers and authorities. 'Root' (*noune*) indicates that Chaos is grounded and not floating freely (97: 29; cf. *Ap.John* II 30:19, 27). The expression implies a conceptual metaphor based on plants – COMPLETE ABSTRACT SYSTEMS ARE PLANTS (Kövesces 2002: 98-101). Another plant metaphor is employed when the tractate says later that from Chaos 'every kind of divinity sprouted up' (98: 32), which depends on the conceptual metaphor PEOPLE ARE PLANTS (here also involving mythological entities). A blending of the two metaphors takes place when the tractate predicts what will happen at the end, when 'the deficiency will be plucked out by its root down into the darkness. And the light will withdraw up to its root' (127: 3-5). The deficiency includes the chaotic cosmological system and its demonic mythological entities. Plucking out by its root associates the chaotic world and its deficiency metaphorically with weeds, and connects the beginning of Chaos to its end.

The light of creation

The text takes its point of departure from something that all people allegedly agreed on (*symphonein*), which is that Chaos is darkness (*kake*) (97: 30-98: 2). But cleverly the tractate immediately makes the observation that darkness must derive from a shadow (*haibes*), which is called 'darkness' (98: 2-3). Apparently darkness is a lack of something, not the real thing, and definitely not the first beginning. Two important moves have been made: (1) Chaos and darkness are identified with shadow (*haibes*), and (2), because a shadow always relates to something else, there must exist a thing that casts shadow. In this way, the tractate peers behind the Chaos-cum-shadow-cum-darkness and discovers something more

[8] *Ap.John* 30: 19, 27, 29; 31: 19

[9] *Hyp.Arch.* 87: 6; 94: 32; 95: 25; 96: 11, 14; 97: 26, 29

primordial, a 'product' (*ergon*) that has existed since the beginning (98: 4-5). Note that this does not mean that the product is eternal. On the contrary, it means that it is created. In this description the tractate applies a craft metaphor (cf. Painchaud 1995a: 224-225).

Naturally the tractate wants to focus on 'the first product' (98: 7-11). This 'product' did not come into being by itself, but was willed into existence:

> When the nature (*physis*) of the immortal beings had been completed out of the infinite, then a likeness (*eine*) called Sophia flew out of Pistis. She (the likeness) had a desire (*ouosh*) and a product (*ergon*) came into being, similar to the primeval light. And immediately her (Sophia) desire (*ouosh*) revealed itself as a likeness of heaven, having an unimaginable greatness. It was situated between the immortal beings and those that came into being after them, like what is above(?). She (Sophia) served as a veil separating human beings from those that were above.
>
> (98:11-23)

According to the passage quoted above, a mythological entity called Sophia is a likeness of Pistis, and this likeness becomes an imitation of the primeval light. This imitation is the 'first product' and constitutes a veil. On the one hand, we are talking about light, flowing out of something, and of likenesses – phenomena connected to light, reflection and vision. On the other hand, we are talking about a female entity and her *ouosh*, which means 'desire, love' and may connote sexual lust. According to Hippocratic medicine, the desire of the mother is necessary to produce a foetus. In this description of the primeval creation there is a blending of two metaphorical models, a dominant model of creation based on light and another model, which is known from similar texts, based on a female entity's desire to procreate (cf. Gilhus 2008b 2015). In *On the Origin of the World*, the last model is only suggested in this passage.

In the next passage (98: 23-99: 2), the tractate makes two interrelated points: 1. The transcendental world has no shadow outside it (*pefbol*) because the light without limit exists everywhere within it; 2. Its outside (*pefsa nbol*) is shadow. This means that the veil, which is an image of the immortal realm, is the origin of the shadow, and that the shadow was *not* caused by the immortal realm itself. Light does not cast shadow, things do. From Chaos a force appeared that presided over the darkness. The forces that came into being afterwards called the shadow 'Chaos since it was limitless' (98: 31). The sentence signals a discrepancy between Chaos conceived of as unlimited by its descendants and it in reality being limited, because it was derived from something else and because it will be dissolved in the end.

The narrative has now arrived at the point where Hesiod begins his description of creation – with a Chaos that produces all sorts of entities and divinities. In fact, throughout the tractate there are several references to the authorities of Chaos, the powers of Chaos, the gods of Chaos and the heavens of Chaos. Chaos is accordingly not a state of the past but a constitutive presence in the world.

Creation as birth

The shadow turns out not to be a mere lack of light, but an entity that is thinking, feeling and acting, an entity that perceives that something exists that is mightier than itself. Then it feels envy (*koh*), becomes pregnant on its own and engenders envy (*koh*) (99: 2-6). This was the beginning (*arche*) of all envy (*koh*) in all aeons and worlds, which means that it is the principle of envy and that envy is a basic emotional stratum in the constitution of the world. The envy, however, was found to be 'an abortion (*ouhe*) without any spirit in it' (99: 9-19). This characteristic is repeated a few lines further on. Here it is 'the matter of Chaos which had been thrown away like an abortion since there was no spirit in it' (99: 23-26, see below). Envy and matter are different things, but the same picture of creation as an abortive birth is used in both cases.

According to Mark Turner, kinship proliferation is a metaphor or model for the unfolding of the universe. Hesiod's *Theogony* is the most famous example, but the model is well known from Ancient Near Eastern mythology as well. It accounts for newness, the unfolding and multiplying of a universe, offspring inheriting qualities from parents and the existence of family resemblance, and for sympathies and hostilities between family members that are used to explain the dynamics and conflicts in the universe (Turner 2000: 101). This model is in full bloom in *On the Origin of the World* when the chaotic cosmos is gradually filled with superhuman entities. Their creation is described as a kinship proliferation. Turner points to CAUSATION IS PROGENERATION as the most used conceptual metaphor for mental creation and notes that in mental creation there is only one parent (Turner 2000: 82-83, 153). This fits the description of the creation of envy in the tractate. The stress on envy also shows, as Andrew Crislip has pointed out, that the tractate 'engages in this common Christian pastime of identifying the passion at the heart of evil' (Crislip 2011: 285).

The abortion came into being 'like a shadow in a great watery substance' (99: 10-11). Where does the watery substance come from? We have just been told that Chaos is darkness. Now it is water as well. The darkness of Chaos is found in Hesiod (124) and was a standard description that also appeared in Roman authors like Ovid, Virgil and Seneca. Chaos, however, was not only darkness, it was sometimes also described as water, for instance in Stoic thinking as well as in Near Eastern mythology and especially in Genesis (cf. Gen 1: 2). Genesis is an authoritative intertext in *On the Origin of the World* as it is in NHC II in general.

The watery substance is connected to the vision model, because of its potential for creating reflections. This is apparent when later the world creator, Ialdabaoth, sees the likeness of Pistis in the water (100: 21-22). But the watery substance is also connected to the birth model as the amniotic fluid (99: 18, *perisson*), a point recently made by Ursula Ulrike Kaiser (Kaiser 2011). She has pointed out the close connection between the abortion, who is envy personified and the ruler of darkness; the afterbirth, which is matter; and the amniotic fluid, which connotes to the waters of Gen 1: 2 (Kaiser 2009: 34).

The concept of envy appears as the basic emotional stratum of the material world. It is closely connected to bile and anger. Bile (*cholé*) comes into being from the shadow, and is thrown out into a part of the Chaos. It has been suggested that bile – *cholé* – could be a distortion of *hylé*, 'matter', which is in line with the description in *Hyp.Arch.* (94:12). Painchaud suggests a distortion of *chorion*, which means 'foetal membrane' (Painchaud 1995a: 239, 244ff.).[10] This restitution is in line with the tractate's interest in the products of birth. However, the only textual witness we have has *cholé*. This is what the readers read, and it makes sense. Crislip explains convincingly that the presence of *cholé* in the tractate is a metonym for anger in line with how bile and anger were connected in later Greek and Roman emotional thought (Crislip 2011: 297-98). He shows further that there is a close connection between envy and anger in three episodes in *Orig.World* (Crislip 2011: 300-303). Envy and anger accordingly belong to the original emotional equipment of the chaotic cosmos.

What happens in this water is like a woman giving birth to a child and like her afterbirth and amniotic fluid flowing out. Matter is then expelled like an aborted foetus without spirit. The Coptic word used, *nouje ebol*, is a translation of the Greek *ekballein*, which covers both birth and abortion (Perkins 1980: 37). There is a certain ambiguity in the tractate as to whether the topic is mythological women and abortions or whether women and abortions are used metaphorically to describe something else. On one level we are dealing with metaphors, and with a text that describes reality by means of images. Its generous use of *nthe* – 'like' – indicates that it talks by means of metaphors and similes. On another level, the distinction between metaphors and what they refer to breaks down, and the metaphors seem to be fused with the reality they presume to describe. In other words, it is undetermined whether the tractate talks about realities in a metaphorical way or whether the metaphors have in fact become realities in their own right. One could ask, with reference to Max Müller, whether this confusion between, or rather blending of, metaphor and reality – by Müller called 'disease in language', a phrase for which he has been endlessly

[10] *chorion* may mean the membrane around chicken in the egg or around a foetus in the womb; cf. NHC I 47: 17 (*The Treatise on the Resurrection*) and NHC VII 5: 26 and 28 and 7: 14 (*The Paraphrase of Shem*).

ridiculed – is rather typical for religious language. In any case, in the description of creation in *On the Origin of the World*, a birth model appears alongside a light model. According to the light model, Chaos is shadow and darkness. According to the birth model, Chaos functions as a cosmic receptacle or rather a uterus in which the abortion, the superfluous matter and the amniotic fluid appear. The two models are mixed with each other.

Further on, the abortion without spirit is animated and becomes a hybrid being who resembles a lion. A similar two-stage creation takes place in relation to Adam, who in a similar way is described as an abortion without spirit in his first stage of creation (115: 4-5).

The chaotic womb

In antiquity, Chaos varied between being conceived of as empty space, either material or immaterial, and as a mixture of the potential that is in all types of matter (Kratzert 1998). The term 'Chaos' is derived from *chasma*, 'gap'. In Hesiod the stress is on Chaos as a gap (Kirk and Raven 1966: 31, 1983: 38ff.). Later, it came to mean 'lack of order', the opposite to cosmos (*kosmos*), which implies 'order'. In passing, it is interesting to note that in *On the Origin of the World*, the cosmos with its heavens and powers is repeatedly characterized as Chaos.

The tractate shows its erudition when it relates, directly or indirectly, to the different varieties of Chaos – the Egyptian *nun* (*noun* in Coptic) the Greek Chaos and Tartarus. Tartarus is mentioned only once. In Greek tradition Tartarus was part of Chaos (Johnson 1999). Its meaning in *On the Origin of the World* is traditional and in line with contemporary developments. It is a place of punishment where an enigmatic entity called 'the troublemaker' is thrown (*Orig.World* 102: 26-34, cf. *Hyp.Arch.* 95: 8-13). This is probably a reminiscence of the fight against the Titans thrown into Tartarus, originally described by Hesiod – a widely spread myth in antiquity, found, for instance, in the Jewish *Book of Watchers* (cf. Bremmer 2004; Bull 2017).

The concept of *nun* is tricky. It is an Egyptian word and refers to an Egyptian mythological entity (Finnestad 1971). In *On the Origin of the World* it is probably a translation from the Greek ábyssos, a feminine word. This partly explains why it is conceived of as feminine, in contrast to the Egyptian *nun*, who, besides being connected to the primordial chaotic waters of the origin, was personified as a male god. In LXX, the void (*tehom*) is translated as ábyssos, which means that *nun* in *On the Origin of the World* also refers to Gen 1: 2.

Nun is first mentioned in a sentence that is corrupt and hard to understand. It either says that it (the shadow), deriving from Pistis, appeared in the abyss (*nun*), or that the abyss itself derived from Pistis (99: 1-2). Independently of whether the text actually says that *nun* existed before Sophia's creation or not, there is a tendency to describe *nun* in line with Plato's *chora* as if it was pre-existent.

The next time *nun* is mentioned is when Pistis blew into the face of 'her disturbance', which was a 'fearful product' 'in the abyss (*nun*) which is below all the heavens' (99: 31-100: 1). Later Pistis predicts that the world creator Ialdabaoth will be destroyed and 'descend to your mother, the abyss (*nun*), along with those that belong to you' (103: 23-24). Also, in relation to Ialdabaoth's repenting son, Sabaoth, *nun* is spoken of as mother: Sabaoth 'hated his father, the darkness, and his mother, the abyss (*nun*), and loathed his sister, the thought of the prime parent' (104: 10-12). In the last case, darkness and abyss (*nun*) appear as two different entities, respectively male and female.

As we saw, the tractate refers to *nun* in a destructive way when it says that Ialdabaoth will go into the abyss (*nun*). In a similar way, it says that Sophia will cast the gods of Chaos (*chaos*), whom she created together with Ialdabaoth, 'down into the abyss (*nun*)' (126: 20-22), and 'they will fall into the abyss (*nun*), and the abyss (*nun*) will be overturned' (126: 34-35).[11] In the abyss the evil forces will ignite each other, like volcanoes, and finally perish. The abyss does not actively destroy them, but furnishes a space in which

[11] In the *Hyp.Arch.*, abyss (*nun*) is described as the mother of Ialdabaoth (87: 6-7), and he is eventually bound and cast down 'into Tartaros below the abyss (*nun*)' (95: 11-13).

they will self-destruct. Accordingly, *nun* has two main functions in *On the Origin of the World*. It serves as a principle of origin and is characterized metaphorically as mother. It is further presented as a place of punishment, which includes Tartarus. Chaos and *nun* could be conceived of as partly overlapping, *nun*/ ábyssos being the depths of Chaos. At the same time, *nun* has, to a more specialized degree, connotations of the motherly receptacle, known from Hesiod and Plato, an eternal principle, where all things and beings are formed.

It is likely that the description of the basic cosmological mechanisms in this tractate is indebted to Plato, or rather to a third- or fourth-century interpretation of him. In the *Timaeus*, Plato introduces three principles of origin: 'the Becoming, that 'Wherein' it becomes and the source 'Wherefrom' the Becoming is copied and produced' (50 C-D) – in other words: Being (*to on*), Space (*chora*) and Becoming (*gignomenos*). The Hesiodic Chaos conception lies, most likely, behind the space conception in Plato (Kratzert 1998: 100). Chaos in Hesiod and *Chora* in Plato both have motherly functions. Plato says that 'it is proper to liken the Recipient to the Mother, the Source to the Father, and what is engendered between these two to the Offspring' (50 D), and he characterizes *chora* as 'wet nurse' (*thene* 49 A) and 'receptacle (of seed)' (*upodoche* 49 A).[12] Plato characterizes *chora* in this way: 'and a third kind is ever-existing place (*chora*) which admits not of destruction, and provides room for all things that have birth.... it is somehow necessary that all that exists should exist in some space and occupying some place' (52 A-B).

In *On the Origin of the World* the transcendental world is identical with Being, while the creation of Pistis, including Chaos, is equivalent to Becoming, but *nun* and Chaos partly also function as a receptacle à la Plato.[13] *Nun* is explicitly called mother, but Chaos too has motherly functions because it is the place where the abortion and the 'superfluities' were created.

In Plato, *chora* is ontological and not perceptible. It is noetic space, not material space. Later philosophers, however, identified the receptacle with matter. In *On the Origin of the World* it seems to be conceived of as empty space, but later appears as material space filled with 'bottomless water'. Accordingly, there is a play on a more abstract and a more anthropomorphic view of Chaos and between a metaphorical and non-metaphorical conception of it. Similar to the Platonic *chora*, and more than the Hesiodic *Chaos*, *nun* and *Chaos* are mythologically gendered and appear as female.[14]

Conclusion

On the Origin of the World presents a dominant model of creation based on vision and light and a supplementary model based on a female desire to procreate. The abyss (*nun*) connotes to a motherly receptacle known from Homer and Plato, but also to a chaotic womb and its destructive forces. The tractate refers to Chaos and Tartarus as well as to the abyss. A variety of concepts, creation models and metaphors interact with each other in a language that is emotionally charged. The tractate invites the readers to struggle to grasp the meaning of this chaotic creation and its consequences for their lives.

References

Bull, Christian. (2017). Women Angels, and Dangerous Knowledge: The Myth of the Watchers in the *Apocryphon of John* and its Monastic Manuscript-Context. In: Ismo Dunderberg, Outi Lehtipuu, Ivan Miroshnikov, and Ulla Tervahauta (eds) *Women and Knowledge in Early Christianity.* (Supplements to Vigiliae Christianae 144): 75-107. Leiden: Brill.

Bussanich, John. (1983). A Theoretical Interpretation of Hesiod's Chaos. *Classical Philology* 78/3: 212-219.

[12] On the relationship between *meter* and *upodoche*, see Ashbaugh (1988: 100).

[13] John D. Turner points out: 'The function of the maternal member of the Sethian triad, Barbelo, is similar to that of Plato's Mother and Nurse of becoming: she embraces 'the All' as its 'Womb' (the Apocryphon of John BG 54 1-19 II 5, 5)' (Turner 2001:252), and he adds that the other 'Mother' figure, Sophia, also takes on characteristics of the Platonic Receptacle – becoming agitated (ibid.).

[14] 'Hinsichtlich des Geschlects ist die platonische Raumverstellung stärker mytisch überfrachtet als das hesiodische *chaos*' (Kratzert 1998: 100).

Crislip, Andrew. (2011). Envy and Anger at the World's Creation and Destruction in the *Treatise without Title 'On the Origin of the World'* (NHC II,5). *Vigiliae Christianae* 65: 285-310.

Dunning, Benjamin H. (2009). What Sort of Thing Is This Luminous Woman? Thinking Sexual Difference in *On the Origin of the World*. *Journal of Early Christian Studies* 17/1: 55-84.

Finnestad, Ragnhild Bjerre. (1971). *Nun: En studie i det egyptiske kaos- begrep*. Hovedfagsoppgave: Universitetet i Bergen.

Gilhus, Ingvild Sælid. (1984). *The Nature of the Archons: A Study in the Soteriology of a Gnostic Treatise from Nag Hammadi (CG II, 4)*. Wiesbaden: Otto Harrassowitz.

Gilhus, Ingvild Sælid. (2008a). Hva er kaos? Om verdens opprinnelse i kodeks II fra Nag Hammadi. *Chaos. Dansk-norsk tidsskrift for religionhistoriske studier* 49: 43-54.

Gilhus, Ingvild Sælid. (2008b). Sexuality, Marriage and Knowledge in the Apocryphon of John. In: Martti Nissinen and Risto Uro (eds) *Sacred Marriages: The Divine-Human Metaphor from Sumer to early Christianity*: 487-510. Winona Lake: Eisenbrauns.

Gilhus, Ingvild Sælid. (2015). Why is it better to be a plant than an animal? Cognitive poetics and ascetic ideals in the book of *Thomas the Contender* (NHC II, 7). In: P. Pachis and D. Wiebe (eds) *In the Sights of History and the Cognitive Sciences: Chasing Down Religion*: 99-114. Sheffield: Equinox.

Jenott, Lance. (2013). Recovering Adam's Lost Glory: Nag Hammadi Codex II in its Egyptian Monastic Environment. In: Lance Jenott and Sarit Kattan Gribetz (eds) *Jewish and Christian Cosmogony in Late Antiquity*: 222-36. Tübingen: Mohr Siebeck.

Johnson, David. (1999). Hesiod's description of Tartarus (*Theogony* 721-819). *Phoenix* 53: 8-28.

Kaiser, Ursula Ulrike. (2009). Geburt im Chaos und Belebung im Wirbelwind. Zwei neue Deutungsvorschläge zu NHC II, 5. *Zeitschrift für Antikes Christentum* 13/1: 29-37.

King, Karen L. (2006). *The Secret Revelation of John*: 191-214. Cambridge (MA) and London: Harvard University Press.

Kirk, G. S. and J.E. Raven. (1983). *The Presocratic Philosophers. A Critical History with a Selection of Texts*. Cambridge: Cambridge University Press [first edition: 1966].

Kövesces, Z. (2002). *Metaphor*. Oxford: Oxford University Press.

Kratzert, Thomas. (1998). *Die Entdeckung des Raums. Von hesiodischen chaos zur platonische chora*. Amsterdam/ Philadelphia: B.R. Grüner.

Layton, Bentley (ed.). (1989). *Nag Hammadi Codex II, 2-7 together with XIII,2*, Brit. Lib. Or.4926(1), and P. Oxy.1, 654, 655. Volume Two*. Leiden: Brill.

Lundhaug, Hugo and Lance, Jenott. (2015). *The Monastic Origins of the Nag Hammadi Codices*. Tübingen: Mohr Siebeck.

Mansfeld, J. (1981). Hesiod and Parmenides in Nag Hammadi. *Vigiliae Christianae* 35/2: 174-182.

Miller, Patricia Cox. (2001). *The Poetry of Thought in Late Antiquity. Essays in Imagination and Religion*. Aldershot: Ashgate.

Oeyen, Christian. (1975). Fragmente einer subachmimischen Version der gnostischen 'Schrift ohne Titel'. In: M. Krause (ed.) *Essays on the Nag Hammadi Texts in Honour of Pahor Labib*: 90-109. Leiden: Brill.

Painchaud, Louis. (1995a). *L'Écrit sans titre. Traité sur le l'origine du Monde*. Louvain/Quebec: Peeters/Les presses de l'Université Laval.

Painchaud, Louis. (1995b). The Writing without Title of Nag Hammadi Codex II: A Redactional Hypothesis. *The Second Century* 8: 217-34.

Perkins, Pheme. (1980). On the Origin of the World (CG II,5): A Gnostic Physics. *Vigiliae Christianae* 34: 34-46.

Schenke, Hans Martin. (1959). Vom Ursprung der Welt: Eine titellose gnostische Abhandlung aus dem Funde von Nag Hammadi. *Theologische Literaturzeitung* 84: 243-256.

Turner, John D. (2001). *Sethian Gnosticism and the Platonic Tradition. Bibliothèque Copte de Hag Hammadi*. Québec/Paris: Les Presses de l'Université Laval/Peeters Press.

Turner, Mark. (2000). *Death is the Mother of Beauty: Mind, Metaphor, Criticism*. Rochester: Cybereditions [first edition: 1987].

Wintermute, Orval. (1972). A Study of Gnostic Exegesis of the Old Testament.' In: James M. Efird (ed.) *The Use of the Old Testament in the New and other essays: studies in honor of William Franklin Stinespring*: 241-264. Durham NC: Duke University Press.

Liquid Images and the poetics of vision in ancient Greece

Jørgen Bakke
University of Bergen

The notion that vision is a form of physical contact was deeply rooted in ancient Greek culture. In this article, I will discuss the idea of interactive vision from the Archaic through to the Hellenistic period. Euclid's optical theory is an important reference for this discussion. My focus will, however, be on pre-Euclidean cultural optics as it can be documented by visual culture and early Greek literature rather than on a close reading of Euclid. I first address some theoretical aspects of early Greek poetics of vision, and then I will discuss a selection of examples from early Greek mythology and visual culture, including the myth about the Theban princess Semele and her love affair with Zeus, as well as the image of the lethal gaze of the gorgon Medusa.

In modern art historical terms, I will approach vision in ancient Greece as a part of what art historians like Svetlana Alpers referred to as 'visual culture' back in the late 1980s (Alpers 1983: 8). Very much inspired by cultural anthropology (Geertz 1976), Alpers regarded physical images, everyday use of visual objects and scientific theories about vision (optics), as well as experimental practices and scientific instruments, as integrated elements in a specific geohistorical visual culture.

While I have labelled my approach to interactive vision in ancient Greece a poetics of vision, this should be understood more in a classical (Aristotelian) rather than in a modern sense. I will not attempt to describe a literary theory of vision, or discuss poetry about vision. Vision will be viewed as an activity (πράξις) that involves the external world, the instrument of vision (the eye), the medium of vision and the mind where vision is processed. This is how Aristotle approached vision in *De sensu* (Aristotle and Ross 1906: 437a 19-439a6; 47-54). The place of images in the Aristotelian model is complex because an image can be something external like a painting or a sculpture and it can be a mental image. In the ancient Greek poetics of vision, external and mental images are, as we will see, closely interconnected. According to Aristotle, it is this process of interconnecting external and mental images that makes up the activity of vision. It is also from Aristotle that I have adopted the notion of the liquid image. I aim to demonstrate that far from being the theoretical construction of Aristotle, the notion of the fluidity of the imaging process can be found in the epic tradition, in the Pre-Socratics as well as in ancient Greek religious culture.

Interactive Images and the Poetics of Vision

In Euclid's *Optica*, human vision is described as a form of physical contact between the observing subject and the observed object. Euclid described the nature of this physical contact as 'discrete rays of vision' (αἱ προσπίπτουσαι ὄψεις), rays that cannot be seen, but that establish unbroken connections between the eye and the object of vision (Euclid and Heiberg 1865: 1.3, 2). In Euclid's model the eye is the active agent in this process. He believed that these rays emanate from the eye (extramission) rather than from the object of vision (intromission). Euclid's *Optica* is first and foremost a discussion of the mathematics of vision. He has very little interest in the physics of the rays of vision or, indeed, in the physiology of the eye itself.

Euclid's extramission theory is clearly based on a traditional concept, the so-called 'theory of intraocular fire' (Lindberg 1981: 5), which can also be found in Plato. In the *Timaeus* this is described as a mild form of fire, a 'gentle light' (φῶς ἥμερον) that flows through the eye, coalesces with daylight and reaches the object of vision in a straight line from the eye (Plato 1990: 45b-d, 76). Plato does, in fact, say a lot more about the physics of the rays of vision than Euclid, and he is also fascinated by the physiological mechanics of the instrument of vision:

> [The gentle fire] is making the whole fabric of the eyeball, and especially the central part, smooth and close in texture, so as to let nothing pass that is of coarser stuff, but only fire of this description to filter through pure by itself. (Plato 1990: 45b-c, 76; Cornford 1997: 152).

Different versions of the theory of intraocular fire and a similar interest in the physiology of the eye can be found in the Pre-Socratics. According to Aristotle, the Sicilian Empedocles (ca. 493-433 BC) compared the eye with a lantern placed around a flame to protect it against the weather:

> [...] it divides the blasts of the rushing winds, but the light, the finer substance, passes through and shines on the threshold with unyielding beams; so at that time [when Aphrodite created eyes] primeval fire, enclosed in membranes, gave birth to the round pupil in its delicate garments which are pierced through with wondrous channels. These keep out the water, which surrounds the pupil, but let through the fire, the finer part (Diels 1906: fr. 84, 194; Aristotle and Ross 1906: 437b28-438a3, 48; Guthrie 1965: 235).

In his translation of this passage William Guthrie inserted the expression 'when Aphrodite created eyes' (Guthrie 1965: 235), which is not actually there in the Greek text but which makes perfect sense because it is inspired by another fragment of Empedocles (Diels 1906: fr. 95, 196) where he mentions that the goddess Aphrodite crafted the eyes of men 'with her own hands' (ἐν παλάμῃσιν). In fragment 84, cited by Aristotle in his discussion of vision in *De sensu*, Empedocles's more technical explanation is presented. Empedocles believed that it was rather the first fire that broke through the membrane of the eye that created the perfect circularity of the pupil. Empedocles thus regarded the pupil not as the agent of vision, but rather as an element in the medium of vision, because the fire of vision passes through it. It is the fire of vision that designs the pupil rather than the pupil that generates vision.

Another theorem of Empedocles is that the eye itself was made of water. Rather than extinguishing the fire of vision, the water of the eye was ingeniously diverted away from the pupil by channels in the eye designed by Aphrodite, and so the water of the eye protects the fire of vision like a lantern protects a flame.

Unlike the traditionalists Empedocles and Plato, Aristotle accepts neither the concept of extramission nor the idea of the corporeal nature of vision. In *De anima* he states that vision 'is neither fire, nor in general any body, nor an emanation from any body' (Aristotle and Hett 1957: 2.7. 418b14-16, 105). Aristotle has a long list of critical remarks about earlier theories of vision, and he is especially sceptical of the view presented in the *Timaeus* (Aristotle and Ross 1906: 437a19-439a6, 47-55). One might say that there are two basic, and typically Aristotelian, counter-arguments to Pre-Socratic and Platonic optics. First, even though sense perceptions are physical, the senses represent a form of local consciousness. As the most important of the senses, vision has a special role in Aristotle's thinking. For him the eye is not just fascinating for its remarkable physiological mechanics that his predecessors had ascribed to the handicraft of Aphrodite:

> The reason for these contentions is that consciousness, or the psychical faculty of sense perception (τῆς ψυχῆς τὸ αἰσθητικόν), does not reside on the surface of the eye, but evidently within; this is why the interior of the eye must be transparent and receptive of light (Aristotle and Ross 1906: 438b9-13, 52-53).

The eye is important for Aristotle because it is inside the eye that the faculty of visual perception is located. This view also implies that vision, unlike taste, is not a form of touch. Touch and taste belong to the warm senses because they 'are close to the heart' (Aristotle and Ross 1906: 439a1-5, 52-53). Vision is believed by Aristotle to be the sense that is closest to the brain, and accordingly it is regarded as the coldest of the senses: 'The origin of the eyes is of the same fashion [as odour]; they derive their composition from the brain, the coldest and most watery of the bodily members.' (Aristotle and Ross 1906: 438b30-32)

It was probably Aristotle's understanding of the brain as the coldest and most watery part of the body that led him to accept one traditional theorem of vision, namely that the eyes are made up of water (Aristotle and Ross 1906: 438a5-6, 50-51). In accepting this theorem, Aristotle also makes his most important reinterpretation of traditional poetics of vision by focusing not on vision itself, but rather on the medium of vision. In order for vision to function, according to Aristotle, a transparent continuum must be present between the object of vision and the faculty of vision that is located inside the eye (Aristotle and Hett 1957: 2.7. 418a32-b3, 103). According to Aristotle, air and water are the only two possible candidates that meet the requirements for such a continuous medium. Since Aristotle has already accepted the traditional notion that the eye consists of water, he argues that it is the water of the eye that permits it to participate in the transparency of the continuous medium between the object and the interior of the eye.

Aristotle accepted the theory that the eye consists of water and that it is this quality that permits it to participate in the medium of vision (Aristotle and Ross 1906: 438a13-17, 50-51). Most importantly, Aristotle continues, this theory can also be supported by experience:

> Thus this theory is true that the sightorgan consists of water [...] The facts themselves make this clear (δῆλον); what issues from the eyes when they are seriously hurt is evidently water (Aristotle and Ross 1906: 438a13-19, 50-51).

The eyes can connect with the transparent continuum due to their ability to actively release some of their moisture. It is interesting that Aristotle presents the secretion of tears both as evidence of the liquid composition of the eye, but also as an analogy, and even as something very close to a paradigm, of the act of vision itself. Like the secretion of tears is a result of a strong emotional movement in the watery substance of the eye, vision itself can be regarded as an inversion of the process of crying. Vision, thus, is understood by Aristotle as an internal movement in the watery substance of the eye caused by an external visible object. The watery substance of the sense organ of the eye thus generates visual impressions, liquid mental images, by taking on the form, colours and volumes of the objects of vision. By means of this inverted crying, the sense organ of vision 'becomes the sensible object' as was once formulated by Harold Cherniss (Cherniss 1935: 320).

Aristotle's approach to vision is a radical reinterpretation of the traditional fifth-century poetics of vision. The example of Euclid demonstrates, however, that Aristotle's distinction between touch and vision remained controversial in the later phases of ancient science. Because Euclid's optics was the basis of medieval optics, the traditional view has been that the Euclidean notion of the corporeality of vision was first challenged by neo-Aristotelians in the thirteenth century (Lindberg 1981: 132-139). The implication of recent attempts to question the corporeality of vision in the Byzantine tradition for the history of optics is currently an open debate (Betancourt 2016; Peers 2012). From the classical to the early modern era, optical theorists disagreed about whether the rays emanated from the object (intromission) or from the eye (extramission), but the idea of vision as a form of invisible physical contact appears to be the most stable theorem in the pre-modern history of optics (Lindberg 1981). With a few exceptions, Aristotle being the most important, vision in ancient Greece was always regarded as a form of physical interaction, between men, between men and gods, and between men and monsters, as we shall soon see. The modern expression 'It was just something I saw' would be incomprehensible in ancient Greece because vision is never innocent and always physical. Ancient Greek mythology is rich in stories about how the physical contact of vision can be dangerous and even lethal.

Semele: The Divine Paradigm of Intraocular Fire

That the imaging functionality of the sensory organ of the eye is closely connected to its ability to physically interact makes vision a very powerful tool for interaction with supernatural entities. An important paradigm for the power of divine vision in ancient Greece is the story of the Theban princess Semele and her fatal love affair with Zeus. When Semele convinced Zeus to show his true nature to her, the rays of Zeus's eyes (to speak in Euclidean terms) burned his lover so hard that nothing remained of her but ash (Ovid 2004: 3.300-310; 107). Zeus's child by Semele, Dionysus, was thus 'delivered by the fire of lightning' (λοχευθεῖσ' ἀστραπηφόρῳ πυρί, Euripides and Dodds 1986: 3; 3) that also consumed his mother but made him immortal. In Dionysus's monologue in the prologue of Euripides's *Bacchae*, Semele's home in Thebes, where Zeus burned her to ashes, was kept as an 'unapproachable ... sacred precinct' (ἄβατον ... σηκόν, Euripides and Dodds 1986: 11, 3.); 'And the ruins of her home smoulder with the yet living fire of Zeus' (Δίου πυρὸς ἔτι ζῶσαν φλόγα, Euripides and Dodds 1986: 3; 3 and 64). What Euripides referred to as a 'memorial of Dionysius's mother' (μητρὸς μνῆμα, Euripides and Dodds 1986: 6; 3) was still there when Pausanias visited the site in the second century AD. Pausanias referred to it as one of 'the ruins of bridal chambers' (θαλάμων ἐρείπια, Pausanias and Jones 1979: 9.12.3, 222). According to Pausanias's guides, this precinct was held in the highest regard and it was 'still unapproachable' (ἔτι ἄβατον, Pausanias and Jones 1979: 9.12.3; 222).

All sites, and indeed also persons (Euripides and Way 1962: 937, 204), in ancient Greece that were struck by lightning were held in the same especially sacred regard signified by the Greek word ἄβατος ('unapproachable, not to be trodden'). Pausanias does not say anything about a perpetual fire at the μνῆμα of Semele in Thebes, but he does mention that together with the strike of lightning that hit Semele, another miraculous item was deposited there from heaven:

> There is also a story that along with the thunderbolt hurled at the bridalchamber of Semele there fell a log (ξύλον) from heaven. They say that Polydorus adorned this log with bronze (τὸ ξύλον τοῦτο χαλκῷ ἐπικοσμήσαντα) and called it Dionysus Cadmus. Near it is an image (ἄγαλμα) of Dionysus; Onasimedes made it of solid bronze (Pausanias and Jones 1979: 9.12.4; 222-225).

The log (ξύλον) that fell from heaven can best be related to a word that is more commonly associated with early Christianity, namely the ἀχειροποιήτος (Mark 14.58), the image (or building) that is miraculously made ‹without the use of human hands›. Especially in the study of the Byzantine Christian tradition, the ἀχειροποιήτος has provided a paradigm for the view that Christian images reach out to the beholder (Nelson 2000). Recently this view of Byzantine cultural optics has been contested (Betancourt 2016; Peers 2012). In ancient Greece, the ἀχειροποιήτος was regarded as an early form of cult image (Burkert 1985: 90; Vernant 1991: 154). Many of these logs were probably carved with simple iconic features, or adorned with metal plates as described by Pausanias. Such simple 'wooden images' are usually referred to as ξοᾶνα. When Pausanias uses the term ξύλος ('wood, log') rather than ξοᾶνον ('image made of wood'), his choice probably indicates that the item in question was a simple aniconic wood fragment wrapped in a, possibly iconic, bronze plate. The distinction between the aniconic and acheiropoietic ξύλος that was adorned with bronze and the massive bronze ἄγαλμα (‹statue, image') is, however, one of degree rather than essence: they both represent Dionysus, but the acheiropoietic ξύλος is, despite its lack of visual resemblance, of a higher degree of unity with the divinity it represents than the mimetic ἄγαλμα.

The story about the lightning-stricken Semele and her offspring Dionysus can be read as the mythological origin of divine vision: Semele is burning with an impossible desire. She wants to see her divine lover. In Euripides's *Bacchae*, Semele's brother Pentheus is faced with a similar problem. He tries to spy on the female followers of Dionysus (Euripides and Dodds 1986: 981; 40). The problem that the two siblings of the House of Cadmus share is that it is impossible to see a god without being spotted, without being looked back at. When he is discovered, Pentheus is torn to pieces by his own mother (Euripides and Dodds 1986: 1125-1136; 46) and reduced to a mask (πρόσωπον, Euripides and Dodds 1986: 1277; 52), a mere image as his mother returns to Thebes with his head on a stick. His sister Semele was killed by divine vision itself. The gaze of Zeus is nothing like the gentle light (φῶς ἥμερον) that Plato assigns to interactive human vision. It is pure energy that consumes anything terrestrial in its way.

As an extreme version of it (sic), the incinerating fire of divine vision also serves as a paradigm for the theory of intraocular fire. Human vision is shaped in the image of divine vision, so to speak, but with downgraded effect. An important detail in the myth about Semele is that the power of Zeus's vision presupposes interactive vision. What triggers the incineration is, in fact, not the gaze of Zeus, nor the gaze of Semele, but the interactive exchange of gazes between them. It is when Semele meets the true gaze of Zeus with her own that she becomes completely incinerated.

This story about the πράξις of divine vision also offers a possible medium for the interactive exchange of vision between men and gods, and that is through the visual traces, the residue (ἐρείπια) of divine vision. The image of the supernatural in the form of a mimetic statue (ἄγαλμα) of a god is obviously one example of such a medium, but the most powerful medium is the visually least impressive, the actual, physical traces that are left behind from Semele's encounter with divine intraocular fire. These traces are made up of 'the ruins of Semele's bridal chamber' (θαλάμων ἐρείπια), but the most important trace is the ‹aniconic wooden fragment' (ξύλος) that fell down from the sky in the process of the burning of Semele. Now according to the myth, the terrestrial body of Semele was completely incinerated, and the only residue of that process was the foetus of Dionysius that Zeus incorporated in his leg. Since the log that fell from the sky was also a result of the interchange of vision between Zeus and Semele, the log is, like the foetus of Dionysus, also a residue of this process. It is thus similar to the remains of the house of Semele, but of a higher order, because it is born, like Dionysus himself, of the very incinerating process of divine vision.

Medusa: If looks can kill, how do they go about doing it?

Another expression of the malevolent power of supernatural vision in Greek mythology is the gorgon Medusa, but the interactive vision of Medusa works in a very different manner to Zeus's incinerating bolt of lightning. The gorgon's head is described as the most hideous appearance, with a mask-like face, snake hair, a mouth with gnashing teeth that create the most terrible sound and large, wide-open eyes (Vernant 1991: 116-118). In early Greek visual culture, the head of Medusa (Figure 1) is always portrayed in the frontal position facing the unfortunate passer-by. Unlike Zeus, who tries to avoid making a true visual appearance before the eyes of humans, Medusa actively pursues man with her true and terrible image.

Figure 1. Head of Medusa. Detail from late archaic Attic hydria found in Tarquinia, Italy. British Museum m.n. 1867,0508.1048. Published under the Creative Commons Attribution-NonCommercial-ShareAlike 4.0 International (CC BY-NC-SA 4.0) licence.

Just the sound of her teeth or the poisonous bite of the snakes that make up her hair would probably kill whatever adversary anyway, but these receptacles are superfluous because her gaze is lethal. According to the legend, anyone who met the eyes of the gorgon would be turned into stone (Vernant 1991: 144). The multi-sensorial impression caused by an encounter with Medusa is literally petrifying. Her ugly and frightening appearance reaches out through the continuum of vision and creates a horrible image, and sound, in the mind of the beholder. With the burning force of supernatural vision, the gaze of Medusa shoots through and evaporates the fluctuating continuum of living vision. When the lightning flame from Medusa's eyes meets the eyes of a living man, death will immediately occur in a most instant and terrible way.

In early Greece, the living body is described as warm and infused with liquid αἰῶν, 'the stuff of life' (Homer and Monro II 1902: 14.24-28; 32). As already pointed out by Richard Onians, αἰῶν should not be understood primarily as the abstract temporal concept lifespan as it is often translated, but rather as the concrete and liquid stuff of life associated with tears, sweat and sexual activity (Onians 1988: 200-205). There were very specific ideas about how αἰῶν was supposed to leave the body during a normal death, which included the performance of funeral rituals, handling of the body and communal mourning (Onians 1988: 272-274). Being turned into stone in a split second by the supernatural gaze of Medusa is, however, anything but normal. Such a death threatens the very social order of ancestral memory culture (Vernant 1991: 149). What remains after an encounter with Medusa is not even a body (σῶμα), but a dry, inanimate image (ἄγαλμα) of the body in stone. If you look at the image of Medusa, you will yourself be reduced to nothing more than an image, a memorial in carved stone (μνῆμα) like so many other grave markers in stone in an ancient Greek cemetery. The gaze of Medusa does not completely incinerate the human beholder but reduces him to a dead ruin (ἐρείπια), a mere visual residue, an image of the living body.

Despite her lethal character, the Argive hero Perseus eventually manages to kill Medusa, but he requires a lot of help and preparation. What is so special about Perseus's equipment and preparation is that it is all about making him a superhero of optical deception. Like Achilles is equipped with new armour crafted by Hephaestus the god of metallurgy, Perseus is aided by the god of rhetoric and optical deception Hermes to obtain the most spectacular stealth technology (to use a term from modern military technology) available to the Greek gods. To get hold of this technology Perseus must first fight off the sisters of the gorgons, the Graiai. Only the Graiai know the route to the nymphs that are the keepers of the optical talismans that he needs to approach the gorgon Medusa (Vernant 1991: 145). Like their sister Medusa, the Graiai are also optical monsters. Their monstrosity is a form of collective defect since they possess only one eye between them (Aeschylus and Mazon 1931: 795; 189). By stealing their common eye 'as one was passing it on to the other' (Ovid 2004: 776; 169) Perseus forced them to reveal the route to the nymphs. The most important talisman he obtained from the nymphs is the κυνέη (Hesiod and Evelyn-White 2002: Sh. 227, 236), Hermes's magical cap of invisibility. Perseus is also equipped with another instrument of optical deception, a mirror (Vernant 1991: 135). This permits Perseus to attack Medusa undetected while looking indirectly at her weakened reflection in the mirror. A third optical device that Perseus is equipped with is the κίβισις (Hesiod and Evelyn-White 2002: Sh. 224, 236), the pouch that he will use to hide the head of Medusa in. Blacking out the gaze of Medusa is crucial because even though the body of Medusa is mortal, her lethal gaze is immortal. This is also why the image of the frontal mask-like face of the gorgon with its wide-open eyes (Figure 1) is such a popular and powerful symbol of interactive images in ancient Greek visual culture. Even though the monster is dead, her eyes still retain their lethal power; even the image of her gaze has an effect on whoever meets it with their own eyes.

The scene with Perseus and Medusa was popular in early Greek visual culture, in monumental temple decoration (Figure 2) as well as in vase painting. In the Selinunte metope from the mid sixth century, Perseus is typically looking away from Medusa as he beheads her. There are four figures squeezed into the narrow pictorial space of the metope: Athena, Perseus, Medusa and Pegasus. All three main characters are portrayed in a frontal pose with gazes oriented directly towards the spectator. This is not an uncommon phenomenon in early Greek temple sculpture, and is usually regarded as an apotropaic device (Stewart 1990: 115). The most powerful apotropaic image, of course, is the head, and especially

Figure 2. Perseus killing Medusa with Athena and Pegasus. Limestone metope from Temple C at Selinus, ca. 550 BC. Archaeological Museum of Palermo. Photo: Giovanni Dall'Orto. Published under the Creative Commons Attribution-ShareAlike 2.5 Generic licence.

the eyes, of Medusa. Even though her body is dead, her mask-like image has preserved its death-infusing powers. The parallel direction of the gazes also makes sense within the non-linear visual representation of the plot. The three main characters are locked in a silent optical dialogue with Perseus caught in the middle. Perseus can't look at Medusa because he will be dead if he does. Because she is a god, it would also be an act of hubris for Perseus to look at Athena. If he did try to look directly at Athena, he would be making the same kind of tragic optical error as the Theban siblings Semele and Pentheus. Perseus is, in other words, not just looking away from the gaze of the gorgon. He is caught between the gazes of two supernatural entities.

The way that the marble workers at Selinunte compressed the story into one metope draws the spectator approaching the sanctuary into a disturbing optical dialogue: he can't see Perseus holding up a mirror, but the parallel and frontal gazes of the three main characters enable the interpretation that the mirror is outside the image. In that case, could it be the reflective surfaces of the eyes of the spectator that are drawn into the place of the mirror? The marble workers at Selinunte have, in that case, chosen a particularly disturbing display of this mytheme; it would have been less disturbing if the spectator was not looking directly at the gaze of the gorgon: she would be already dead, and her ugly head hidden in Perseus's κίβισις. The depicted moment is rhetorically efficient in reminding the spectator about the particular optical monstrosity of Medusa: as Perseus beheads her, she dies, but the lethal power of the gaze on her mask-like face does not die. It is merely enclosed in Perseus's κίβισις. The most terrifying power of the monster is the capacity of its image, its face, its mask to preserve its lethal effect even

Figure 3. Perseus, Medusa and Hermes. Red figure scene by the Amasis Painter on late archaic Attic Olpe. British Museum m.n. 1849,0620.5. Published under the Creative Commons Attribution-NonCommercial-ShareAlike 4.0 International (CC BY-NC-SA 4.0) licence.

Figure 4. A man riding a hippalectryon (cock-horse) flanked by two gigantic eyes. Detail of late archaic Attic Eye Cup found in Vulci, Italy. British Museum m.n. 1836,0224.65. Published under the Creative Commons Attribution-NonCommercial-ShareAlike 4.0 International (CC BY-NC-SA 4.0) licence.

after the monster is dead. Fortunately, we might think, we are not turned into stone because we are not actually looking at Medusa. We are looking at the image of Medusa in the reflective surface of the carved stone relief, but then we forget that the image of Medusa is not simply an image. It is an animated mask that has preserved the lethal power of the dead monster. The sculptural composition is accordingly threatening to reverse the very optical process, as though it is not we who are looking at Medusa's image, but rather the lethal and immortal gaze of Medusa that is looking at us as though we are mere images, reflective surfaces, objects, dead stones.

The interaction between Perseus and Athena is, of course, very different from his interaction with Medusa. Athena is there to help him, not by directly interfering in the plot, but by assisting Perseus with the particular kind of practical knowledge (μῆτις) that he needs to fight Medusa (Detienne and Vernant 1978: 179). Perseus's approach to divine vision is a much cleverer approach than Semele's and Pentheus's. He is not struck by an impossible desire to see what he should not see. He is rather patiently listening to instructions from Athena (and from Hermes), and he uses the practical knowledge he obtains from them to defend himself against the supernatural vision of Medusa. This approach is supported by the design on an olpe attributed to the Amasis Painter (Figure 3) from the second half of the sixth century. Here Medusa is placed in the centre of the scene in a frontal pose. Perseus stands to the left of her and is just about to behead the monster. Here his gaze is turned to the left and away from Medusa. To the right of Medusa stands Hermes, messenger staff lifted, mouth wide open and with his right hand gently lifted as though he is speaking, instructing perhaps his pupil Perseus. Note that here Perseus is dressed up as Hermes's double with the κυνέη and winged boots, the instruments of optical deception that he obtained from the nymphs (Vernant 1991: 146).

The kind of optical deception that Perseus is made capable of with the help of Athena and Hermes, and with the devices obtained from the nymphs, is, of course, a lot more sophisticated than the simple optical devices known in early Greek culture such as the ὕαλος, an optical lens used for making fire that

Figure 5. Pair of eyes of bronze, marble, frit, quartz and obsidian. Classical period of unknown provenance. The Metropolitan Museum of Art. Ac.n. 1991.11.3a, b. Photo: The Metropolitan Museum of Art's photograph studio.

is mentioned in Aristophanes's *Clouds* (Aristophanes and Dover 1968: 765-772, 47; Pasquale 2004: 56-57) or the optical quality rock crystal lenses perhaps used by Greek craftsmen to work with fine details that have been documented by archaeologists already from the Bronze Age (Sines and Sakellaris 1987). Importantly, Perseus also uses a common optical device, the mirror, to fight Medusa. Polished bronze mirrors were common in Greco-Roman antiquity. The story about a mirror in a sanctuary at Lykosoura mentioned by Pausanias confirms the belief that a mirror could be used to view the visual appearance of supernatural entities 'in their full clarity' (ἐναργῶς, Pausanias and Jones 1979: 8.37.7; 88) without the same fatal effect as viewing its true appearance.

The story about the killing of Medusa and the remains of her mask-like head are reminders of a most particular feature of ancient Greek poetics of vision, namely the interactive and potentially lethal power of images, and perhaps of images of stone in particular. The economic resources and technical skills invested in the visual arts in ancient Greece are closely linked with a strong cultural desire to interact visually with the supernatural. This desire to visualize the supernatural perhaps also explains the ancient Greek obsession with the visual, with vision, with instruments of optical deception, with optical theory and, first and foremost, with the gaze and with eyes.

Moist eyes, wet landscapes, funerary libations and liquid images

Eyes were popular motives in archaic Greek vase painting (Figure 4), and the topsides of every Greek ship were equipped with eyes designed to frighten off the enemy. In Greek sculpture the eyes were the most elaborately decorated features. Often made in precious material and crafted with great technical precision, inlaid eyes are seldom preserved in Greek sculpture. The mid-fifth-century Riace Bronzes are rare examples (Sparkes 1987: 162-163). A beautiful pair of eyes (Figure 5), probably also from the mid fifth century, is in the collection of the Metropolitan Museum in New York (Picón 2007: 127, 433). The whites of these eyes were made of a kind of glass paste that is also preserved in one of the Riace Bronzes.

Irises were made of coloured quartz, and a polished piece of black volcanic glass, obsidian, was placed at the centre of each eye. In pristine condition this would have created a similar reflective surface to the natural pupil of the eye. Both eyes were mounted in a frame of beautifully crafted eyelashes in bronze. The making of eyes for sculpture was certainly a work for jewellers, and since Aphrodite was believed to be the original designer of eyes it is not that strange that the finest craftsmanship would be involved in making the eyes the most beautiful, lifelike and seductive feature of the sculpture. Literary descriptions such as Pausanias's ekphrasis of the eyes of a statue of Athena in the sanctuary of Hephaestus in the Athenian Agora are reminders of this almost completely lost art of vision:

> When I saw the statue (ἄγαλμα) of Athena [in the temple of Hephaestus] had blue eyes I found out that the legend about them [Athena and Hephaestus] is Libyan. For the Libyans have a saying that the Goddess is the daughter of Poseidon and Lake Tritonis, and for this reason has blue eyes like Poseidon (Pausanias and Jones 1992: 1.14.6, 74).

Pausanias's description of the ἄγαλμα of Athena is not a description in the modern sense, but rather an ἔκφρασις (Webb 2009), a rhetorical-literary device aimed at generating visual impressions in the psychical faculty of visual perception of the audience/reader, to use Aristotle's terminology. The rhetorical purpose of the description is thus to set into motion the production of liquid images without an act of vision actually occurring. When the gaze of the ἄγαλμα of Athena meets the gaze of the second-century AD academic tourist Pausanias it is as though she reveals hidden truths to him, as though he can see what he cannot really see. The eyes of the statue turn the meeting into an epiphany, and Pausanias's description into a true eyewitness account (αὐτοψία), a term that in ancient Greek is used as much about visions of supernatural entities as in a modern forensic meaning. Looking into the reflective surface of the beautifully crafted obsidian pupils of Athena's eyes, all kinds of liquid images take shape in the mind of the beholder.

The eyes of gods and supernatural monsters can interact visually with men in a number of different ways, and this visual interaction is crucial for the reception of images of the supernatural in ancient Greece. What, then, about the eyes of ordinary, and not so ordinary men (heroes)? The most potent way that the eyes of humans can physically interact is through the secretion of tears. In Homeric anthropology, tears were considered to be a release of αἰών, the very stuff of life (Onians 1988: 201), and Aristotle, as we have seen, considered the secretion of tears to be both a paradigm and evidence of the liquid character of the medium of vision. In the funeral ritual, crying was considered a compulsory form of expression, not just because crying was an appropriate social expression of personal mourning, but also because the tears of the attendants were considered to have a special role in consolidating the interactive visual relationship between the dead and the living. The secretion of tears was believed to open a continuum between the world of the living and the world of the dead. Communicating with the dead is accordingly a process where the poetics of vision is very much involved. A very precise literary description of this process is provided in the 11th song of the Odyssey where Odysseus pays a visit to the gate of the Underworld (Bakke 2010).

In order to get to the passage to the Underworld, where no living man, hero or god can pass, Odysseus must travel through a wet, subterranean landscape. Homer's description of the Underworld is very much a literary visualization of a wet, almost liquid, landscape. It is very difficult to manoeuvre in this landscape dominated by intersecting streams and overlaid with thick mist. The route to the Underworld is described as streams and channels (Homer and Allen III 1917: 10.505-534, 185-186) similar to the description of the liquidity of the medium and instrument of vision that we have seen from the Pre-Socratics to Aristotle. In order to pass safely through the liquid continuum of vision beyond life Odysseus can't travel alone. There is no mention of Hermes in the 11th song of the Odyssey. Probably in analogy with Perseus's hunt for Medusa, an Athenian fifth-century vase painter added Hermes as the companion of Odysseus's journey to the Underworld.[1] In order to view beyond life, and pass through the liquid landscape to the Underworld, Odysseus, like Perseus on his journeys, also needs all the stealth technology that he can get from Hermes.

[1] See classical Attic red figure pelike painted by the Lykaon Painter with Odysseus, Elpenor and Hermes in the Underworld.. The Museum of Fine

When Odysseus eventually reached the gate of the Underworld he performed a sacrifice with honey, milk, wine and water (Homer and Allen III 1917: 11.26-8, 190), exactly the kind of liquid sacrifices, libations, that would normally be offered to the dead in ancient Greek funeral rituals (Onians 1988: 271-274; Burkert 1985: 71-72). The circumstances that Odysseus found himself in, still alive looking into the chasm of Erebus, are, however, anything but normal. In order to attract the souls of the dead, Circe has instructed Odysseus to pour blood from a sacrificial animal into the chasm. The shadows of people from Odysseus's past rise from the 'mist and clouds' (Homer and Allen III 1917: 11.15, 189) that surround it, and just like the undead vampires of modern popular culture, the blood gives the departed souls strength to communicate with Odysseus (Bakke 2010: 29).

In the dialogue between Odysseus and the soul of Elpenor, a recently deceased member of Odysseus's crew, the details of the early Greek poetics of vision beyond life are described: Elpenor had met a most unfortunate death. Dead-drunk, he had fallen asleep on a cliff, and when he woke up confused and hung-over, he tripped, fell down and broke his neck. Because Odysseus and his crew were in a hurry to leave the island of Circe, they did not have time to perform the burial rites for Elpenor, but left his body, as Homer says, 'unwept (ἄκλαπτον) and unburied (ἄθαπτον)' (Homer and Allen III 1917: 11.53-54; 191). It is obvious from the dialogue with Elpenor's soul that Odysseus had forgotten all about the incident. When he is reminded of it he is overcome with emotions: 'When I saw him I wept, and my heart had compassion for him (Homer and Allen III 1917: 11.55, 191; Bakke 2010: 31).'

Another reason why Odysseus becomes so emotionally touched by the first encounter with the soul of Elpenor is that it (his soul) is in a very bad state. Elpenor's visual appearance is unclear, without proper form, a ψυχῆ, a ghost (Onians 1988: 202). After Odysseus has seen this blurred phantom of Elpenor, he has an emotional and physiological reaction that leads to the secretion of tears, and it is those tears – the ultimate expression of the physics of optical communication – that cause the visual appearance of the soul of Elpenor to change. The tears of Odysseus physically touch Elpenor's blurred phantom, and actively mend it. It is as though a leak in the continuum of vision beyond life that has made it weaker is repaired and so the continuum is rehabilitated. After Odysseus's reaction, the soul of Elpenor is no longer described as a blurred phantom (ψυχῆ) but as a clear and well-proportioned image, an εἴδωλον (Bakke 2010: 32). The physiological response of Odysseus's optical instrument gives Elpenor a proper form, referred to with a word that in later Greek literature is used, among other things, to refer to visual art. This is probably the reason why the specific visual form that is given to Elpenor's ghost in a fifth-century vase painting is that of a sculpture of a male nude by Polycleitus, the ultimate contemporary expression of artistic beauty in the mid fifth century (Bakke 2010: 38; Osborne 1998: 169).

The idea that the secretion of tears as an emotional response to encounters with the dead is critical in forming a clear, aesthetical form to the images of the dead is, I believe, important in order to understand the particular ancient Greek practice of erecting grave markers with images of the deceased at the site of the grave. This practice is documented as early as the eighth century, for example with the famous so-called Dipylon vases, found in the Kerameikos cemetery outside the Dipylon (Double Gate) in the city wall of Athens. The most elaborately decorated examples are large craters (Figure 6), bowls for mixing wine and water, which were probably used to mark aristocratic warrior tombs (Boardman 1998: 25-26). Typically, the body of these vessels is decorated with two separate pictorial friezes, and the upper section of the vessel is crowned with a broad, continuous meander band. The upper figural band is made up of a funeral scene: a body is stretched out on a raised platform, surrounded by both large and small human figures and animals. On each side of the funeral scene, rows of attendants stand upright with arms raised to the head, a conventional pictorial gesture of grief, emotional outburst and crying. The lower figural scene, also a continuous band going all around the vase, shows wagons pulled by four horses and warriors with shields.

Arts, Boston: http://www.mfa.org/collections/object/jar-pelike-with-odysseus-and-elpenor-in-the-underworld-153840 (visited 11.12.17).

Figure 6. Dipylon Krater. Late Geometric Attic black-figure krater with burial scene. The Metropolitan Museum of Art. Acc.n. 14.130.14. Photo: The Metropolitan Museum of Art's photograph studio.

The still accepted, traditional interpretation of the funeral scene is that it represents one particular stage in the funeral ritual (Ahlberg 1971: 285): of the lower figural band that it is a conventional representation of warriors, and of the upper meander that it is simply a decorative band with no specific cultural meaning. I believe that the entire design should be connected very closely with the 11th song of the Odyssey, and that the pictorial logic that we see in practice here is precisely the same as described in the 11th song of the Odyssey. The continuous meander in the upper band of the vase decoration is a landscape reference to the shape of a surface river, and it reminds the attendants of the world of subterranean rivers that the soul of the deceased has entered. The continuous lower band of warriors is a reference to the continuous stream of warrior souls that approached Odysseus in the Underworld. There is something very characteristically Homeric about the material culture of war in this scene – anachronistic fighting techniques (wagons) and shields with a characteristic shape that can be found in images from the Mycenaean period (Grethlein 2008). In the eighth century, these images appear as portraits of mythical battles in a constructed past: this is the pictorial equivalent of the anachronistic language of the Homeric dialect.

The central scene does not merely describe a specific stage of the funeral ritual, but is rather a reminder of the necessary liquids for the soul of the deceased to transform from the blurred phantom referred to in Homer as ψυχῆ into a clear and well-proportioned image, an εἴδωλον. The intimate scene close to the deceased probably represents the family preparing the libations that will be offered at the funeral ritual. The crying attendants are, however, most important here, because they emphasize the critical element in the αὐτοψία of the deceased: the vision of the clear and well-proportioned image, the εἴδωλον of the deceased, is only possible through the most potent physical expression of the instrument of vision.

In early Greece, crying at the funeral of a family member was not just regarded as an appropriate social ritual, but as a necessary act of establishing a memory image (μνῆμα) of the deceased. Like the physical traces of the incineration of Semele, the μνῆματα of ancestors are physical traces of their lived lives. These μνῆματα are mental images preserved in the minds of the family of the departed, but they are also physical images made of pottery or stone, interactive images like the εἴδωλον of Elpenor maintained in the liquid continuum of vision beyond life through the secretion of Odysseus's tears. In this ritual production of memory images the tears of the attendants are not simply exterior, physiological signs of grief. Tears are physical agents of vision that actively take part in finding and shaping μνῆματα of the dead by rehabilitating the liquid continuum between the world of the dead and the world of the living. Like fingers of the eye, tears reach out into the misty void left behind by departed ancestors and shape their fuzzy shadows into recognizable and memorable sharp resemblances (εἴδωλα).

Concluding remarks

Based on the Platonic notion of vision as a reflection of rays emanating from the eye, Euclid's optical theory should also be seen as part of a more ancient tradition in Greek culture. In this tradition, human vision was regarded as most powerful when it was accompanied by emotional involvement, especially if the emotional involvement was directed towards supernatural entities (gods and monsters) or deceased ancestors. Lamenting lost friends and relatives was not just considered to be a vital element in social and psychological life, but also an active instrument in the cultural poetics of vision. The active power of tears is that they can generate images, liquid images, of the dead. Without the tears of Odysseus his dead comrades and relatives are nothing but shadows and smoke. By turning on the taps of his optical instruments Odysseus makes a stream of clear, liquid images flow out of the shadows of the Underworld and thus mend the leak in the liquid continuum between the dead and the living. Nowadays, we tend to think about tears of grief as, first of all, psychologically important, as a therapeutic aid in the physical process of grief. In ancient Greece, crying over dead ancestors was first of all considered to be of physical importance for the soul of the deceased. When the Pre-Socratics and Aristotle in the fifth and fourth centuries emphasize the liquid nature of the instrument and the medium of vision, they lean heavily on this traditional early Greek poetics of vision. Aristotle may have been critical of the traditional notion of the corporality of vision, but his understanding of the mental power of vision in generating liquid images can also be regarded as an interpretation of the poetics of vision beyond life already described in the 11th song of the Odyssey.

References

Aeschylus and Mazon, P. (1931). *Prométhée enchainé. In Eschyle. Tome I. Texte* établi *et traduit par Paul Mazon*: 161-199. Paris: L'Association Guillaume Budé.

Ahlberg, G. (1971). *Prothesis and Ekphora in Greek Geometric Art*. Göteborg: Paul Åströms förlag.

Alpers, S. (1983). *The Art of Describing. Dutch Art in the Seventeenth Century*. Chicago: Chicago University Press.

Aristophanes and Dover, K. J. (eds) (1968). *Clouds*. Oxford: Clarendon Press.

Aristotle and Hett, W. S. (trans.) (1957). *On the Soul, Parva naturalia, On Breath*. Loeb Classical Library. Cambridge (MA): Harvard University Press.

Aristotle and Ross, G. R. T. (trans.) (1906). *Aristotle De Sensu and De Memoria. Text and Translation with Introduction and Commentary*. Cambridge: Cambridge University Press.

Bakke, J. (2010). The Tears of Odysseus. Memory and Visual Culture in Ancient Greece. *ARV. Nordic Yearbook of Folklore* 66: 21-42.

Betancourt, R. (2016). Tempted to Touch: Tactility, Ritual, and Mediation in Byzantine Visuality. *Speculum* 91 (3): 660-689.

Boardman, J. (1998). *Early Greek Vase Painting. 11th-6th Centuries*. London: Thames and Hudson.

Burkert, W. (1985). *Greek Religion*. Cambridge (MA): Harvard University Press.

Cherniss, H. (1935). *Aristotle's Criticism of Pre-Socratic Philosophy*. Baltimore: The John Hopkins Press.

Cornford, F. M. (1997) [1935]. *Plato's Cosmology. The Timaeus of Plato*. Indianapolis: Routledge.

Detienne, M. and Vernant, J.-P. (1978). *Cunning Intelligence in Greek Culture and Society*. Chicago: The University of Chicago Press.

Diels, H. (1906). *Die Fragmente der Vorsokratiker. Griechish und Deutsch*. Berlin: Widemannsche Buchhandlung.

Euclid and Heiberg, I. L. (ed.) (1865). *Euclidis Optica, Opticorum recensio theonis, Catoptrica, sum scholis antiquis*. Leipzig: Teubner.

Euripides and Dodds, E. (ed. et com.) (1986). *Euripides Bacchae. Edited with Introduction and Commentrary*. Second Edition. Oxford: Clarendon Press.

Euripides and Way, A. S. (trans) (1962). *Euripides in Four Volumes. Volume III*. London: William Heineman Ltd.

Geertz, C. (1976). Art as a Cultural System. *Modern Language Notes* 91: 1475-1476.

Grethlein, J. (2008). Memory and Material Objects in the Iliad and the Odyssey. *Journal of Hellenic Studies* 128: 27-51.

Guthrie, W. K. C. (1965). *A History of Greek Philosophy*, vol. 2. Cambridge: Cambridge University Press.

Hesiod and Evelyn-White, H. G. (trans.) (2002). *The Homeric Hymns and Homerica with an English Translation*. London: William Heinemann.

Homer and Allen, T. W (ed.). (1917). *Homeri Opera. Volumes III–IV (The Odyssey. Greek text and critical notes)*. Oxford: Oxford University Press.

Homer and Monro, D. B. and Allen, T. W. (eds). (1902). *Homeri Opera. Volumes I–II (The Iliad. Greek text and critical notes)*. Oxford: Oxford University Press.

Lindberg, D. C. (1981). *Theories of Vision from Al-Kindi to Kepler*. Chicago and London: Chicago University Press.

Nelson, R. S. (2000). To say and to see. Ekphrasis and vision in Byzantium. In: Nelson, R. S., (ed.) *Visuality Before and Beyond the Renaissance. Seeing as Others Saw*: 143-168. Cambridge: Cambridge University Press.

Onians, R. B. (1988). *The Origins of European Thought about the Body, the Mind, the Soul, The World, Time, and Fate. New Interpretations of Greek, Roman and Kindred Evidence Also of Some Basic Jewish and Christian Belief*. Cambridge: Cambridge University Press.

Osborne, R. (1998). *Archaic and Classical Greek Art*. Oxford: Oxford University Press.

Ovid and Raeburn, D. (trans.) (2004). *Metamorphoses. A New Verse Translation*. London: Penguin Books.

Pasquale, G. (2004). Scientific and technological use of glass in Graeco-Roman antiquity. In: Beretta, M. (ed.) *When Glass Matters. Studies in The History of Science and Art from Graeco-Roman Antiquity to Early Modern Era*: 31-76. Florence: Leo S. Olschki.

Pausanias and Jones, W. H. S. (transl.) (1992) [1918]. *Pausanias Description of Greece with an English Translation. Vol. I*. Loeb Classical Library. Cambridge (MA): Harvard University Press.

Pausanias and Jones, W. H. S. (transl.) (1979) [1935]. *Pausanias Description of Greece with an English Translation.* Vol. IV. Loeb Classical Library. Cambridge (MA): Harvard University Press.
Peers, G. (2012). Object relations: Theorizing the late antique viewer. In: Johnson, S. F. (ed.) *The Oxford Handbook of Late Antiquity*: 970-987. Oxford: Oxford University Press.
Picón, C. A. (2007). *Art of the Classical World in the Metropolitan Museum of Art: Greece, Cyprus, Etruria, Rome.* New York: The Metropolitan Museum of Art.
Plato (1990). *Timaios. Kritias. Philebos. Bearbeitet von Klaus Widdra* (Platon Werke in acht Bänden. Griechish und Deutsch). Siebter Band. Darmstadt: Wissenschaftliche Buchgesellschaft.
Sines G. and Sakellaris, Y. A. (1987). Lenses in Antiquity. *American Journal of Archaeology* 91 (2): 191-196.
Sparkes, B. A. (1987). Greek Bronzes. *Greece & Rome* 34 (2): 152-168.
Stewart, A. (1990). *Greek Sculpture. An Exploration.* New Haven: Yale University Press.
Vernant, J.-P. and Zeitlin, F. I. (eds) (1991). *Mortals and Immortals. Collected Essays.* Princeton (NJ): Princeton University Press.
Webb, R. (2009). *Ekphrasis, Imagination and Persuasion in Ancient Rhetorical Theory and Practice.* Farnham: Ashgate.

Umm Gumyāna and the *Zār*

Richard Johan Natvig

Introduction

Among the many *zār* songs Enno Littmann (1875-1958) published in his *Arabische Geisterbeschwörungen aus Ägypten* [Arabic spirit incantations from Egypt] (Littmann 1950), there is one that invokes a female character named, in his transliteration, 'Umm Gumyāna'. Based on clues in the text, Littmann reasoned that we are here dealing with a Christian demon ('eine christliche Dämonin'), but he was at a loss trying to explain the name 'Gumyāna'. He pointed to the fact that the name 'Ǧumāna' (*Jumāna*) was in use in Old Arabic. 'Here, however, Umm Gumyāna is supposed to be a Christian, and this form of the name is otherwise unknown to me' (Littmann 1950: 67).[1] Actually, the religion of the spirit ought not to be a problem, since the Arabic female name Jumāna, meaning 'pearl', occurs among Christians as well as Muslims. The problem was rather, and remains: who is 'Umm Gumyāna'? This question is important since any interpretation and analysis and, in the end, translation depend upon a correct identification of who it is that the song invokes. Obviously, the understanding of a text will be radically different if the invoked being is understood to be a god, a saint, an angel or a demon.

The purpose of this paper is firstly to identify the main character of the song. I will argue that she is a *zār* spirit double of a well-known Coptic saint, in fact one of the most popular Egyptian Coptic saints over the centuries, and, according to Febe Y. Armanios, the most widely revered female saint after the Virgin Mary in today's Egypt (Armanios 2003: 101). This insight in turn leads me to the second purpose of the paper, which is to present a new reading and understanding of the song. First, however, a few words about the *zār*.

The *zār*

The complex of religious beliefs and rituals called in research literature '*zār*' or '*zār* cult' is concerned with a category of spirits collectively called '*zār*', spirits that are quick to afflict human beings with illnesses or other misfortunes if offended. *Zār* rituals are aimed at appeasing the spirits so that they will withdraw the affliction. *Zār* is found in North-East Africa, the Arabian Peninsula and southern Iran, but in regional and local variants. The Egyptian *zār* can be distinguished as one such regional variant, with local variations, especially between rural and urban areas. In Egypt it is practised mainly among Muslims, but sometimes and in some places Christians are known to take part in the rituals.[2]

Songs are essential in the Egyptian *zār* and have various functions, but first of all they are a means of communication with various non-empirical powers. One category of songs is those that address the *zār* spirits, invoking and inviting the individual spirits to the ritual gathering, praising and flattering them, and promising that their demands will be met. The songs, which typically have a call and response structure, are accompanied by music and a certain beat that attract the particular spirit called upon. The one who is possessed by this spirit will feel a compulsion to rise and dance, or move the body in certain ways, when he or she hears the spirit's beat. This is a sign that the spirit is taking over the body, 'clothing' itself in or 'mounting' its human subject, enabling a two-way communication. The belief is that the spirit world reflects the human world with, for instance, Muslim and Christian spirits, Upper Egyptian, Ethiopian and foreign (i.e. European, *khawājāt*) spirits, occupational spirits, male and female spirits, and so on. The possessed person will act out the characteristics of her or his spirit, usually in a stereotypical

[1] 'Hier aber soll Umm Gumyāna eine Christin sein, und diese Form des Namens ist mir sonst nicht bekannt.'
[2] The literature on *zār* is extensive. See, for instance, Makris and Natvig (1991) and Rouaud and Battain (2002).

and exaggerated manner, through the way of speaking, gestures and bodily movements, and may also put on clothes and brandish an object symbolizing that particular spirit.

Another category of songs calls on and praises Allah, the prophet Muhammad and saints. Typically, a *zār* ceremony, or *ḥaḍra*, is opened with such *madāʾīḥ*, praise songs, thereby mobilizing the assistance of these benevolent powers in achieving the aim of the *zār* rituals, which is the healing of illnesses caused by the possession of *zār* spirits. Invoking these powers creates a beneficial frame for dealing and negotiating with the ambivalent and potentially dangerous *zār* spirits who must be persuaded to withdraw the symptoms they have caused.[3]

The distinction between categories or genres of songs, between spirit songs and *madāʾīḥ*, and the distinction between the various non-empirical powers invoked in the *zār*, have not always been appreciated in research literature. Saints such as Ahmad al-Badawi, Ibrahim al-Dasuqi, Umm Hashim, Ahmad al-Rifaʿi and many others are called upon not because they are believed to be possessing spirits (e.g. Kriss and Kriss-Heinrich 1962: 147; El-Adly 1984: 658), nor in a conscious or unconscious attempt to 'Islamize' the *zār* (e.g. Sengers 2003: 105), but for the help they can give in the healing process or in solving other problems (see also El Hadidi 2006: 165).

The song for Umm Gumyāna

Enno Littmann's *Arabische Geisterbeschwörungen aus Ägypten* contains his edition and translation of two Arabic manuscripts he termed 'Text A' and 'Text B', both written by Mahmud Sidqi, a former copyist at the Khedivial Library with whom Littmann often collaborated in his studies and publications of Cairene folk literature. Sidqi's two manuscripts in turn were based partly upon his own investigations and talks with *zār* leaders, and partly on some printed Egyptian sources (see Littmann 1950). In Littmann's book the texts of the manuscripts were reproduced partly in Arabic script, partly in transliteration, and were translated and commented upon by Littmann.

The song for Umm Gumyāna is found in Littmann's edition of the 'Text B' manuscript. Mahmud Sidqi wrote 'Text B' in 1930 for the German orientalist Franz Taeschner (1888-1967), who presented it to Littmann in 1941. The songs in this manuscript were, as pointed out by Littmann, transcribed from a small publication, *Kitāb bidaʿ al-fujjār fī ḥaflat al-zār* [Book of the heresy of the godless in the *zār* assembly], by Kamil Afandi Darwish, with only minor variations noted by Littmann. The 48-page booklet contains no publication place nor date, but Kamil Darwish himself dates his text to 1911; these songs therefore go back to at least that year (Darwish, n.d.: 47).

The variations between Kamil Afandi Darwish's Umm Gumyāna text and that of Sidqi's in Littmann's *Arabische Geisterbeschwörungen* are insignificant and of no consequence for the interpretation and translation of the song. For instance, in Darwish's booklet the song has the heading *dawr ṣaʿīdī*: 'An Upper Egyptian (musical) number' (Darwish, n.d.: 12). Sidqi changed this into *ghayruh ṣaʿīdī. ʾumm gumyāna naṣrānīya*: 'Another Upper Egyptian one. Umm Gumyāna. A Christian' ('Eine anderes, aus Oberägypten. Umm Gumyāna. Eine Christin', Littmann (1950: 23 [translation], 103 [transliteration])). The reference to Upper Egypt has to do with the musical style, and not the song's protagonist. Here follows the song in Littmann's transliteration (1950: 103):

yā sâkin il-barârīyā	*ʾumm gumyâna*
yā ṣafṣafyā	*ʾumm gumyâna*
ʾuḫt is-salāṭînyā	*ʾumm gumyâna*
ġêrik mā raʾêtyā	*ʾumm gumyâna*
ḥusnik mā bašûfuyā	*ʾumm gumyâna*
wiʾiftĕ fi d-dôryā	*ʾumm gumyâna*

[3] For more information, see, for example, Natvig (2014) and Natvig (2013).

nišrab fi l-ḫumûryā *ʾumm gumyâna*
ʾinta mâsik iṣ-ṣalîbyā *ʾumm gumyâna*[4]

Littmann transliterated the texts according to Egyptian 'popular pronunciation' ('volkstümlichen Aussprache', Littmann (1950: vii)). Thus he transliterated the word wiqiftu in line 6 as wiʾiftĕ, in order to reflect the usual Lower Egyptian pronunciation of qāf as hamzah or glottal stop. In line 5, Mahmud Sidqi wrote, probably unintentionally, confused by the mā on the previous line, ḥusnik mā bashūfu instead of Darwish's ḥusnik lam bashūfu, which does not change the meaning. This is how Littmann translated the song:

O Wüstenbewohnerin O Umm Gumyāna!
O weite Wüste! O Umm Gumyāna!
Schwester der Sultane! O Umm Gumyāna!
Ausser dir sah ich keine! O Umm Gumyāna!
Deine Schönheit sah ich irgends, O Umm Gumyāna!
Ich hielt an im Kloster, O Umm Gumyāna!
Wir tranken die Weine, O Umm Gumyāna!
Du hieltest das Kreuz, O Umm Gumyāna!

In English this would be, excluding the refrain: 'O desert dweller / O wide desert! / Sister of the Sultans! / Except for you I saw no one! / Your beauty I saw nowhere else, / I stopped in the monastery, / We drank the wine, / You held the cross'.

As a more or less literal translation this makes perfect sense, with the possible exception of the word *dūr* on line 6, which Littmann translated as 'monastery': '*dôr* soll hier 'Kloster' bedeuten; das passt in den Zusammenhang' ('here *dôr* must mean 'monastery'; this fits in with the context', Littmann (1950: 103, n. 6)). I have not been able to verify the occurrence of *dūr* as an Egyptian colloquial variant of the word *dayr*. It is possible that it was a misprint in Darwish's book (there are several others), *d-ū-r* instead of *d-y-r*, but this is not very likely since the learned Mahmud Sidqi almost certainly would have corrected the mistake in his transcript. Moreover, *dūr* rhymes with *khumūr* on the next line. Another possibility is that we are dealing with the plural *dūr*, of *dār*, 'house', referring to the complex of buildings and a court (Hinds and Badawi 1986: 310; Lane 1984: 931) that make up a monastery.

sākin al-barārī on line 1 can be translated as 'one who dwells in the desert', although *barārī*, pl. of *barriyya*, does cover a wider semantic field: 'desert; a waste; a spacious tract of ground without herbage' (Lane 1984: 177); 'desert, wilderness' (Spiro 1923: 55); 'open country; steppe, desert' (Wehr 1976: 49); 'open land, wasteland' (Hinds and Badawi 1986: 64).

The noun *ṣafṣaf* on line 2 can be translated as 'desert', but that word, too, has a wider semantic field: 'A level or an even tract of land or ground [...] having in it no herbage [...] A desert, or waterless desert' (Lane 1984: 1694). Hans Wehr lists the adjective *ṣafṣaf*, which he translates as 'even, level; waste, desolate, barren, empty', with an example of its use in '*qāʿ ṣafṣaf*': 'wasteland, desolate area' (Wehr 1976: 518). Martin Hinds and El-Said Badawi translate the verb *ṣafṣaf* as 'to become depleted or whittled away' (Hinds and Badawi 1986: 505). Curiously, in a different song, Littmann chose to treat *ṣafṣaf* as a personal female name (Littmann 1950: 31). We shall return to that song in a little while. For now it should be noted that '*Ṣafṣaf*' is also a nickname for the woman's name Safiyya. In Out-el-Kouloub's *Trois Contes de l'amour et de la mort*, it is the name of a Coptic woman (Out-el-Kouloub 1940: 98), and in Annie van Sommer and Samuel M. Zwemer's *Our Moslem Sisters*, it is the name of a Muslim woman who had converted to Christianity (Sommer and Zwemer 1907: 56f.). Hinds and Badawi list *Ṣafṣaf* as a nickname for both the male Mustafa (the chosen one) and the female Safiyya (the pure one) (Hinds and Badawi 1986: 505); both names are derived from the same root, *ṣ-f-ū*.

[4] In Littmann's transliteration, *ḫ=kh*, *ġ=gh*, *š=sh*.

Questions remain: who is this beautiful lady of noble birth ('sister of sultans'), who dwells in the desert, and what is she doing in a monastery? The clue lies in the name 'Umm Gumyāna', which Littmann failed to recognize. The song's beautiful lady appears in fact to be the Coptic saint Sitt (Lady) Dimyāna, much celebrated among Egyptian Christians and respected and sometimes called upon for help by Muslims as well. Her name has nothing to do with the Arabic *jumāna*, 'pearl', but is an Egyptian vernacular variation of the saint's name Dimyāna.

Sitt Dimyāna aka Sitt Gimyāna

According to Sitt Dimyāna's hagiography, she was born to Murqus, the Roman governor of the Nile Delta province of Burullus, Zaʿfarana and Wadi al-Sisban in North-East Egypt. She was raised as a devout Christian, much loved by her father, and she was well mannered and very beautiful. When she was 15 her father wished her to marry a nobleman, but she refused, declaring that she had dedicated herself to Christ. Her father accepted her refusal, and also built her a palace outside the city where she withdrew to worship and to lead an ascetic way of life, accompanied by 40 female virgins (Armanios 2011: 70).

These events took place during the reign of the Roman emperor Diocletian (r. 284-305), infamous for his persecution of Christians. When Dimyāna's father Murqus complied with Diocletian's order that the officials should worship the Roman gods to demonstrate their allegiance to him, he was severely lectured and set straight by his daughter. Accordingly, when he in turn reprimanded the Emperor, he was executed. Learning that Dimyāna was the instigator of Murqus's subordination, Diocletian sent soldiers to punish her. After a number of gruesome tortures and repeated deaths from which she was revived each time by divine intervention, she was beheaded along with her 40 virgin companions and thousands of people who had witnessed Dimyāna's example and converted to Christianity (Armanios 2011: 70f.).

According to the hagiography, the bodies of Dimyāna and her 40 companions were later found by Helena, the mother of Emperor Constantine (r. 306-37), and by his order their unharmed and uncorrupted bodies were collected and placed in a crypt, and Dimyāna's shrine was built on top of her demolished palace (Armanios 2011: 71).

The prologue to the hagiography names Abba Yuhanna, Bishop of Burullus, possibly of the fourteenth century, as the one who transcribed the story of Dimyāna from an earlier possibly Coptic or Greek manuscript into Arabic. Until the 1930s, when the story was included in a publication of the Coptic Synaxarion, Dimyāna's hagiography existed, as far as is known, only in Arabic, predominantly in the Egyptian colloquial language, making the text easily accessible (Armanios 2011: 71f.). Febe Armanios characterizes Dimyāna's hagiography as a 'best-seller' among Copts in Ottoman Egypt; it 'ranks among the most widely copied and read hagiographies of that period' (Armanios 2003: 101).

It was in the Ottoman period that the cult of Dimyāna grew in popularity, as suggested by Otto Meinardus (Meinardus 1969: 54ff.) and corroborated by Febe Armanios's research (Armanios 2011: 77). A church in Akhmim in Upper Egypt dating to the sixteenth or seventeenth century was named after her, and a monastery in Balyana, also in Upper Egypt, adopted Dimyāna as its patron saint sometime after the fifteenth century (Armanios 2011: 77). From the seventeenth century onward several travellers through the north-east of Egypt (see below) have attested to the popularity of her *mūlid*, which took and takes place at the monastery built at the site of her grave and named after her, Dayr Dimyāna, a few kilometres north of Bilqās in Daqahliya. One visitor, the protestant missionary John Lieder, who attended a few days of the *mūlid* in May 1833, compared its importance for the Copts with the significance of the *mūlid* of Sayyid Ahmad al-Badawi in Tanta for Muslims, and just as those Muslims who could not perform the pilgrimage to Mekka would visit Ahmad al-Badawi, so would Copts who were unable to undertake the pilgrimage to Jerusalem visit Saint Dimyāna ('Gemiana'). Illustrating (among other things) the importance of the cult of Saint Dimyāna throughout Egypt, Lieder also mentioned pilgrims from Upper Egypt: 'The Christians from Saïd (Upper Egypt), in particular, take earth with them for their friends; of which they make precious presents, even to Mahomedans [...]' (Lieder 1834: 178).

Lieder referred to the saint as 'Sette Gemiana', and in a letter from 1829 he explained: 'Gemiane is a faulty pronunciation of the Copt' (CMS Archives: C M 048/42). However, 'Gemiane' and variants are neither faulty nor Coptic, but rather a regional, vernacular version of the name with the 'd' of the Dimyāna name form exchanged for the 'j', or hard 'g' as it would be in Egyptian dialectical pronunciation. In fact, this form of the saint's name goes far back in time.

The first known mention of Dimyāna's monastery near Bilqās in Dakhaliyya province in the Delta is from the pre-Ottoman Mamluk era, when the Egyptian historian al-Makrizi (1365-1442) mentioned '*Dayr Jimyāna*' as one in a group of four Coptic monasteries in the area, in his monumental *al-Khiṭaṭ* (Maqrizi 2003: 1050). Many travellers in Egypt from the seventeenth century and onwards knew the saint under this name, pronounced with the hard 'g', as Gemiane and similar. Johann Michael Wansleben, who visited the monastery in 1672, wrote the name 'Gemiane' (Vansleb 1677: 156ff.), and Claude Sicard, who visited the place in 1714, called her 'sainte Gemianne' (Sicard 1810: 57ff.). Richard Pococke, who passed through the area in 1738, wrote of the monastery of 'St. Geminiani' (Pococke 1743: 129, probably a printer's mistake for 'Gemiani'), and Carsten Niebuhr, writing of the eastern part of the Delta, mentioned an old church dedicated to 'Gemiâne' that the Copts visit annually (Niebuhr 1774: 97f.).

The name form *Jimyāna* is also used on an eighteenth-century icon of Dimyāna and the 40 virgins in the Muᶜallaqa church in Cairo, signed by Ibrahim al-Nasikh (Atalla 1998, vol. i: 100) and dating from 1773,[5] and on another by Hanna al-Armani in the same church, from 1776 (Skalova and Gabra 2006: 234-5). Two nineteenth-century icons of Saint Dimyāna by Astasi al-Rumi (Eustathius the Greek) also use the *Jimyāna* form (see Meinardus 1969: 60 and 62 (Figures 2 and 4) and 61-5; Atalla 1998, vol. i: 95). Other nineteenth-century attestations of this name form are the already mentioned John Lieder, and John Gardner Wilkinson who wrote about the monastery of 'Sitte Gamián' (Wilkinson 1843: 393, 410).

Moving on to the twentieth century, the Jesuit missionary Michel Jullien mentioned that some say 'Djimiane' (Jullien 1903: 189). Élie Sidawi, with no comment, wrote 'Dimiana ou Guimiana' (Sidawi 1917: 81). 'Guimiana' is also the form of the name used in a popular song that he quoted. This song will be further referred to later in this paper. Joseph McPherson, who spent many years in the early part of the twentieth century in Egypt and who had a great interest in Egyptian religious customs, especially the *mūlids*, wrote of Sitt Dimyāna: 'Many Delta people stoutly maintain that her name is Gemiana' (McPherson 1941: 179, n. 1). The Egyptian anthropologist Fatima al-Misri, in a list of religious characters (*rijāl al-dīn*) who figure in *zār* songs (such as saints, Jesus, the prophet Muhammad, etc.), included 'Umm Gimyāna' (Misri 1975: 69). Finally, Gérard Viaud also knew both forms: 'Saint Damienne ou Sitt Guimyânah' (Viaud 1979: 21).

Thus the name form Gimyāna (with slight variations) is well attested as an alternative name for Dimyāna, from the fifteenth century to the present. The reason Littmann vocalized the name with a *ḍamma* instead of a *kasra*, Gumyāna instead of Gimyāna, may very well be that he never heard a native speaker pronounce the name in the *zār* song, and did not recognize it as the name of this Coptic saint, and therefore assumed it had to be related to the word jumāna, 'pearl'.[6]

Gimyāna in the *zār* song

Does rereading the *zār* song with the saint Gimyāna/Dimyāna in mind as the one who is or appears to be invoked instead of some unknown desert-dwelling Christian spirit make a difference? To begin with, the invocation on the first line, *yā sākin al-barārī*, which Littmann translated literally as 'O Wüstenbewohnerin' ('O desert dweller'), is an invocation of the Coptic saint. The Arabic text below the main picture of one of the two nineteenth-century icons by Astasi al-Rumi mentioned above reads, in Meinardus's translation, 'The holy martyr Sitt Gimiana, dwelling in the deserts' (Meinardus 1969: 62). It is just possible to discern

[5] Ibrahim inscribed on the icon both the Hijri year 1187 and the Coptic A.M. (anno martyrum) year 1489. I am grateful to Alexandros Tsakos for discussing the reading of the dates with me.

[6] I have come across only one instance of the saint's name transliterated with a *damma*, 'Dumyana', in Guirguis (2008: 44 and 89), and no instances of 'Gumyana' other than Littmann's.

the Arabic '*sākin al-barārī*' on the poor-quality reproduction of the icon that accompanies Meinardus's article (1969: 60, Figure 2). In the popular song for the saint quoted by Élie Sidawi, mentioned above, she is called upon, in Sidawi's transliteration, as '*Guimiana saknet al-berria*' and '*Guimiana saknet el-barari*', *berria* (*barriyya*) being the singular of *barārī*. In a line from a *zār* song quoted by Fatima al-Misri, we find the phrase '*yā umm dimyāna saknat al-barārī yā umm dimyāna*' (Misri 1975: 261). Finally, her monastery near Bilqās in the Delta is called Dayr al-Barārī (Viaud 1979: 21-3). When 'our' *zār* song invokes the *sākin al-barārī* it is in fact calling upon the dweller of the *monastery* 'Barārī': Dimyāna/Gimyāna.

It should be noted that the translation of barāri as 'desert(s)' in this context is misleading since the area in question is not a desert. In the seventeenth-century description by Sicard, it was a plain covered by vegetation as the Nile flooded and fertilized it, creating grazing grounds for oxen and sheep (Sicard 1810: 57ff.). Lieder commented in his journal from 1833 that '[t]he large tract of land, in the midst of which the convent stands, cannot properly be called a desert: it is good land, every year watered by the overflow of the Nile; and although much saltpetre is contained in it, yet the attempt made here and there to cultivate it succeeds very well' (Lieder 1834: 178; see also Armanios 2011: 81). As noted earlier, the word has a wider semantic field, including land as opposed to sea, open country, wild and wilderness.

Turning to the next line, Littmann chose to translate *yā ṣafṣaf* as 'O weite Wüste' ('O wide desert'). In another song, however, he opted for *Ṣafṣaf* to be a woman's name, probably influenced by the heading Sidqi had made. Again it is a short song that Sidqi had copied from *Kitāb bidaʿ al-fujjār fī ḥaflat al-zār* by Kamil Afandi Darwish, this one with no changes except for the heading *dawr ṣaʿīdī*, where Sidqi added *al-sitt Ṣafṣaf*, translated by Littmann: 'Ein Lied aus Oberägypten. Die Herrin *Ṣafṣaf*' ('A song from Upper Egypt. The Lady Ṣafṣaf') (Littmann 1950: 31 [translation], 111 [transliteration]). The song goes:

ṣafṣaf yā ṣafṣaf	*yā bint al-amāra*
yā ʿāyiqa yā ṣafṣaf	*yā bint al-naṣāra*
yā ʿāyiqa yā hānim	*yā bint al-amāra*
(Darwish n.d.: 34).	

Ṣafṣaf, o *Ṣafṣaf*,	o daughter of the nobles!
O proud one, o *Ṣafṣaf*,	o daughter of the Christians!
O proud one, o Lady,	o daughter of the nobles![7]

In spite of Sidqi's helpful hint in adding *sitt*, 'lady', to the name in the heading, Littmann was in the dark as to who this *Ṣafṣaf* might be, and in his general introduction to *zār* ('Allgemeines über den *Zār*') he placed her in his category of 'Naturgeister', 'nature spirits', and explained *Sitt Ṣafṣaf* as 'die Herrin 'Wüstenebene', 'the Lady desert plain' (Littmann 1950: 55). Yet, the *Ṣafṣaf* of this song is characterized as being a Christian (*bint al-naṣāra*), just like Umm Gimyāna. She is of noble birth (*bint al-amāra*), like Umm Gimyāna (*ukht al-salāṭīn*), and this is underscored by invoking her as a *hānim*, the Turkish title for a woman of the upper class, and as *ʿāyiqa*, a word that here can mean 'proud', which is how Littmann translated it, elegant in clothes and manners (the word will be discussed below). Umm Gimyāna, in our song, is so beautiful that the singer can only look at her, on lines 4 and 5: 'Except for you I saw no one! / Your beauty I saw nowhere else'. In the line from a *zār* song quoted by Fatima al-Misri, mentioned above, the same word *ʿāyiqa* is used to describe Umm Dimyāna, along with *saknat al-barārī*: '*yā ʿāyiqa wa taʿālā yā umm dimyāna saknat al-barārī yā umm dimyāna*': 'O proud one, come o Umm Dimyāna, o dweller of (the monastery) al-Barārī, o Umm Dimyāna'.

My conclusion is that Ṣafṣaf in both songs refers to Umm Gimyāna; it is another epithet used to invoke her: 'Ṣafṣaf o Ṣafṣaf, o Gimyāna'. It is also clear, I believe, that there is some sort of link between the song's Umm Gimyāna and the saint Gimyāna so venerated by the Copts, and who is invoked not only by Copts

[7] Littmann: '*ṣafṣaf yā ṣafṣaf yā bint il-ʾamâra / yā ʿây*ʾ*a yā ṣafṣaf yā bint in-naṣâra / yā ʿây*ʾ*a yā hânim yā bint il-ʾamâra*' - '*Ṣafṣaf*, o *Ṣafṣaf*! O Tochter der Fürsten! / Du Stolze, o *Ṣafṣaf*! O Tochter der Christen! / Du Stolze, o Dame! / O Tochter der Fürsten!' (Littmann 1950: 111 and 31)

but sometimes also by Muslims for help in cases of illness and infertility.[8] But how are they connected, and how did *Sitt* Gimyāna become *Umm* – 'Mother' – Gimyāna? Is it really the venerable virgin saint Dimyāna/Gimyāna who is called upon in this song?

From Sitt Gimyāna to Umm Gimyāna, from saint to spirit

There are indeed clues in the song that suggest that, despite the name, invocation and characterization of her as a noble lady, Umm Gimyāna is different from Sitt Gimyāna. Firstly, what is not in the text: totally missing in the song(s) are perhaps the most common epithets for the saint: 'virgin', 'martyr' and *al-qadīsa*, 'the holy', used for a (female) Christian saint. Secondly, the choice of the word *ʿāyiqa*, briefly touched upon above, to describe her in the *Ṣafṣaf* song and in the song quoted by al-Misri: the root *ʿ-y-q* has a wider semantic field than the translation above ('O proud one') suggests. The adjective ʿāyiq has the meaning of 'dandified', 'foppish'; the noun *ʿāyiq* can be translated as 'dandy'; the verbal form *itʿāyiq* means 'to show off, behave ostentatiously'; and finally, the noun ʿāyqa is translated by Spiro as 'patroness of a brothel', and Hinds and Badawi explain: '[obsol] madam of a brothel' (Spiro 1895: 421; Hinds and Badawi 1986: 613).[9] That the latter sense is unlikely in this context is suggested by its use in other *zār* spirit songs in Darwish's booklet where it seems to be used rather in the sense of showing off, striding dandylike (also Galal 1937: 149: 'O élégante dame'). The word is used only in describing spirits, both male and female, and not saints, in the instances that I have found. In any case, the notions evoked by the use of the term *ʿāyiqa*, whether in the sense of 'dandy, show off' or 'madam of a brothel', do not fit in at all with the respected saint Sitt Gimyāna.

Thirdly: after the first five lines of the song discussed so far, invoking Umm Gimyāna and praising her beauty, follow the three lines (excluding the refrain) 'I stopped in the monastery, / We drank the wine, / You held the cross'. They are standard phrases used in *zār* songs that call on Christian spirits, and we find them with variations in other spirit songs. For example, *dakhalnā 'l-dayr fī niṣf al-layl ṭiliʿnā 'l-ṣubḥa sakārā*, 'we entered the monastery in the evening, we left it in the morning, drunk' (Darwish, n.d.: 33), and *shīl al-ṣalīb*, 'lift up the cross' (Darwish, n.d.: 34; for other examples see Galal (1937: 149), Elder (1927: 94-6) and Nabhan (1994: 293-5)). Stopping in, visiting or staying overnight in a monastery (or a church), the drinking of wine or other alcoholic beverages and holding up a cross or a rosary are standard characteristics of the Christian *zār* spirits. I suggest that the fact that drinking wine is not only allowed for Copts but is also a vital ritual element in the Mass (the Eucharist), in stark contrast to the Muslim total prohibition, is being exploited to the fullest in the *zār* in its exaggerated stereotypical image of the Christian spirits' inclination to drinking and drunkenness.

What we are dealing with here is a spirit version of the saint Dimyāna, a spirit reflection or double. It is not the saint that is called upon but a spirit clearly modelled upon her.

So why is she called Umm? Sitt Gimyāna or Dimyāna is not, obviously, among the Coptic Church's 'mother saints' (see, for example, Meinardus 2003: 49-50), who at least in some instances are called 'mother', such as 'Umm Rifqah (Rebecca)' and 'Umm Dulagi' (Stene 1991: 47, 50-1). She is called 'Mother of 40 virgins' in Coptic hymns,[10] but to my knowledge, the saint is never called Umm Dimyāna/Gimyāna. Perhaps invoking the spirit as Umm has the twofold function of endearing the spirit, connecting with it as to a mother, while at the same time clearly signalling that it is not the saint. To call her Umm is perhaps an insurance that one does not call upon the saint in vain. The pattern for this name construct exists with other female *zār* spirits (Umm al-ghulām, Umm Wallāj, Umm al-Warāyid).

[8] See, for instance, Leeder (1918: 145): '[...] Moslems, as well as Copts [...] respect this saint considerably, and believe that she is the means of granting them most important benefits, when they address themselves to her. Moslems are usually heard singing to her name, calling her *Ya Sitt ya bint el wali* [...]', that is: 'o Lady, o daughter of the governor.'

[9] In modern usage, in spite of Hinds and Badawi's marking it as obsolete, it is found to mean 'prostitute' in the indefinite form, and 'madam of a brothel' when in the definite. I am grateful to John Erik Sætren for discussing this term with me.

[10] See, for example, in the Coptic book of liturgical hymns, nos 168 and 169, at http://St-Takla.org ('Lyrics of Songs & Hymns: Psalmodia (Tasbeha)'), accessed 22.08.2016.

Rereading the song for Umm Gumyāna

The *zār* songs are not unchanging liturgical texts, but are made up of a number of more or less set phrases that are drawn upon, can be varied upon, and are put together and used in the ritual when appropriate, typically with a call and response structure where the lead singer sings a phrase (for instance, praising the spirit in question), and the assistants respond with a refrain (for instance, 'O ... [the spirit's name]'). The songs do not describe what goes on in the ritual, but are part of the ritual procedure. This means that in order for us to understand the song for Umm Gimyāna, we need to attempt to resituate it in the *zār* ritual from which it was decontextualized at one time:

O dweller of (Dayr) al-Barārī!	O Umm Gimyāna!
O *Ṣafṣaf*!	O Umm Gimyāna!
Sister of the Sultans!	O Umm Gimyāna!
Except for you I saw no one!	O Umm Gimyāna!
Your beauty I saw nowhere else!	O Umm Gimyāna!
I stopped in the monastery!	O Umm Gimyāna!
We drank the wine!	O Umm Gimyāna!
You held the cross!	O Umm Gimyāna!

The scene we need to 'audiovisualize' is the musicians playing a certain rhythm and melody connected with the spirit Umm Gimyāna, and the lead singer invoking her by her appellations 'dweller of al-Barārī' and '*Ṣafṣaf*' (lines 1-2), praising her as a noble lady of head-turning beauty (lines 3-5), the other singers responding, here and throughout the song, by calling on her by her name. What we also have to imagine is the one who is possessed by Umm Gimyāna getting up to dance, perhaps elegantly dressed, moving in a stately manner like a lady, drawing everybody's attention to herself because she is so beautiful. The words are directed as much to her as to the spirit, since she is the spirit. Since she is a Christian spirit and dweller of the monastery, the singer imagines a visit there, drinking wine with the spirit/the possessed person, and the spirit/possessed person wielding a cross (lines 6-8). What we need to visualize is the possessed person drinking (or pretending to be drinking) wine and carrying a cross while she dances. The lines of the song may be repeated and varied and the song goes on until the possessed person enters into a trance when the *zār* leader can supposedly speak with the spirit Umm Gimyāna herself.

Zār songs are, of course, not meant to be transcribed and published. Publishing gives the songs a misleading aura of constancy, and suggests that the songs have a meaning in themselves that can be extracted from the text. However, the *zār* spirit songs are not narratives that tell us a story; they are not informative in themselves. The process of recording the words of the songs and what is said in the ritual starts a process of divorcing and alienating the words from the very context in which they have a meaning and a function, and indeed in which they came to be. The only way to fully understand a *zār* song is to go back to its context, the lived ritual, as I have tried to do here.

References

Armanios, Febe Y. (2003). Coptic Christians in Ottoman Egypt: Religious Worldview and Communal Beliefs. Unpublished PhD dissertation, The Ohio State University.

Armanios, Febe. (2011). *Coptic Christianity in Ottoman Egypt*. Oxford: Oxford University Press.

Atalla, Nabil Selim. (1998). *Coptic Icons*. 2 vols. Cairo: Lehnert & Landrock.

CMS Archives. Revd [John] R. Th. Lieder's Journal of his journey to the Delta; Damietta, Rosetta, Alexandria, and back to Cairo, from the 25th of July to 16th Sept. 1829. Archives of the Church Missionary Society, Special Collections, University of Birmingham Library, United Kingdom. CMS/B/OMS/C M 048/42.

Darwish, Kamil Afandi. (no date). *Kitāb bidaʿ al-fujjār fī ḥaflat al-zār* [Book of the Heresy of the Godless in the zār Assembly]. Published at the expense of Mahmud Ahmad Al-ʾUzi, no place.

El-Adly, Saber. (1984). The 'Zar'. In: Szilárd Biernaczky, ed., *Folklore in Africa Today. Proceedings of the International Workshop Budapest, 1-4, XI 1982* (Artes populare 10-11). 2 vols.: vol. 1: 655-686. Budapest: Department of Folklore, Eötvös Loránd University, African Research Program.

Elder, E. E. (1927). *Egyptian Colloquial Arabic Reader*. London: Oxford University Press.

El Hadidi, Hager. (2006). Survivals and Surviving: Belonging to *Zār* in Cairo. Unpublished PhD dissertation, University of North Carolina at Chapel Hill.

Galal, Mohammed. (1937). Essai d'Observations sur les Rites Funéraires en Égypte Actuelle. *Revue des Études Islamiques* 2 (2-3): 131-299.

Guirguis, Magdi. (2008). *Armenian Artist in Ottoman Egypt: Yuhanna al-Armani and His Coptic Icons*. Cairo: American University in Cairo Press.

Hinds, Martin and Badawi, El-Said. (1986). *A Dictionary of Egyptian Arabic: Arabic-English*. Beirut: Librairie du Liban.

Jullien, Michel. (1903). Quelques anciens couvents de l'Egypte. [First part] I. – Le couvent de Sainte-Dimiana. In: *Les Missions Catholiques. Bulletin Hebdomadaire Illustré de l'Oeuvre de la Propagation de la Foi* 35: 188-190.

Kriss, Rudolf and Kriss-Heinrich, Hubert. (1960 and 1962). *Volksglaube im Bereich des Islam*, 2 vols. Wiesbaden: Harrassowitz.

Lane, Edward William (1984). *Arabic-English Lexicon*. 2 vols. Cambridge: The Islamic Texts Society. Facsimile of original edition in 8 vols. (1863-93). London: Williams and Norgate.

Leeder, S. H. (1918). *Modern Sons of the Pharaohs: A Study of the Manners and Customs of the Copts of Egypt*. London: Hodder and Stoughton.

Lieder, John. (1934). Voyage to Parts of the Delta [May–June 1833]. *Church Missionary Record* 5, 9: 177-183.

Littmann, Enno. (1950). *Arabische Geisterbeschwörungen aus Ägypten*. Leipzig: Harrassowitz.

McPherson, Joseph Williams. (1941). *The Moulids of Egypt (Egyptian Saints-Days)*. Cairo: Nile Mission Press.

Makris, G. P. and Natvig, Richard. (1991). The Zar, Tumbura and Bori Cults: A select annotated bibliography. In: I. M. Lewis, Ahmed al-Safi, and Sayyid Hurreiz (eds) *Women's Medicine: The Zar-Bori Cult in Africa and Beyond*: 233-282. Edinburgh: Edinburgh University Press.

Al-Makrizi, Taqiyy al-Din Ahmad b. 'Ali b. 'Abd al-Qadir. (2003). *Al-mawā'iẓ wa'l-i'tibār fī dhikr al-khiṭaṭ wa'l-athār*. vol. IV/2. Ed. Ayman Fu'ad Sayyid. London: Al-Furqan Islamic Heritage Foundation.

Meinardus, Otto. (1969). A Critical Study on the Cult of Sitti Dimiana and her Forty Virgins. *Orientalia Suecana* 18: 45-68.

Meinardus, Otto. (2003). *Coptic Saints and Pilgrimages*. 2nd printing. Cairo: The American University in Cairo Press.

Misri, Fatima al-. (1975). *Al-Zār: Dirāsa nafsiyya taḥliliyya anthrūpūlūjiyya* [Zar: A Socio-Psychological Study]. Cairo: Al-Hayʾa Al-Misriyya Al-ʿAma Li'l-Kitab.

Nabhan, Muna. (1994). *Der zār-Kult in Ägypten: Rituelle Begegnung von Geist und Mensch. Ein Beispiel komplementärer Gläubigkeit*. Frankfurt am Main: Peter Lang.

Natvig, Richard Johan. (2013). Umm al-Ghulam: *Zār* Spirit or Half-Forgotten Saint? Making Sense of an Egyptian *Zār* Song. *Folklore*, 124 (3): 289-306. Published online: http://www.tandfonline.com/doi/full /10.1080/0015587X.2013.812417.

Natvig, Richard Johan. (2014). 'I Saw the Prophet in My Dream': Prophet Songs from a *Zār* Ceremony in Lower Egypt. *British Journal of Middle Eastern Studies* 41 (3): 306-21. Published on-line: http://dx.doi.org /10.1080/13530194.2014.888263.

Niebuhr, Carsten. (1774). *Carsten Niebuhrs Reisebeschreibung nach Arabien und andern umliegenden Ländern*. Volume 1 (of 3). Kopenhagen: Friedrich Perthes.

Out-El-Kouloub. (1940). *Trois Contes de l'Amour et de la Mort*. Paris: Corrêa.

Pococke, Richard. (1743). *A Description of the East and Some Other Countries*. Volume 1 (of 5): Observations on Egypt. London: W. Bowyer.

Rouaud, A. and Battain, Tiziana. (2002). *Zār*. In *Encyclopaedia of Islam*, 2nd edition. Vol. 11. Leiden: Brill.

Sengers, Gerda. (2003). *Women and Demons: Cult Healing in Islamic Egypt*. Leiden: Brill.

Sicard, Claude. (1810). *Lettre du Père Siccard [sic!], Missionnaire en Egypte, à son Altesse Sérénissime Monseigneur le Comte de Toulouse*. Vol. 5 of Lettres Édifiantes et Curieuses. Écrites des Missionnaires de la Compagnie de Jésus. Mémoires du Lévant. Toulouse: Noel-Etienne Sens.

Sidawi, Élie. (1917). Moeurs et Traditions de l'Égypte Moderne: Sitti Dimiana, sa Légende, son Mouled. *Bulletin de la Société Sultanieh de Géographie* 8: 79-99.
Skalova, Zuzana and Gabra, Gawdat. (2006). *Icons of the Nile Valley*. 2nd edition. Cairo: Egyptian International Publishing Company - Longman.
Sommer, Annie van and Zwemer, Samuel M. (eds) (1907). *Our Moslem Sisters: A Cry of Need from Lands of Darkness Interpreted by Those Who Heard It*. New York, Chicago, Toronto, London, Edinburgh: Fleming H. Revell Company.
Spiro, Socrates. (1895). *An Arabic-English Dictionary of the Colloquial Arabic of Egypt*. Cairo: Al-Mokattam.
Spiro, Socrates. (1923). *Arabic-English Dictionary of the Modern Arabic of Egypt*. Cairo: Elias' Modern Press.
Stene, Nora. (1991). 'Fordi barn er som engler ...' En religionshistorisk studie av barn i Den koptisk-ortodokse kirke i Egypt. Unpublished MA dissertation, University of Oslo.
Vansleb [Johan Michael]. (1677). *Nouvelle Relation en Forme de Journal, d'un Voyage Fait en Egypte par le P[ère] Vansleb, R. D. en 1672 et 1673*. Paris: Estienne Michallet.
Viaud, Gérard. (1979). *Les Pèlerinages Coptes en Egypte d'après les Notes du Qommos Jacob Muyser*. Cairo: Institut Français d'Archéologie Orientale du Caire.
Wehr, Hans. (1976). *A Dictionary of Modern Written Arabic (Arabic-English)*, edited by J. Milton Cowan. 3rd edition. Ithaca (NY): Spoken Languages Services.
Wilkinson, [John] Gardner. (1843). *Modern Egypt and Thebes: Being a Description of Egypt*. Volume 1 (of 2). London: J. Murray.

Trade and religion in the Central Sahara. The Ibāḍīs and Kawar

Knut Vikør

The trans-Saharan trade route from Tripoli to Lake Chad was an important channel for culture contact from at least the medieval period until the middle of the nineteenth century. Salt, slaves and other goods were exchanged in a complex network of interlocking local and regional trade networks (Miège 1975; Ahmida 2011). But religions were also exchanged, and by tracing the trade, we can also say something about religious developments in this area.

To give an example of the relation between the two spheres, we may look at the history of one of the most remote spots in the world, a string of oases located in the absolute centre of the Sahara, where one must travel several hundred kilometres of desert in all directions before hitting another settlement, i.e., the oasis of Kawar, today in the north-eastern corner of the Republic of Niger (Le Coeur 1985; Vikør 1999).

This could thus be called the 'ultimate periphery'. Yet, it could not possibly have supported its population of about 3,000 scattered over about a dozen villages along a mountain range (Vikør 1999: 33-51) if it had not been for their geographical location. Furthermore, its location also meant that it had changed its identity over the centuries, in terms of which centre it was a periphery to. During the medieval period – it is possible to trace its history at least back to the ninth century – it was culturally and politically a part of the Maghreb (North Africa; Vikør 1987). It then constituted the southernmost reach of Maghrebi culture. However, in the later Middle Ages, the North African states went through a period of crisis, while new strong states or empires grew south of the desert in the Sudanic Belt. As a result, the Maghrebi oasis of Kawar changed to become an extension of central Sudanic[1] culture, and became part of West African history rather than that of North Africa.

Clearly, such a change of apparent identity may simply be a reflection of a change in our sources on the oasis. We only get detailed sources from the Lake Chad region itself from about the same period, the eleventh or twelfth century, and evidently these sources emphasize their own control and interest in the Saharan oases, while new and original Arabic geographical works on this part of the Sahara largely disappear from that time. So each source could depict Kawar as being influenced by *their* culture and being an element of their 'sphere of influence'.

However, there are also local sources that would seem to substantiate that there was a change of emphasis in the later Middle Ages. There are no written sources from Kawar, and oral sources are clearly influenced by the extensive contacts with the south over the last few centuries. More lasting, and more revealing, however, are the place names of the oasis (Vikør 1999: 51-60, 165-70). There are now about a dozen villages in Kawar. Several of the most important of them have names that, while they appear in a form influenced by the local Kanuri or Teda languages, are of evident Arabic origin. Thus, the important village of Gasabi or Guedsebi-Gassar is clearly the town mentioned in Arabic sources as al-Qaṣaba (*Qaṣaba-qaṣr*; Lange and Berthoud 1977), described as the central village of the oasis alongside Bilma, and the outlying village of Jado has taken its name from the town of the same name in Tunisia (Rottier 1924; Chapelle 1957: 100-8; Le Rouvreur 1999). Segedin village between Kawar and Jado was said to contain a mosque, so its name is most likely derived from Arabic *Sāqī al-Dīn*, 'The well of [the place of] religion' (Gentil 1948: 39-41; Carl and Petit 1954: 29ff.).[2] The medieval sources also speak of Qaṣr Umm 'Īsā; this name cannot be identified

[1] 'Central Sudan' and 'western Sudan' here refer to regions of the Sudanic belt south of the Sahara (Central Sudan being the regions on either side of Lake Chad, including Hausaland, Bornu and Kanem), and are not to be confused with the modern Republic of Sudan ('Nilotic Sudan', and 'Sudanese', not 'Sudanic') further east.

[2] Other etymologies include *Ṣaqī al-Dayn*, the 'well of perdition'. A stronger religious connection between *sajada*, 'to prostate oneself in prayer',

today, so the village could have been abandoned later, or possibly changed its name, for example when new Teda immigrants came to Kawar in the later Middle Ages.

The persistence of the Arabic names into modern Kanuri and Teda usage shows the importance of the Arabic-speaking Muslim cultural influence and population in the earlier periods. It supports the descriptions of the village in the medieval sources as a town populated by Muslim Arabs and Berbers, with traders coming from all over the Maghreb. The local population, al-Idrīsī wrote in 1154, 'have adopted the customs of the whites in wearing wool, cotton and soft cloth', and veiled their faces like modern-day Tuareg, indicating a Berber culture (al-Idrīsī 1970: 116-19).[3]

The modern population of Kawar is Sudanic, related to two distinct ethnicities: in the northern part of the oasis, settled Teda ('Toubou') dominate an economy of date cultivation and maintain contacts with Saharan Teda groups in Tibesti to the east (modern Chad). The southern villages are populated by Kanuri speakers, related to the main population of Bornu and Kanem around Lake Chad in the south. It is here that Kawar's main export, salt, is produced, exclusively by Kanuris. The advent of these groups in the oases is not clear; Kanem sources talk of a 'settlement' of Kanuri slaves in the Middle Ages,[4] and local myth speaks of earlier Sudanic peoples such as the So and Koyam (Le Sourd 1946: 5; Fuchs 1989: 119-20; Vikør 1999: 38-43). However, it is reasonable to assume that the Kanuri are the earlier of the two present-day groups and most likely constituted the salt-producing segment of Kawar in the medieval period we speak of here. The Teda probably arrived towards the end of the medieval period and later, after the shift to a 'Sudanic identity' we postulate here, but there may have been a smaller Teda trading population already in place earlier (Vikør 1999: 46-8).

The evidence thus shows that the dominant medieval population of Kawar was Muslim, at a time when the new Kanem kingdom east of Lake Chad and the other central Sudanic states had only a fleeting contact with this new religion. Arabic sources seem to indicate that Islam and Maghrebi culture was not limited to the immigrant traders but also spread among the local Sudanic population who had 'adopted' the northerners' ways.[5] This then, allows us to try to place the religious identity of Kawar in a regional context, where trade is the dominant factor and constitutes the material basis for the settlements of this distant oasis region.

The importance of Kawar was that it was situated in two trading networks. One was regional and directed southwards, and was based on Kawar's production of salt, which was consumed on the desert edge to the south. There is clear archaeological evidence of this production even before the medieval period, though we do not know how far back it goes. The actors in this trade were Sudanic traders from the south, and it is reasonable to assume that the critical factor was ecological, that is, the degree to which the alternation between wet and dry periods provided water sources between Kawar and the consumer areas for traders to stop at, in particular on the road directly south to Lake Chad (Lovejoy 1986: 182-9; Vikør 1999: 79-139). We do know that there were populated villages on this route as late as the seventeenth century, and it is reasonable to think that the people of these villages, the Koyam, played a part in the salt trade. But we do not know how far back, and we do not know much about the culture and nature of this trade before the Tuareg came and took over from the eighteenth century onwards.

The other trading network was inter-regional or 'international', going north-south from the Mediterranean and other parts of North Africa to Lake Chad and the central Sudanic belt. This trade was distinct from the regional salt trade in the post-medieval period, and Kawar was most important here as the main halting place on this very difficult and dangerous road, not least for the slave trade. However, medieval

and '*sagadin*' is less likely, given the consonant shift in the region, *g* more often replacing Arabic *q*.

[3] Cited in Vikør (1999: 295-6). The latter work contains the relevant Arabic sources for Kawar, while a wider collection of Arabic sources for West African history is Levtzion and Hopkins (1981).

[4] Or, rather, Kanembu of Kanem. A distinct Kanuri ethnicity is probably only usefully established around the rise of the Bornu empire some centuries later, but for the purpose of this article, we will use 'Kanuri' for people ethnicity linked to the Kanem-Bornu region without distinction. The settlement story is from Palmer (1936: 143); see below.

[5] See the sources in Vikør (1999: 283-301).

Arabic sources also talk of trade in a number of goods taking place in Kawar, including 'alum', by which is probably meant salt used for medical or other purposes; the description of production fits what we know from modern salt production in Kawar (Lange 1982; Vikør 1999: 101-7). This was exported to the north as well in considerable quantities, according to al-Idrīsī, that is, in the mid 12th century.

It was thus the trading network going to the north that brought Muslims and Islam to Kawar. But what kind of Islam did these traders, and thus the Kawar Muslims, practise?

The most expansive medieval sources from the twelfth and thirteenth century do not specify that beyond saying they were 'Muslim'. However, as the religious influences in Kawar came from their northern neighbours, we must look at what Islam these northerners practised. And everyone to the north of Kawar in the period from the eighth to about the twelfth century belonged to the 'third branch' of Islam, the one that is neither Sunni nor Shi'i, *Ibāḍism*.

The Ibāḍī branch of Islam

The Ibāḍīs are today completely dwarfed by their two rival denominations of Islam, and now account for less than one per cent of all Muslims. The only place where they have a dominance is in the sultanate of Oman, where they constitute about a half of the population (the other half being mainly Shāfiʿī Sunnis), including the sultan and the leading aristocracy of the country. Small communities have also existed on the East African coast since the Omanis settled there, but the largest distinct communities of Ibāḍīs in Africa are in some remote regions of the Maghreb, such as Mzab in Algeria, Jerba Island in Tunisia and Jabal Nafusa in Libya, each place numbering no more than 20-30,000 at most (Lewicki 1971a 1971b).

The Ibāḍīs are today considered a peaceful and tolerant minority. However, their origin is linked to the early current called the *khārijīs*, those who leave or rebel against established authority. The name stems from the first civil war in Islam between the fourth caliph ʿAlī ibn Abī Ṭālib and his enemy, the Damascus governor Muʿāwiya, and the Battle of Ṣiffīn in 657 (Muʿammar 2007; Prevost 2010; Wilkinson 2010). There, Muʿāwiya proposed that the conflict should be settled by arbitration, and ʿAlī agreed to this. One group of his followers protested against this and left his camp, *kharaja*, giving them the nickname 'leavers', *khārijīs*. A few years later, one such Khārijī murdered ʿAlī, thereby ending the war and leaving the way open for Muʿāwiya and his Umayyad dynasty to claim the caliphate.

Over the following century, a number of revolts against the Umayyads were described as Khārijī revolts. Many of these may not have had anything to do with the religious current, but some were claimed (at least by their enemies) to be based on the simple dichotomy that only their particular group were real Muslims, thus everyone else were infidels, and true Muslims should fight infidels. Hence, a war against everyone. From this, the term *khārijī* came to be used for a 'fanatic extremist'. Excluding other Muslims from the community of believers is commonly known as *takfīr* (to call a Muslim a *kāfir*, infidel), and the term *khārijī* came to be used for a similar attitude towards fellow Muslims.[6] Today, *takfīr* is a term normally applied to radical Salafi or jihadist groups such as IS or al-Qāʿida, who justify *jihād* against other Muslims by their not being 'real Muslims'. However, these groups themselves reserve the term *khārijī* for attacks on each other, meaning a group that is even more extreme than themselves.[7]

Clearly, today's peaceful Ibāḍīs want above all else to distance themselves from this sordid description, and it is today a fundamental tenet of Ibāḍī belief to reject that they are today's Khārijīs and play down the link to the historical precedent (Hoffman 2012: 3-4). They do accept that their intellectual ancestors left ʿAlī's camp, but not that they at any point took part in any campaign against him. Instead, they highlight that when a group of those who had left the battlefield gathered in a place called Nahrawān in Iraq, ʿAlī sent an army and massacred a large number of them without provocation. ʿAlī's murderer acted

[6] The 'leaving' is thus also extended to refer to *kharaja ʿalā*, 'to revolt against someone', or even *kharaja min al-dīn*, 'to leave the faith'.

[7] E.g. Abu Hamza Al-Misri, *Khawaarij and Jihad*, Birmingham n.d. [2000], the 'Londonistan' preacher attacking the Algerian GIA; also the IS magazine *Dābiq*, for example.

in revenge of Nahrawān, but had no connection to the main group that had gathered peacefully in Baṣra. It was several decades later that some of the Basra group became a distinct religious group that came to be known as Ibāḍīs, from an early leader, ʿAbd Allāh ibn Ibāḍ.

Exactly why they took this name (or why the name was given them) is not clear, as Ibn Ibāḍ is not considered the founder of the current. That role is normally given to the scholar Jābir b. Zayd (d. 712).[8] Neither Ibāḍī sources nor modern scholars can explain why they are then named after this mysterious Ibn Ibāḍ, whose existence is not certain, but may have been a scholar of the movement living perhaps half a century after Jābir. Some scholars suggest that the name Ibāḍī was originally a pun that the group later took to using themselves and gave it an etymology: two of the other main groups of Khārijīs in Baṣra were known as the Azraqīs and Ṣufrīs, linked to the colours blue (*azraq*) and yellow (*aṣfar*), while 'ibāḍī' may with some imagination be seen to stem from *abyaḍ*, white.[9]

Anyway, these early Ibāḍīs did not have any political ambition, although a group under Ṭālib al-Ḥaqq (d. 748) in Hadramawt (eastern Yemen) revolted in 747, at the very end of the Umayyad period. They briefly conquered Mecca and Medina before being pushed back into Hadramawt, where an Ibāḍī presence remained for about three centuries (Prevost 2010: 7-9).

The main group of Ibāḍīs had then already, from the beginning of the eighth century, began a partially forced transfer from Baṣra to Jābir's native Oman, where they already had support from a number of tribes, and established an imāmate there in 793. That first imāmate in Oman lasted less than a century, until 886, and internal divisions weakened them for centuries, but they retained the support of the local tribes, and returned to power later, and also influenced Arabian trading colonies in East Africa. However, it was in the Maghreb that the Ibāḍī presence was most important in a short hectic period from the middle of the eighth to the beginning of the tenth centuries.

Berber Ibāḍī states in the medieval Maghreb

Ibāḍī missionaries first appeared in Tripolitania around 745 AD (Lewicki 1957; Rebstock 1983: 56-138). They quickly gained the support of Berber tribes of the Maghreb who had converted to Islam less than two generations earlier, and who probably found the Ibāḍī theology of equality in Islam preferable to the Arabism then dominant in mainstream Islam. In around 760, a Persian general, Ibn Rustam, settled in the town of Tahert in present-day Algeria, and created an Ibāḍī state that over the next half century came to dominate most of North Africa from eastern Morocco to Tripolitania (western Libya today; Dangel 1977; Zerouki 1987; Savage 1997). Only the northern parts of Tunisia were under the control of a governor loyal to Baghdad. This probably represents the height of Ibāḍī power at any time in Islamic history. However, dynastic and theological strife caused different factions to split from the 'Wahbī' Rustamids of Tahert, with several of them settling in Tripolitania. This province remained predominantly Ibāḍī through the ninth century, but escaped direct control from the Rustamids of the west for much of that time. The Ibāḍīs carried out considerable trade across the Sahara towards the Western Sudan (Lewicki 1960; 1962; 1964; Vikør 2002a).

From Tripolitania, Ibāḍī groups also ventured south to the region of Fezzan, which constitutes the northern border of the Sahara Desert. They established a town, or state, called Zawīla (Lewicki 1957: 340-1).[10] This may have been independent from the older Fezzani centre of Jarma, ancient Garama of the Garamantes. Jarma appears to have remained loyal to the Rustamid state of Tahert, while Zawīla may thus have been dominated by another Ibāḍī branch, or the distinction may have been tribal, Zawīla being

[8] Wilkinson, however, believes that Jābir's role was also more modest, and suggests the Ibāḍīs as a group were formed about 60 years later (Wilkinson 2010: 154-210).

[9] See my discussion of this in 'What's in a name? The third branch of Islam and its naming' (forthcoming). It was the Azraqīs that were the militant rebels, who, it is claimed, had the Manichean view that everyone else were infidels.

[10] See a discussion about the date of Zawīla's establishment in Vikør (1999: 156n49) and Vikør (2000b). Recent archaeological research has found the remains of an early, no doubt Ibāḍī, mosque at Zawīla, probably dating from the early ninth century (Mattingly, Sterry and Edwards 2015: 44-52).

dominated by the Berber Hawwāra tribe. It is recorded in history as being ruled by an ʿAbd Allāh al-Ibāḍī in 763 (Ibn ʿIdhārī 1983: i, 73; Lewicki 1957: 341; Rebstock 1983: 99), and Ibāḍī sources retain the memory of several scholars of this branch in Zawīla in the ensuing centuries.

The heyday of Ibāḍī power in the Maghreb came to an end with the arrival of the Shīʿī Fāṭimids in Tunisia from 909. The Ibāḍī states had been weakened over time, not least through internal struggles, and the Fāṭimids quickly gained the support of important Berber tribes in the region. In a series of campaigns, they crushed both the Rustamids and the other smaller states as far as today's Morocco. There were still many tribes who remained loyal to Ibāḍī thought, however, and the tenth century saw a number of local revolts against the Fāṭimid rulers. However, when their final major challenge was defeated at the Battle of Bāghāya in 969 (Prevost 2006; Prevost 2008: 146-52), the Ibāḍī military and political ambitions in the Maghreb came to an end, even though the Fāṭimids turned their attention eastwards to Egypt in that same year.

Instead, the Ibāḍīs began to withdraw to more remote areas where they could try to survive both politically and also increasingly as a religious minority. Sunnism began to make its way into the Maghreb with the disappearance of Fāṭimid control, and not least through the eleventh-century large-scale immigration of Arab tribes to the formerly Berber Maghreb, and the Arabization of Berber tribes in the centuries that followed. The Ibāḍīs withdrew basically in two directions: one was into mountainous regions or islands in the north, primarily Jabal Nafūsa in Libya and Jerba Island in Tunisia; the other, which was the larger and more important move, was southwards to the desert edge or to oases in the desert.

This was important, because the Ibāḍī Berber states and tribes had trans-Saharan trade as their main economic basis throughout their period of dominance. From Sijilmāsa in Morocco (ruled by Ṣūfrites, another Khārijī branch, but with an Ibāḍī trading community) to Fezzan, all trading centres on the northern side of the desert were Ibāḍī, and so were the traders that went to Gao, Tegdaoust, Tademekka and other southern entrepôts and settled in this period. They also established religious communities of Ibāḍism in the south. Thus the Islam that first reached West Africa, at least where these Ibāḍī traders dominated, such as Gao and Kanem, must have been an Ibāḍī Islam in this period.

When the Ibāḍī tribes thus withdrew southwards, they moved along these trade routes and settled in desert-side cities such as Wargala, Ghat and Ghadames (Lethielleux 1983; Haarmann 1998: 52-65).[11] In this way, they still controlled the trade routes, and could probably for quite some time remain the obvious source of reference for Islamic knowledge south of the desert. Only from the eleventh century onwards do we begin to find clear indication of a Sunni presence in Gao – distinguishable by the presence of Muslim funeral epigraphy, as Ibāḍīs do not seem to have marked their graves with names or other identifying marks; these appear only in the later Sunni period.[12]

The northern desert-side region of relevance for the Kanem-Tripolitania route that passed through Kawar was Fezzan. In this region, the fleeing Ibāḍīs were able to maintain an Ibāḍī state with Zawīla as its capital. From 918, it was ruled by the Berber dynasty of Banū Khaṭṭāb, who remained an autonomous power for two and a half centuries until 1176 (Lavers 1979). This thus became an Ibāḍī refuge, and also apparently somewhat of a scholarly centre. It was during this period, probably in the latter half of the eleventh century, that the first kings of Kanem converted to Islam, and as its trading connection went through Kawar to Fezzan, that must thus also have been an Islam in its Ibāḍī form (Lavers 1971: 28; Levtzion 1978: ii, 682; Vikør 1999: 174-6).

However, the expansion of Sunni power in the north must soon have been felt also into the south. While the Banū Khaṭṭāb retained power through much of the twelfth century, they were clearly weakened. Eventually, the dynasty was forced from power by an Armenian *mamlūk* linked to the Ayyubids of Egypt, thus a Sunni military power grab (Rossi 1968: 614; Pellat 1978). At this time, it is likely that Ibāḍīs, Sunnis

[11] See also the survey of Ibāḍī remains in the Sahara in Van Berchem (1960).
[12] P. F. de Moraes Farias, personal communication; see also Farias (2003).

and perhaps even some remnants of Fāṭimid supporters were vying for influence in the region. That the Ibāḍīs were still present after the fall of the Banū Khāṭṭāb can, however, be seen in that the aggressively Sunni Almoravid movement from the western Maghreb raided the region, attacking Ibāḍī heretics in around 1185.[13]

The weakening of Fezzan enabled a new and unexpected power to appear. East of Lake Chad, Kanem had become an empire, and its ambitions followed the trade route northwards. Kanemi sources claim that the pagan *mai* (king) Arku settled 300 slaves in Kawar and at Traghen in Fezzan towards the middle of the eleventh century (Palmer 1936: 143; Lange 1977: 133). This statement is clearly meant to indicate control. This was at a time when the Banū Khaṭṭāb still ruled in Zawīla. The garrison at Traghen was probably not permanent, but a century later, after the Banū Khaṭṭāb had fallen, another Kanemi force arrived, killed the master of Zawīla (the son of the Armenian *mamlūk*) and established themselves in Traghen as masters of the Fazzan for a period of just over a century (Julien 1970: 111-24; Martin 1977: 7; Lavers 1979: 15-19).[14] This, then, marks the end of a distinct period in the history of the central Sahara. With Fezzan under Sudanic control, Kawar was from then on never again to be considered a Maghrebi outpost, but a more or less autonomous dependency of the Sudanic powers of the south.

That is about as much as we know of this clearly tumultuous period of transition. The rest, how this religious transformation played out in Kawar and how to interpret it, must remain a matter of conjecture. The Arab sources fall silent – or rather, they copy the information given by the more voluminous geographers of the earlier period – and the Sudanic sources only speak of Kanemi expansion and are in any case not very informative regarding the finer detail of Muslim theology in these early days. To try to understand what the effect of the religious distinctiveness of the Ibāḍīs may have been on the society in this period, and thus on the trading communities, we must turn to look briefly at Ibāḍī thought, and in particular how the Ibāḍīs conceived of the 'Other', the relationship between themselves, the true believers, and those Muslims who differed from them.

Exclusive theology and trade with the others

The caricature of *khārijī* thought was thus that they were the only true Muslims and everyone else was an infidel, and as such a target for *jihād* and destruction.[15] This simple dichotomy is rejected by the Ibāḍīs. Nevertheless, the issue of how to consider other Muslims is an important one for their identity formation. Distinctiveness is crucial, focused on the Quranic term *walāya wa-barā'a*, 'closeness [to the 'ingroup'] and distance [from the 'outgroup']'.[16] This has both a religious, pious element, to favour solidarity among those of the faith, and also a legal side in a society regulated by the Sharīᶜa: different rules apply in interactions between Muslims than in those between Muslims and *kuffār*, non-believers. So, the issue of who is a Muslim is essential in defining how you interact with other people. This becomes even thornier when you consider yourselves to be the true Muslims, but live as a tiny minority in a sea of others who also consider themselves Muslims.

The way the Ibāḍīs settled this was to go beyond the simple Muslim/unbeliever dichotomy and to use three categories: the only true Muslims are those who accept the Ibāḍī faith. Those who are not Ibāḍīs are indeed *kuffār*, infidels. But there are many categories of *kuffār*. Apart from the 'book people' (Christians and Jews), who have their own place under the Sharīᶜa, there is also a distinction between the 'hypocrites' and the 'heathens'. The former believe themselves to be Muslim (although they are, as non-Ibāḍīs, actually not), but they pray towards Mecca, and are thus called *ahl al-qibla*, 'the people of the

[13] On the Almoravids, see, for example, Farias (1967).

[14] This was then a rare example of a 'black' African state colonizing a 'white' Arabic/Berber country in the north. A remnant of this colonization may be seen in the presence of Sudanic groups in the Fezzan and Kufra in southern Libya today, although these are Teda and not Kanembu.

[15] More distinctly, this view is said to have been held by the Azraqīya branch of the Khārijīs, who split off from the Basra group and raised militant revolt from southern Fars (Iran) in the late 700s. They also included the Ibāḍīs among the infidels, as they also did not agree with them. As usual, we do not have any texts from the Azraqīs themselves to prove they really did hold this view, but the Ibaḍīs do use the Azraqīs as a counterpoint when explaining their own, more sophisticated viewpoint.

[16] Or 'association and dissociation', as it is often more briefly translated.

prayer direction'. They are *kuffār al-nifāq*, unbelievers of hypocrisy, and are totally distinct from those who reject both Islam and the other scriptures, the heathens or *kuffār al-shirk*, polytheists who have no place in the Muslim society.

The major distinction was that the *ahl al-qibla* retained all the legal rights as Muslims, in spite of their sin, and only the *kuffār al-shirk* were completely outside the legal community.

The non-Ibāḍīs are all sinners, and as such destined for Hell in the next life without exception or hope of salvation. All those who reject the true Ibāḍī faith will receive their due punishment by God in the hereafter. But in *this* life, they are legally to be considered as Muslims, in spite of their sins. This is the main point: while the *ahl al-qibla* are in Ibāḍī theology not Muslims, they are in Ibāḍī law to be considered as Muslims and retain all legal rights as such under the Sharīʿa. Thus, there is no impediment for an Ibāḍī to trade or make contracts with them. Ibāḍīs may even marry non-Ibāḍīs, although views on this varied in Ibāḍī law over time and between circumstances. In social reality, intermarriage was probably an exception rather than the rule, as the Ibāḍī communities, be they tribally based or not, avoided marriage outside the group without necessarily referring to religion.[17] In general, the Ibāḍīs should keep interaction with non-Ibāḍī sinners to a minimum, and it was only well into the twentieth century that Ibāḍī women were allowed to leave the safe haven of Ibāḍī-dominated Mzab for the wider Algerian world (Vigourous 1945; Holsinger 1980; Prevost 2010: 95-6). Male traders could venture there, but stayed in close-knit diasporas and were called back to the homeland at regular intervals. Ibāḍīs could and must trade with other Muslims, but they should only trust their own.

The practicalities of these rules clearly relate to the changing contexts that Ibāḍī communities faced. Until the late nineteenth century, the Mzab oases in particular were independent of any outside authority and could remain a closed community with fully regulated interaction with the outside world, even though they still relied on commerce with non-Ibāḍīs for their survival. It was only with French colonial rule that Ibāḍī integration into the wider Algeria became an issue, when Sunni Algerians entered the Mzab while Ibāḍī traders from there settled in the outside world (Holsinger 1986). Thus, we cannot draw immediate conclusions from this modern situation to that of the declining years of Ibāḍī presence in the late medieval Sahara. Some intriguing reflections can, however, be made.

We must assume that the Berber traders who first settled in Kawar in the Middle Ages were predominantly Ibāḍī, and that whoever was in control of Kawar, be it as an independent Muslim chieftain of local origin, as Idrīsī writes, or as a dependant on Fezzan, was an Ibāḍī. However, if it is true that 'traders came from all lands' came to Kawar to trade in alum or other goods, there must also have been non-Ibāḍī Berber or Arab Muslims visiting the town, as there also were in other Ibāḍī trading towns.

Apart from these statements concerning local Muslim rule and clothing culture (among the wealthy?), we have no way of knowing how far the Islamic faith had penetrated into the local Sudanic population. The Teda immigrants who entered Kawar during the medieval period probably settled gradually, mainly in the northern part of the oasis. It is thus conceivable that the north-south ethnic and economic distinction in the oasis, with the northern villages more concerned with trans-Saharan trade and the southern, Kanuri villages with the regional salt trade, was then already in place, and that the northern villages were more influenced by the outside traders. Nevertheless, Kawar is a very small place, and in the course of several centuries we must assume that the dominant religion had spread and become internalized by the people who lived there, irrespective of economic divisions.

A more intriguing question is whether the exclusiveness and distinctiveness we now see in modern Ibāḍī communities were also present at that time. In other words, whether the Ibāḍī Berber groups would have welcomed non-Berber Sudanic Muslims into their religious community, or whether these would have been more influenced by a less exclusivist theology that they may have picked up from traders

[17] The concept of *kafāʿa*, social and other equality between the spouses as a requirement for a legal marriage, is, for example, very useful when avoiding alliances without specifying why you do so.

coming from Egypt or other lands. We have no way of knowing this. But one may conjecture that the degree to which Ibāḍīs restricted contact with other Muslims varied with the strength of their community. The Rustamids at the height of their power were said to have welcomed traders and travellers from all sides without restriction, while the modern marginalized Ibāḍī communities are very protective against outsiders. Perhaps medieval Ibāḍīs in a remote trading community like Kawar would waver between the two attitudes. Exclusiveness may not have had to be so strictly enforced in the earlier period when they were the only Muslims present, while a more significant presence of non-Ibāḍī traders towards the end of the period may have caused a clearer division between insiders and outsiders. This is only the case, of course, in so far as the inhabitants of this remote oasis were aware of, and concerned with, the theological differences at play. Clearly, religious and ethnic/political identity was linked, and rivalries between the Berber tribes may well have been seen as irrelevant for the Sudanic peoples who stood outside them. But this is, of course, conjectural.

So far, no archaeological remains of an early Muslim presence have been found in Kawar, in fact it may be the last major Saharan trading centre not yet systematically explored archaeologically. Even in other Sudanic towns and cities of this early period, however, such remains are also scarce.[18] One reason for this is, as mentioned, that we do not have epigraphic inscriptions from graves before the Sunni period. Kanemi sources mention a mosque existing in the Kawar village of Segedin when their forces came there in the eleventh century, that is, before Kanem itself was Islamized (Lange 1977: 26, 67). This may have been built for a permanent or semi-permanent settlement of Muslim traders, or it could have been for a local population who had embraced Islam. Such a mosque we must assume to be in the Saharan style known from Air, Ghardaia and elsewhere, but, without continuous maintenance, any such structure disappeared without trace over the centuries.

Do these speculations of what Muslim life may have been in distant times matter? We are unlikely to ever find answers to the questions we raise. However, bearing in mind that we are only dealing with conjecture here, it may still be useful to try to imagine how such a possible scenario could have played out in the turbulent twelfth and thirteenth centuries in the central Sahara.

One question is how these changes affected the trade of Kawar. If we draw conclusions from what we know of later periods, we must assume that they had little impact on the all-important trade in salt flowing southwards from Kawar to the Sudanic region. This would have been affected by disturbances in the south, but climatic changes, such as a desiccation that dried out water sources between Kawar and Lake Chad, would be far more important than internal conflicts in the Fezzan and Kawar.[19] If anything, the rise of Kanem would have improved conditions as well as the market for salt products there. However, medieval sources speak also of salt-related exports going to the *northern* side of the desert, using the term *shabb*, alum rather than salt. There is no indication of such a northern export of salt or salt-derived products in later times. If the Arabic sources are to be trusted with this information – and they put heavy emphasis on it – that might indicate that as Kawar was more linked to the northern markets in the medieval period than later, and as an effect of the 'Maghrebi identity' we have indicated, traders came there not just as a way station en route to Lake Chad, but for picking up products that Kawar itself produced, unlike in modern times. It is quite reasonable to link the end of this trade – which found other, more accessible sources elsewhere – with the changes that Kawar went through in this period. If Kawar's links to the north weakened and any Berber settlement there disappeared when political conditions in Fezzan became less stable, there would have been less incentive for alum traders to have gone to Kawar to look for this product. Of course, other factors, like availability, price and many others, may also have been a cause for moving the trade away, but it is certainly possible to conjecture that a political and cultural 'identity factor' played a role as well.

[18] But see, for example, the work of Paulo Farias (e.g., 2003) for what we know of early Muslim presence in the more western centres of Gao, Tademekka and others.

[19] Environmental data and historical sources seem to indicate a transition towards a drier climate perhaps from the thirteenth-fourteenth century onwards, and certainly from the sixteenth. Several smaller oases or inhabited sources between Kawar and Lake Chad were abandoned over this period (Abadie 1927: 52-4; Le Rouvreur 1948; Lovejoy and Baier 1975: 570).

But Kawar is far away from the Fezzan. Are we overinterpreting the importance of the political and religious strife we know of in Fezzan for remote Kawar in the desert? It really depends on a number of factors we do not know, such as, for example, if there was a permanent or semi-permanent Berber Ibāḍī community settled in Kawar. We know of such communities in other parts of the southern Sahara such as Tademekka and Tegdaoust, and if Kawar hosted such a community, then certainly troubles in the homelands of those Berbers would have had direct influence on life in the oasis, as they of course maintained contact with the north. Kawar's small size may be an argument to the contrary, but it is not unreasonable to believe that a smaller or larger community did exist, perhaps on a semi-permanent or seasonal basis, in one or another of Kawar's oases, in particular those that were, and still are, known by Arabic names. Building on this assumption, we may hazard a guess that the conflicts in Fezzan of the twelfth century were known and had a direct effect on social and political life in the oasis.

We may thus draw a conjectural and hypothetical picture of medieval Kawar along these lines: from the ninth century onwards, Berber Ibāḍī tribes of the Fezzan searching for trade in the south discovered the strategic position of Kawar as a halfway halting place. Discovering the properties of the salt Kawar already produced for the southern market, these traders began taking some of it north, causing others to seek it out. Some traders settled in a few of the villages of the oasis, probably separately from the local Kanuri, building a mosque and actively or passively spreading their religion, causing the local Sudanic population with its local chieftain (or rather 'chieftain clans', the leading families that shared power) to adopt an Islam that must have been Ibāḍī, a century or more before a similar process began to take place among their Kanemi/Kanuri relatives in the south. Most likely, this local political 'elite' spoke Berber and Arabic in addition to their native language.

As trade grew, wider contacts with the Maghreb must have developed, and perhaps from the tenth and certainly eleventh century, Muslims from regions outside the Ibāḍī heartland must have begun to visit Kawar as well, if we are to believe the Arabic geographers. An awareness grew that there were distinctions between these branches of Islam, at least with the decline of Ibāḍī influence in the Fezzan from perhaps the end of the eleventh century or beginning of the twelfth. Kawar, still Muslim, began to move away from identification with the Ibāḍīs. In what way and when would be just guesswork, and would depend perhaps on the relative strength of the Berber tribes that still dominated the region, and with what speed they abandoned their Ibāḍī identity for the increasingly dominant Sunni one. But the process could have taken place in the century between 1050 and 1150, the last generations of Ibāḍī rule in the Fezzan. As that power dwindled, the Berbers who may have settled in Kawar left for the Fezzan, or for larger Ibāḍī communities in Wargala or Ghadames further west. Their villages were taken over by Teda from Tibesti, Islamized or not, who began to enter Kawar in larger numbers at the same time, changing from the nomadic lifestyle they knew in the eastern Sahara to one of settlement in villages, and thus, acquiring a separate identity from the 'Tibesti Teda', they were known as *Gezebidas*, literally 'Teda of *al-Qaṣaba*' (Chapelle 1957: 110-11; Fuchs 1961: 119; Le Sourd 1946: 7ff.; Vikør 1999: 47-8).

How far Ibāḍī theology took hold in Kanem itself is debatable. It is likely that a deepening of Islamic thought in that empire only took place after the disappearance of the Ibāḍīs, or rather their reduction to a minority in the north. Thus, Ibāḍism in Kanem may have been fleeting, and Kanemi Islam soon became Sunni. As contacts between Kawar and the Berber Ibāḍīs were broken, and Kanem took control over the trade route, memory of this medieval brand of Islam disappeared; the local elites, now more and more dominated by the newly arrived Teda clans, turned rather to Kanem for contact and inspiration. The mosques that there were fell into disuse, and Kawar turned into the Sudanic periphery it is today.

This is thus conjectural history. Things may have been completely different. But it is a possible history, an example of how it may have been. As such, we should not draw too far-fetched conclusions from it. We may, however, use it as a possible example of the interaction between a local community in a distant corner of the world and the large religious divides that marked the end of the formative period of Islamic thought in the Maghreb.

References

Abadie, Maurice (1927). *La Colonie du Niger*. Paris: Société d'éditions géographiques, maritimes et coloniales.
Ahmida, Ali Abdullatif (ed.) (2011). *Bridges across the Sahara: Social, Economic and Cultural Impact of the Trans-Sahara Trade During the 19th and 20th Centuries*. Newcastle upon Tyne: Cambridge Scholars Publishing.
Carl, Louis and Joséph Petit (1954). *La Ville de sel (du Hoggar au Tebesti)*. Paris: R. Juillard.
Chapelle, Jean. (1957). *Nomades noirs de Sahara: les Toubous*. Paris: Harmattan (2nd edn).
Dangel, Gérard (1977). L'Imamat Ibadite de Tahert (761–909). Contribution à l'histoire de l'Afrique du Nord durant le Haut Moyen Age. Doctorat de IIIe cycle, Université des Sciences Humaines de Strasbourg.
Farias, P. F. de Moraes (1967). The Almoravids: Some Questions Concerning the Character of the Movement During its Periods of Closest Contact with the Western Sudan. *Bulletin de l'Institut Fondamentale d'Afrique Noire* xxix B, 3-4: 794-878.
Farias, P.F. de Moraes (2003). *Arabic Medieval Inscriptions from the Republic of Mali: Epigraphy, Chronicles, and Songhay-Tuareg History*. Oxford: Oxford University Press.
Fuchs, Peter (1961). *Die Völker der Südost-Sahara: Tibesti, Borku, Ennedi*, Vienna: Wilhelm Braumüller.
Fuchs, Peter (1989). *Fachi. Sahara-Stadt der Kanuri*. Wiesbaden: Franz Steiner.
Gentil, Pierre (1948). *Confins libyens. Lac Tchad, fleuve Niger*. Paris: Charles-Lavauzelle (2nd edn.).
Haarmann, Ulrich (1998). The Dead Ostrich: Life and Trade in Ghadames (Libya) in the Nineteenth Century. *Die Welt des Islams* xxxviii (1): 9-94.
Hoffman, Valerie J. (2012). *The Essentials of Ibāḍī Islam*. Syracuse (NY): Syracuse University Press.
Holsinger, Donald C. (1980). Migration, Commerce and Community: The Mīzābīs in Eighteenth- and Nineteenth-Century Algeria. *Journal of African History* xxi (1): 61-74.
Holsinger, Donald C. (1986). Muslim Responses to French Imperialism: An Algerian Saharan Case Study. *International Journal of African Historical Studies* xix (1): 1-15.
Ibn ʿIdhārī (1983). *Al-Bayān al-mughrib fī akhbār al-Andalus wa'l-Maghrib*. Paris /Beirut: *Dār* al-thaqāfa.
al-Idrīsī, Muḥammad (1970). *Nuzhat al-mushtāq fī ikhtirāq al-āfāq: Opus geographicum, sive, 'Liber ad eorum delectationem qui terras peragrare studeant'* A. Bombaci *et al.* (eds): 116-119. Naples: Instituto Universitario Orientale 1970-[84], translated in Vikør 1999: 295-296.
Julien, Charles-André (1970). *History of North Africa*. London: Routledge and Kegan Paul (translation of 2nd edition, Paris 1961).
Lange, Dierk (1977). *Le Dīwān des sultans du [Kānem-]Bornū. Chronologie et histoire d'un royaume africain (de la fin du xe siècle jusqu'à 1808)*. Wiesbaden: Franz Steiner.
Lange, Dierk (1982). L'Alun du Kawar: Une exportation africaine vers l'Europe. *Cahiers du Centre de Recherches Africaines* 2: 21-24.
Lange, Dierk and Silvio Berthoud (1977). *Al-Qaṣaba* et d'autres villes de la route centrale du Sahara. *Paideuma* xxiii: 19-40.
Lavers, John (1971). Islam in the Bornu Caliphate: A Survey. *Odu* n.s. 5: 27-53.
Lavers, John (1979). Fazzan: Sudanic or Saharan state?. Unpublished paper.
Le Coeur, Marguerite (1985). *Les Oasis du Kawar. Une route, un pays. [i:] Le Passé précolonial*. Niamey: Institut de Recherches en Sciences Humaines.
Le Rouvreur, Albert (1948). *Agadem et Djado: Deux aspects du Téda*. CHEAM, Mémoires verts 1324.
Le Rouvreur, Albert (1999). *Une oasis au Niger: Le Djado*. Paris: Harmattan.
Le Sourd, Michel (1946). Tarikh-el-Kawar. *Bulletin de l'Institut Français d'Afrique Noir* (*BIFAN*) viii (1): 1-54.
Lethielleux, Jean (1983). *Ouargla. Cité saharienne. Des origines au début du xxe siècle*. Paris: Paul Geuthner.
Levtzion, Nehemia (1978). The Sahara and the Sudan from the Arab conquest of the Maghrib to the rise of the Almoravids. In: John Fage (ed.) *Cambridge History of Africa* ii: 637-684.
Levtzion, Nehemia and J. F. P. Hopkins (eds) (1981). *Corpus of Early Arabic Sources for West African History*. Cambridge: Cambridge University Press.
Lewicki, Tadeusz (1957). La Répartition géographique des groupements ibāḍites dans l'Afrique du Nord au Moyen-Âge. *Rocznik Orientalistyczny* xxi: 301-343.
Lewicki, Tadeusz (1960). Quelques extraits inédits relatifs aux voyages des commerçants et des missionnaires ibāḍites Nord-Africaines au pays de Soudan occidental et central au Moyen-Âge. *Folia Orientalia* ii (1-2): 1-27.

Lewicki, Tadeusz (1962). L'État Nord-Africain de Tāhert et ses relations avec le Soudan occidental à la fin du viiie et aux ixe siècle. *Cahiers d'Études Africaines* ii (4/8): 513-35.

Lewicki, Tadeusz (1964). Traits d'histoire du commerce transsaharien: Marchands et missionnaires ibāḍites en Soudan occidental et central au cours des viiie–xiie siècles. *Etnografia Polska* viii: 291-311.

Lewicki, Tadeusz (1971a). The Ibádites in Arabia and Africa. *Cahiers d'Histoire Mondiale* xiii: 51-130.

Lewicki, Tadeusz (1971b). Al-Ibāḍiyya. *Encyclopaedia of Islam* (New Edition) iii: 648-61. Leiden.

Lovejoy, Paul and Stephen Baier (1975). The Desert-side Economy of the Central Sudan. *International Journal of African Historical Studies* viii (4): 551-81.

Lovejoy, Paul E. (1986). *Salt of the Desert Sun. A History of Salt Production and Trade in the Central Sudan.* Cambridge: Cambridge University Press.

Martin, B. G. (1977). Ahmad Rāsim Pāshā and the Suppression of the Fazzān Slave Trade 1881–1896. Paper for the SOAS African History Seminar, 23 Nov. 1977.

Mattingly, David J., Sterry, Martin J., and Edwards, David N. (2015). The Origins and Development of Zuwīla, Libyan Sahara: An Archaeological and Historical Overview of an Ancient Oasis Town and Caravan Centre. *Azania* 50: 27-75.

Miège, Jean-Louis (1975). La Libye et le commerce transsaharien au xix[e] siècle. *Revue de l'Occident Musulman* xix: 135-69.

Mu[c]ammar, [c]Alī Yaḥyā (2007). *Ibāḍism in History. Volume 1: The Emergence of the Ibāḍī School.* Ruwi: Ministry of Awqaf and Religious Affairs.

Palmer, H. R. (1936). *The Bornu, Sahara and Sudan.* London: John Murray.

Pellat, Ch. (1978). Ḳarāḳūsh. *Encyclopaedia of Islam* (New Edition) iv: 614. Leiden.

Prevost, Virginie (2006). La Révolte de Bāġāya (358/969): Le dernier soulèvement des ibāḍites maghrébins. *Journal of Near Eastern Studies* 65: 197-206.

Prevost, Virginie (2008). *L'Aventure ibāḍīte dans le Sud tunisien (VIIIe–XIIIe siècle). Effervescence d'une région méconnue.* Helsinki: Academia Scientiarum Fennica.

Prevost, Virginie (2010). *Les Ibadites. De Djerba à Oman, la troisième voie de l'Islam.* Turnhout: Brepols.

Rebstock, Ulrich (1983). *Die Ibāḍiten im Maġrib (2./8. - 4./10. Jh.). Die Geschichte einer Berberbewegung im Gewand des Islam.* Berlin: Klaus Schwarz.

Rossi, Ettore (1968). *Storia di Tripoli e della Tripolitania: Dalla conquista araba al 1911.* Rome: Istituto per l'oriente.

Rottier, Cpt. (1924). Le Sahara oriental: Kaouar, Djado, Tibesti. *Renseignements Coloniaux: L'Afrique Française,* 1-14: 78-88 and 101-108.

Savage, Elizabeth (1997). *A Gateway to Hell, a Gateway to Paradise. The North African Response to the Arab Conquest.* Princeton: Darwin Press.

Van Berchem, Marguerite (1960). Sedrata et les anciennes villes berbères du Sahara dans les récits des explorateurs du XIXe siècle. *Bulletin d'Institut Français d'Archéologie Orientale* 59: 289-308.

Vigourous, L. (1945). L'Émigration mozabite dans les villes du Tell algérien. *Travaux de l'Institut de Recherches Sahariennes* iii: 87-102.

Vikør, Knut S. (1987). The Early History of the Kawar Oasis: A Southern Border of the Maghrib or a Northern Border of the Sudan?. *The Maghreb Review* xii (3-4): 78-83.

Vikør, Knut S. (1999). *The Oasis of Salt. The History of Kawar, a Saharan Centre of Salt Production.* Bergen: Centre for Middle Eastern Studies.

Vikør, Knut S. (2002a). Wisyānī. *Encyclopaedia of Islam* (New Edition) ix: 212. Leiden.

Vikør, Knut S. (2002b). Zawīla. *Encyclopaedia of Islam* (New Edition) ix: 466. Leiden.

Wilkinson, John C. (2010). *Ibâḍism. Origins and Early Development in Oman.* Oxford: Oxford University Press.

Zerouki, Brahim (1987), *L'Imamat de Tahart. Premier état musulman du Maghreb (144/296 de l'hégire).* Paris: Harmattan.

Fluidité et fixité dans les néotextes numériques[1]

Daniel Apollon
University of Bergen

Fixité et fluidité textuelle

La fixité de l'inscription serait synonyme, selon les goûts, de l'invariance, de l'immobilité, de la rémanence, de l'idempotence, ou de la complétude de l'objet-texte. Même si on peut observer qu'il n'en est pas tout à fait le cas. Bon nombre de stèles en écriture cunéiforme, quand elles ne disparurent pas tout court, se délitèrent ne laissant que quelques fragments pour la postérité. Les lacunes des manuscrits furent ' réparées ' de manière routinière par des réécritures tardives dans les scriptoriums. De nos jours, les contenus circulant sur le web ne sont que rarement des reproductions parfaites d'un original mais fréquemment des remixages fugaces d'éléments difficilement identifiables. Malgré cela, de nos jours comme dans le passé, l'idéal d'une ' ipséité scripturale ', extensible aux images fixes ou cinématographiques et aux paroles enregistrées (et souvent remixées) semble encore sous-tendre les attentes des auteurs et des lecteurs de documents physiques ou numériques. Cet imaginaire de la fixité textuelle, donc plus une vue de l'esprit qu'un phénomène avéré, offrirait en quelque sorte un cadre minimum et nécessaire délimitant l'espace des interprétations. Le texte ' fixé ' pourrait être comparé à terrain de sport délimitant un espace normé qui permettrait toutefois une infinie variation de dérivatifs subtils, mais pourtant tous lisibles, exprimant ' le jeu du texte '. Même si les arguments abondent pour mettre en doute la possibilité d'une telle fixité, il n'en reste pas moins que dans les civilisations de l'écriture, l'idée selon laquelle il existerait des manières de comprendre les textes plus licites que d'autres, et que ces lectures seraient organiquement liées à la matérialité et à permanence de l'inscription, est encore tenace.

Nous noterons d'emblée que cette notion de fixité scripturale n'empêche nullement l'émergence de diverses théories qui mettent en avant la multiplicité des interprétations (d'une inscription fixe) et jettent le doute sur la réalité du périmètre de l'entité dénommée ' texte ' en faisant, par exemple, appel à la notion d'intertextualité (Kristeva 1969). De même, il est parfaitement possible de se débarrasser de la fonction d'auteur (Barthes 1984 ; Foucault 1969), qui, par son ' auteurité ‹ (sic), se porterait garant de l'ipséité du texte, et de la remplacer par la fonction moins prestigieuse de ‹ scripteur(s) ‹.

Bien que les termes 'fluidité' et 'variation' semblent indissociablement liées, la notion de fluidité met l'accent sur les déplacements textuels dans le temps (vitesse, accélération, rythmes) et dans l'espace physico-numérique (diffusion, épanchement, dislocation, déversement, propagation des récits, etc.), alors que la notion de variation textuelle met l'accent sur les modifications successives des états textuels. Un texte peut être spatialement et temporellement fluide, attestant une diffusion florissante et une pluralité d'usages et d'interprétations, sans subir de fortes variations scripturales. Mais aussi, comme c'est le cas des manuscrits antiques et médiévaux, la variation textuelle est inconcevable sans une circulation temporelle et géographique d'exemplaires entraînant une perte de contenu et diverses formes de recension et de restitution du texte, ainsi que diverses innovations narratives. La notion de fluidité impliquerait non seulement une suite d'états distincts d'inscriptions d'un contenu (phénomène couvert par le concept de variation textuelle), mais aussi une dynamique (physique ou numérique) de déplacements de ces états du texte dans le temps et l'espace. À ces déplacements du texte (ou des contenus) et de leurs supports matériels s'ajouteraient les déplacements des lecteurs (nouveaux lectorats) et des modes de lectures (nouvelles formes de littératie). Dans le cas des néotextes numériques, la fluidité textuelle caractériserait plus spécifiquement les déplacements et manipulations des contenus opérés par leurs utilisateurs (par ex. le partage généralisé

[1] Les traductions en français de citations publiées originalement en anglais et en allemand sont celles de l'auteur de cet article.

de fragments de textes ou d'hyperliens sur Facebook, les recyclages et remédiatisations de récits par les lecteurs-utilisateurs), ou même, les déplacements ou actions d'éditorialisation opérées par des agents algorithmiques opérant sans intervention humaine (par ex. sur Wikipédia).

Nous approcherons dans ces pages les notions de fixité et de fluidité textuelle en relation avec la matérialité du texte, non pour démontrer une simple relation de cause à effet, mais pour nous demander dans quelle mesure une nouvelle matérialité textuelle, par ex. les documents hyperliés en ligne, induirait de nouvelles formes de lecture, et par là ouvrirait un espace d'interprétations multiples hypothétiquement plus vaste qu'il en a été le cas dans le monde des manuscrits et des imprimés.

Retour sur la notion de fixité textuelle typographique

Un retour sur les travaux d'Elizabeth Eisenstein s'impose. La notion de fixité textuelle est indissociablement liée aux travaux maintenant classiques d'Eisenstein (voir plus particulièrement Eisenstein 1979 et 1983), à qui on doit une réflexion systématique sur le passage du manuscrit à l'imprimé et sur les effets civilisationnels qui suivirent l'avènement de la fixité typographique en Europe. Pour Eisenstein, l'invention de la presse typographique introduisit une nouvelle technologie dont la capacité à reproduire et à conserver l'expression typographique d'une œuvre permit l'avènement de la science moderne.

Il est important de souligner que le regard que porte Eisenstein sur la révolution typographique ne fait pas appel à une tendance présupposée intrinsèque des textes ou des récits à incorporer naturellement une fixité énonciative ou discursive qui motiverait l'emploi de techniques appropriées permettant une reproduction fidèle. Pour Eisenstein, la notion de fixité textuelle signifie essentiellement une fixité typographique qui découlerait, selon elle, de la capacité technique de la presse typographique à produire des séries de caractères, *identiques* d'une copie à une autre. Cette reproductibilité typographique potentiellement parfaite au niveau de l'encodage alphabétique (reproduction de 'a' comme 'a', de 'b' comme 'b', etc.) est une condition essentielle pour assurer une transmissibilité fiable des textes dans l'espace et dans le temps, plus efficace que la transmission orale ou manuscrite, à en croire Eisenstein (nous passerons sur les fluctuations calligraphiques, graphémiques, chromatiques etc.).

Limites de l'approche technocentriste

Les théories d'Eisenstein pourraient alimenter l'espoir d'appréhender d'éventuels processus et mécanismes de transition ayant la faculté d'éclairer les conséquences de la transition de l'imprimé au numérique. Une telle démarche supposerait que le passage de l'*un* à l'*autre* exhibe quelques analogies et répétitions observables, et qu'il existerait un principe sous-jacent qui régirait les caractéristiques de la fluidité et de la fixité textuelle au-delà des ressources et contraintes émanant des supports physiques et logiques. Cependant, l'existence d'un tel principe ou de tels principes sous-jacents peut être contestée. On pourrait, en effet, imaginer que les changements historiques dans les technologies et matériaux d'inscription, ainsi que dans les formes d'encodage des documents (pictogrammes, idéogrammes, alphabets et plus tard balisage des métadonnées textuelles, par ex. XML, HTLML) ne représenteraient que des suites de phénomènes contingents. Rétrospectivement, on pourrait argumenter que l'écriture cunéiforme des sumériens et assyriens était parfaitement reproductible à volonté, comme le démontre l'existence de seaux-cylindres et de tampons dès le IVe millénaire avant notre ère. L'impression de caractères alphabétiques sur des jarres dès le VIIe siècle avant notre ère atteste une forme précoce de typographie à caractères fixes. Il en va de même pour l'écriture logographique en caractères chinois. En effet, en Chine, depuis Bi Sheng au XIe siècle de notre ère, des caractères mobiles auraient été employés (voir Bussotti 2001). Toutefois, même si la technique des caractères mobiles était connue, cette technique a eu une utilisation limitée dans l'Empire du Milieu par rapport à la xylographie :

> La Chine avait le papier dès le début de notre ère, et possédait aussi, avec les sceaux, le principe de la gravure renversée, mais ses sceaux étaient alors gravés en creux. Quand vers l'an 500 on grava les sceaux en relief, la Chine, ayant désormais et le papier et la gravure inversée en relief, aboutit très

> naturellement à la xylographie. Il n'y eut pas besoin d'un inventeur, et les contemporains furent témoins d'un développement progressif si simple qu'il ne les frappa pas. (Pellliot 1953 cité dans Poitou 2009).

Quand les Occidentaux ' découvrirent ' la Chine, cherchant à reproduire son écriture, il se tournèrent naturellement vers la typographie (Bussotti et Landry-Deron 2015) Malgré le fait qu'ils connaissaient déjà de près ou de loin la typographie européenne, les chinois ont préféré la xylographie à l'imprimerie en caractères mobiles jusqu'au XIXe siècle.

Ce détour par la Chine et la xylographie nous servira à conjurer le spectre du techno-déterminisme. On pourrait en effet entrevoir chez Eisenstein les contours d'un principe minimaliste que nous dénommerons ' principe de reproductibilité fiable '. Si Eisenstein ne raisonne pas sur un mode purement techno-déterministe, comme certains de ses critiques l'ont prétendu (voir Baron, Lindqvist et Shevlin 2007: 3 suiv.), elle tend à attribuer aux technologies en général, et plus particulièrement à la technique de la presse typographique jugée vastement supérieure à l'écriture manuscrite, un rôle central et même, selon les interprétations, explicatif. Par contrecoup, Eisenstein, d'après certains critiques, tend à déprécier d'autres technologies discursives et textuelles, et d'après d'autres critiques, à décontextualiser une technologie spécifique, la typographie mécanique, de son contexte sociohistorique et à lui conférer un pouvoir autonome d'agencement.

Cependant, comme le note Love (2007: 140), le fait d'avoir une ' capacité ' n'implique pas qu'elle soit mise en œuvre et qu'elle devienne opérative et déterminante dans n'importe quel contexte historique. Eisenstein se rapprocherait plutôt de la notion moins déterministe d'*affordance,* que nous traduirons dans ce contexte comme une ' potentialité exploitable dans un contexte socioculturel '. On notera que le concept *d'affordance* fut lancé à la même époque par Gibson (1977) sans toutefois qu'Eisenstein qui s'était investie dès 1964 dans ce long projet d'écriture qui durera quinze ans (Williams 2004 : 2) y fasse référence dans son œuvre. La définition plus large donnée par Gaver (' Affordances are properties of the world that make possible some action to an organism equipped to act in certain ways ‹, Gaver 1991 : 81) selon laquelle les affordances seraient des caractéristiques intrinsèques des objets, dans le cas de l'imprimerie, les caractères mobiles, rendant possible certaines actions à certains 'organismes', par ex. les clercs et scribes, est particulièrement applicable à la thèse d'Eisenstein sur la reproductibilité typographique. La révolution typographique n'opèrerait donc pas, en lisant Eisenstein à travers le filtre de Gaver, selon une prédétermination fonctionnelle mais résulterait d'une convergence propice entre les *affordances* des caractères mobiles et le contexte socioculturel de l'Europe de Gutenberg. Nous pourrions aller plus loin et nous demander si l'invention ou la réinvention de l'imprimerie par caractères mobiles n'est qu'un évènement fortuit, ou nous pourrions inverser le raisonnement d'Eisenstein et postuler que la révolution typographique est le produit d'une dynamique socioéconomique plus large. Ce qui, dans ce dernier cas, suggérerait une position résolument socio-constructiviste ou socio-déterministe.

L'utilité de cette réflexion sur la fixité typographique est de démontrer pourquoi une transposition de l'approche technocentriste d'Eisenstein à l'analyse des néotextes numériques, quand bien même tentante, serait néanmoins trop réductrice.

La thèse de la perte de fixité non-typographique

Les stéréotypes exploitant l'idée d'une rupture fondamentale entre d'une part, l'ère du manuscrit et de l'imprimé et, d'autre part, l'inscription numérique, jouissent d'une certaine popularité. Pour alimenter ces stéréotypes divers auteurs sous-estiment les différences fondamentales entre les modes de transmission manuscrite (phénomène compliqué par la présence d'une dimension d'oralité résiduelle dans les littératies comme l'a défendu magistralement Ong 1982) et la diffusion de l'imprimé. Nicholas Carr, un des plus ardents partisans, et de ce fait controversé, de la thèse de la déstabilisation du texte dans les environnements numériques, aligne une série d'observations (Carr 2011 et 2012) qui, selon lui, corroboreraient l'idée d'une perte fondamentale de la ' fixité textuelle '. Ces observations se résument en quatre catégories qui, selon Carr, ne seraient pas de nature typographique :

1. *L'intégrité de la page*, qui date d'avant la machine à imprimer disparaît d'après Carr, dans les *e-books* – les livres électroniques (' The integrity of the page has been so intrinsic to the technology of the book (and of the book's predecessors) ' Carr 2012). La page devient donc, sous format numérique ' malléable ‹ à volonté.
2. *L'intégralité de l'édition*, conçue comme la fixité du contenu dans plusieurs éditions du même texte est vue par Carr comme l'effet direct de la capacité intrinsèque à reproduire fidèlement un texte, ce qui était jusque-là quasi-impossible.
3. *La permanence de l'objet* : malgré leur destructibilité physique, les imprimés subsistent un certain temps. Les supports physiques et logiques des contenus numérisés souffrent, paradoxalement, d'une ' impermanence ‹ constitutive : si leur durabilité et reproductibilité théorique ne peuvent être contestées, les pratiques culturelles et industrielles en vigueur en font autre usage.
4. *Le sentiment de complétude* (*sense of completeness*) est décrit comme une ' qualité perçue ‹ entremêlant acquis culturels, symbolique institutionnelle, et autres représentations amplement partagées par les acteurs du système-livre.

Le mirage de la fixité textuelle au crible de l'histoire

Cette vision, présentée à l'emporte-pièce par Carr, a donné lieu à un fructueux débat en ligne impliquant autant des critiques littéraires, que des documentalistes et des informaticiens. Les critiques ont abondé, et certaines ont été particulièrement virulentes. Tel est le cas de la critique formulée par Anderson (2012) pour qui l'idée que se fait Carr d'une fixité textuelle pré-numérique constitue une exagération fallacieuse et ne serait en fait qu'un ' mirage '. Sur ce point, Anderson rejoint le thème de prédilection de Cerquiglini (1989) sur la variation textuelle à l'ère du manuscrit. Selon ce dernier auteur les divagations scripturales des scribes ne seraient pas dues à une prétendue incapacité technologique mais plutôt à la créativité et à la virtuosité des scribes, ainsi qu'à une conception alors en vogue plus généreuse de l'ipséité textuelle. Prenant l'exemple des antétextes de John Updike, Anderson démontre sans difficulté que les textes du romancier furent l'objet de changements profonds dans leur architecture narrative avant et après leur première parution. Une telle constatation ne devrait pas surprendre les lecteurs avertis, et encore moins les spécialistes de l'édition. Ainsi, l'accès récent aux antétextes de Flaubert, par ex. la collection de fragments du roman inachevé Bouvard et Pécuchet (voir Leclerc et Girard 2013), les travaux de Gabler sur les textes de James Joyce, et l'édition en ligne des écrits posthumes de Wittgenstein (Pichler 2015) ne plaident pas en faveur d'une fixité pré-numérique. Si la critique d'Anderson résumée ci-dessus semble pertinente, elle tombe quelque peu dans l'excès. En effet, même si la variabilité des textes pré-numériques est un fait avéré, facilement illustré par de nombreux exemples tirés de divers genres et supports, Anderson semble ne pas prendre en compte que l'instabilité observable des antétextes de romans, autant que les diverses versions révisées des articles en ligne de n'importe quel quotidien, ou des articles de Wikipédia, peuvent être impulsées par l'imaginaire d'une complétude passée (le texte original perdu) ou d'une complétude à venir (donc une forme d' ' horizon d'attente ' des producteurs de texte).

Inscription fixe ou non, l'œuvre reste ouverte

Parmi les quatre exemples de perte de fixité textuelle numérique énumérés par Carr trois d'entre eux se réfèrent explicitement ou implicitement à la notion d'œuvre. Les caractéristiques d'intégralité, de permanence et de complétude propres aux textes manuscrits et imprimés, déstabilisées selon Carr dans les environnements numériques, correspondent cependant à une représentation plutôt réductrice que l'on peut faire de l'œuvre d'auteur.

En contraste flagrant, la notion d'*œuvre ouverte* proposée par Umberto Eco (1965) se dégageant de la gangue de l'intégralité, la permanence et la complétude (sans s'adonner pour autant au démembrement opéré par la nouvelle critique), fait appel à la réception et à l'interprétation de l'œuvre. Pour Eco, certains textes, tout comme d'autres œuvres par ex. musicales, se noient dans l'exubérance offrant à l'interprète, au lecteur ou aux relecteurs des degrés de liberté vastement exploitables leur permettant de créer des surplus de sens et de sensations les menant très loin de l'intention présumée de l'auteur. Pour Eco, le récepteur de l'œuvre ouverte, ou œuvre en mouvement, se distingue du récepteur de l'œuvre close par l'acception de l'invitation à la participation créatrice de sens. L'œuvre close, en supposant qu'elle existe, ne reste que prétendument close, en ce qu'elle abonde d'ambiguïtés et de possibilités d'interprétation, même si son inscription typographique ou picturale reste, fréquemment, plutôt fixe. Alors que même dans un texte hypothétiquement figé dont l'inscription ne varierait pas d'un iota et au récit des plus austères il résiderait un potentiel d'exubérance interprétative. Somme toute, le monde des œuvres offrirait une *affordance* généralisée pour les interprétations multiples et débordantes. Chaque œuvre, chaque texte, chaque inscription numérique productrice de sens offrirait des ' horizons d'attente ', notion plus restrictive (all. *Erwartungshorizont*) chez Jauss (1991) que celle d'' œuvre ouverte ‹ (Eco 1965).

En conclusion, l'équation à résoudre n'est pas dans quelle mesure une fixité textuelle (illusoire) produit ou présuppose un ' sens objectif une fois pour toute arrêté, immédiatement accessible en tout temps à l'interprète ', comme l'avance Roger Chartier (2015) citant Jauss (1974, 78). Chartier, s'appuyant sur Jauss, pour réfuter les positions de la Nouvelle Critique et du ' New Historicism ', tend à associer la production de sens et l'interprétation de l'œuvre à une quête du Saint Graal qui exigerait non seulement d'avoir trouvé le ' vrai texte ' mais aussi la bonne formule pour le lire. La solution ne réside pas non plus dans une dichotomie aux antipodes du fondamentalisme textuel décrit ci-dessus, qui prônerait une dissociation absolue entre matérialité et interprétations telle que l'a énoncé Wollenberg pour lequel il devient impératif non seulement de dissocier la matérialité du texte, mais aussi sa constitution au sens large (genèse, transmission, édition, etc.) de la production ultérieure de sens (' Ce qui dépasse le texte tangible et dans le domaine immatériel de la conception poétique ressort de l'interprétation ; ceci n'a rien à voir avec la constitution du texte ', Wollenberg 1971: 255). Une position critique, qui nous paraît plus empirique et moins jusqu'au-boutiste, s'interrogerait plutôt dans quelle mesure divers types de variations (pl.) textuelles et présentationnelles ainsi que diverses formes de circulation textuelle (par ex. les néotextes numériques à courte vie) offrent des *affordances* permettant une production de sens à profusion. Ces *affordances* peuvent être considérées non seulement comme des *ressources* permettant aux auteurs, scripteurs et lecteurs d'engager des processus interprétatifs, mais aussi comme des *contraintes* les retenant avec plus ou moins de force à l'intérieur de procédés de production de sens.

Fixité vs ipséité textuelle

Contrecarrant Carr, Owens (2012) s'attaque plus fondamentalement à la notion d'ipséité (' c'est la même chose ‹), insistant sur le rapport difficile des autographes à leurs allographes. Prenant l'exemple des travaux de Werner (2012), Owens insiste sur le fait que ' [q]uand bien même le texte encodé dans deux objets resterait le même [par ex., serait encodé dans deux fichiers comme deux séquences identiques d'octets], il pourrait y avoir quantité infinie d'information textuelle qui pourrait résider dans la matérialité des objets sur lesquels il est encodé [par ex. la configuration physique et logique du support pourrait être différente et exprimer des contextes sociohistoriques et techniques distincts] ‹. S'appuyant sur Kirschenbaum (2008), Owens refuse aux objets numériques une ipséité plus fondamentale que celle de l'écrit ou de l'imprimé qui reposerait sur un principe de la similarité des *bits, octets,* ou de tout autre encodage imaginable, de deux ou plusieurs fichiers. En conséquence, pour Owens et Kirschenbaum, chaque inscription des mêmes octets sur deux supports physiques différents correspond à deux artéfacts distincts impliquant deux contextes différents. Cependant, pour ces deux auteurs, la relation entre autographe et allographe s'avère être notoirement complexe et pleine d'ambiguïtés, autographe et allographe exhibant, selon les cas, divers degrés de parenté et de similarité. D'après Owens, ' l'image physique [angl. *forensic*] d'un disque [par ex., disque dur] est allographique, mais peut conserver les traces autographiques d'un artéfact ‹. En accord tacite avec la nouvelle philologie française (Cerquiglini 1989) et la New Philology anglo-saxonne (par ex., Nichols 1990), Owens insiste pertinemment sur le fait que le ' le support sur lequel un texte est inscrit ainsi que les caractéristiques autographiques d'un scribe particulier ou ressortant du travail d'un imprimeur convoient une quantité d'information intéressante ! ‹. La définition de la fixité textuelle, définie comme l'identité de caractères ou des octets qui les codent, reste foncièrement instable, et repose plus sur des présupposés culturels et institutionnels que sur des critères ‹ forensiques ‹. L'anglicisme ‹ forensique ‹ signifierait dans ce contexte ‹ la valeur d'existence des traces physiques d'une inscription ‹ et par extension légitimerait la véracité légale d'une inscription sur un support physique et logique (Duranti 2009).

Extension de la notion de matérialité

Quelles leçons tirer de ce débat sur la fixité textuelle ? Tout d'abord que la notion de fixité est relativement... fluide, et repose plutôt sur une construction collective et individuelle que sur un phénomène intrinsèque lié à la matérialité des textes, par ex. un codage scriptural particulier. Les arguments se réclamant de la matérialité des textes ou de technologies spécifiques pouvant être réfutés, nous privilégierons une approche plus vaste et plus complexe qui nous permettra d'inscrire la matérialité textuelle et documentaire au sein d'une *littératie* faisant appel aux capacités des individus et des groupes sociaux à produire une cohésion interprétative minimale. Ceci implique l'inclusion de la notion de matérialité textuelle à l'ère du numérique au sein d'un système comprenant cinq types de ressources et contraintes qui opèrent sur la production et la circulation et variabilité des contenus :

1. la *matérialité physique et pratique* du texte et de ses outils de production : ceci réfère non seulement aux supports physiques (stèle, tablette d'argile, papyrus, parchemin, papier, écran, unité de stockages), mais aussi aux outils (burin, stylet, plume, crayon, interfaces, matériel informatique, etc.) et aux pratiques et techniques qui entrent en jeu dans la production, la diffusion et la prise de connaissance des contenus (écriture boustrophédon, dictée, sténographie, reliures, ingénierie des réseaux, agents algorithmiques, moteurs de recherche, etc.) ;
2. les *codages* nécessaires pour inscrire les contenus sur leurs supports physiques et produire les effets de lecture ou d'utilisation escomptés (pictogrammes, alphabets, encodage par XML, conventions paratextuelles, hyperliens, etc.) ;
3. les *techniques et conventions paratextuelles* définissant les modes de description, de présentation et d'accès aux contenus (voir plus bas notre discussion de la paratextualité dynamique) ;
4. les modes d'*organisation sociale* et plus généralement l'économie politique des pratiques éditoriales concrétisant les régimes d'autorité textuelle ;
5. les *systèmes épistémiques* liés aux littératies dominantes.

Pour combiner ces cinq niveaux, la notion de ' technologies de l'intellect ' prônée par Jack Goody, à laquelle nous avons déjà fait appel dans d'autres publications (voir Desrochers et Apollon 2014: xxx-xxxi; Apollon, Bélisle et Régnier 2014: 13 et 85) offre un cadre conceptuel unificateur. Les représentations et normes relatives à la fixité, réelle ou imaginaire seraient indissociablement liées à la littératie que nous interprétons avec Goody comme un système épistémique et interprétatif activé dans un système social spécifique : ' The written word does not replace speech, any more than speech replaces gesture. But it adds an important dimension to much social action. This is especially true of the politico-legal domain, for the growth of bureaucracy clearly depends to a considerable degree upon the ability to control 'secondary group' relationships by means of written communications. ' (Goody 1977: 15-16). Nous noterons que pour Goody le terme 'secondary group' réfère aux groupes extérieurs à la sphère intime qui, d'après Goody, n'a que peu besoin de communication écrite. Les littératies peuvent être analysées comme des formes parmi d'autres de contrôle social sur des groupes secondaires (groupes extérieurs à la sphère intime) exercé à distance sans contact face à face nécessaire. Les attributs d'un support physique et d'un système d'inscription permettent d'exercer ce contrôle mais n'en constituent pas la source, ce contrôle demeurant un fait social. Les représentations et normes relatives à la fixité textuelle varient amplement selon les contextes linguistiques, religieux et géographiques. Ainsi, dans les civilisations monothéistes, la notion de fixité restant indissociable de celle d'autorité religieuse, seul le texte authentique transmis correctement (ou restitué) pouvant être interprété correctement avec plus ou moins de degrés de liberté. Même à l'époque de Wikileaks et de Twitter, les représentations sur la fixité et l'ipséité textuelle subsistent, même quand il s'agit de messages Twitter effacés par leur auteur et au contenu potentiellement dévastateur pour tel ou tel personnage public, mais dont il subsisterait néanmoins une trace. Ironiquement, la *restitution forensique* s'impose alors plus que jamais, dans un environnement au sein duquel les néotextes ont une durée d'existence numériques souvent très courte.

La description des contenus numériques offerte par Carr ci-dessus n'est pas foncièrement erronée, mais mettant tous les types de contenus numériques dans la même besace, ne permet pas d'explorer plus finement la nature de la fluidité dont cet auteur se réclame. De plus, Carr semble ne pas opérer de distinction entre divers niveaux de matérialité des environnements numériques qui pourraient avoir des incidences distinctes sur les phénomènes auxquels Carr se réfère dans sa thèse de la perte de fixité textuelle. Il nous semble, en contraste avec l'approche trop peu nuancée de cet auteur, utile de distinguer entre plusieurs niveaux de matérialité numérique, regroupés en quatre catégories décrites ci-dessous :

1. La *matérialité des artéfacts physiques* impliqués dans la production, diffusion et présentation des contenus numériques (par exemple, unités de stockage, affichage sur écran, réseaux physiques, etc.) ;
2. la *matérialité du codage logique primaire* liée au bits et octets, qui permettent de multiples formes d'encodage de contenus ;
3. la *matérialité des algorithmes, langages et structures* permettant, par abstraction, de spécifier des structures, qui non seulement constituent des matrices pour les contenus, mais en séparant la description des contenus (SGML, XML) de leur présentation (par ex. HTML ; voir Pichler et Bruvik 2014; Huitfeldt 2014) dépassent le stades des *affordances générales* discutées plus haut pour être des machines de production textuelle ouvertes et flexibles.
4. Nous ajouterons, reconnaissant que cette dernière catégorie peut être sujette à discussion, comme dernière catégorie de matérialité, la *dimension paratextuelle*, collection d'objets polymorphes, fusionnant diverses conventions appartenant au tronc commun des cultures de l'écrit (apparat titulaire, note, incipit, liste) avec des mécanismes de circulation spatiale, temporelle, ou réticulaire (écran interactifs, hyperlien) et des métadonnées de conceptualisation (ontologies informatiques).

Dans les tourbillons de la paratextualité

Craig Mod (2011) ne s'oppose pas fondamentalement à Carr, mais explique la prétendue perte de fixité dans le contexte numérique comme le passage d'un stade pré-artéfactuel (par ex., celui de l'auteur et de ses avant-textes) à un stade post-artéfactuel, celui de la lecture partagée, sans plus passer par le stade purement artéfactuel (celui du manuscrit et de l'imprimé immuable et par extension, des maisons d'édition). Selon Mod, le passage au stade post-artéfactuel serait une conséquence directe de nouveaux systèmes d'encodage numérique véhiculés par les réseaux d'hyperliens (le web). Les néotextes numériques (notre expression) exprimeraient ainsi un ' système post-artéfactuel ' qui se serait défait de l'artéfact compact et monumental du livre imprimé. La description, la présentation, la circulation, l'usage et la lecture des contenus en ligne s'appuient, souligne cet auteur, sur une multitude d'ajouts annotatifs, de *marginalia,* somme toute, de *métadonnées* s'empilant les unes sur les autres en ' strates cumulatives ' reliées dynamiquement les unes aux autres par des algorithmes, agents performatif opérés en connaissance de cause par des lecteurs-utilisateurs humain, ou, automatiquement, sans intervention humaine. Mod précise cependant que l'usage qu'il fait du terme ' post-artéfactuel ' ne signifie pas que ces contenus numériques instables ne contiennent pas d'artéfacts, mais plutôt qu'ils impliquent une interchangeabilité et une mutabilité constante d'artéfacts locaux qui, même s'ils sont indispensables, restent eux-mêmes fondamentalement ' marginaux ' (voir aussi le thème de la marginalité livresque chez van Dijk 2014).

La thèse de Mod, résumée ci-dessus reste très motivée par le désir de démontrer et de célébrer la rupture fondamentale avec l'artéfact-livre. Nous noterons que sa vision d'un système post-artéfactuel ne s'appuie pas sur une analyse concrète de divers types de *néotextes* numériques, mais présuppose un système généralisé applicable à tous les contenus en ligne. Mod étant de toute évidence plus un essayiste polémique plus qu'un philologue méticuleux, nous lui pardonnerons volontiers son exubérance rhétorique en reconnaissant la validité de son observation fondamentale : les contenus en ligne sont produits, véhiculés, présentés, consommés et recyclés par une multiplicité de *marginalia* et de métadonnées qui permettent (certains l'espèrent, d'autres le redoutent) de se libérer de la structure (angl. *canvas*) imposée par l'artéfact-livre. Cette nouvelle capacité est décrite par Mod comme 'the ability to construct canvas independent hooks beyond the reading space'.

Nous noterons que, pour Mod, la fluidité n'est plus un attribut fondamental des textes en général, qui seraient congénitalement ' ouverts ' (Eco 1965) ou offriraient à qui le désire des ' horizons d'attente ' (Jauss 1991), ou ne seraient que l'épiphénomène d'interactions au sein d'un continuum textuel universel (Kristeva 1969), mais plutôt l'effet de la manipulation et de l'échange d'ajouts marginaux fonctionnellement liés les uns aux autres par des hyperliens. Il en émergerait un transfert de production de sens vers ces *néotextes* constitués par des associations dans le temps et dans l'espace numérique d'annotations et de renvois, dont les ' textes ' n'en constitueraient plus que la ' matière '.

Il est surprenant que ni Carr, ni Mod, ni les autres critiques de Carr, ne fassent appel au riche concept de paratexte présenté par Gérard Genette (1987), dont je rappellerai très brièvement l'idée maîtresse. Pour Genette ' [l]e récit, le noyau de l'œuvre, n'est pas seul. En fait il ne peut exister seul. D'autres éléments font que le texte est présent, le rendant accessible, appréhendable au lecteur et apte à être ' reçu ' et ' consommé ‹ ‹. Nous connaissons tous ces paratextes, identifiables comme péritextes (apparat titulaire, nom de l'auteur, illustrations, table des matières, index, etc.) ou comme épitextes (interview d'auteurs, analyses de textes, correspondance épistolaire sur le texte, publicité, etc.). Genette insiste sur l'impossibilité de tout texte, voire de tout contenu producteur de sens, d'exister de son propre fait. Qu'on le veuille ou non, le paratexte matérialise le texte et souligne Genette, lui assigne un statut, un rôle et une position dans un espace, et, peut-on dire, configure le texte. Genette parle de ' seuil ‹, de ‹ zone ', de ' bordure ', jouant sur diverses métaphores. Pour lui le paratexte est une ' zone indéfinie ' positionnée ' entre le dehors et le dedans ' qui, dans le monde des manuscrits et de l'imprimé formait d'après Genette un seuil entre le monde du texte et le monde tout court. Le mérite de Genette est de décrire avec de nombreux exemples à l'appui comment, bien avant l'avènement des *néotextes numérique,* les frontières entre texte et paratexte ont été bien plus floues que l'on pourrait se l'imaginer, et que les textes étaient, bien avant le système post-artéfactuel de Mod, configurés et par un système de métadonnées à vocation illocutionnaire et performative.

Les néotextes numériques ne sont pas réifiés comme il est en est le cas de la tablette d'argile assyrienne, des Très Riches Heures du duc de Berry ou de la première édition de tel ou tel roman de gare et sont reconfigurables et recyclables à volonté. Le système stratifié décrit par Mod est en mouvement permanent et implique l'action de divers agents algorithmiques produisant ici et là pour tel utilisateur, non seulement des présentations uniques dans les environnements numériques en ligne, mais aussi des contenus uniques (textes produits par des machines) combinant une diversité d'éléments souvent dissociés de leur contexte d'origine. Les *néotextes* mixant de diverses manières ' textes ' et ' paratextes ' sont ainsi configurés, par un système de *paratextualité dynamique* au cœur de laquelle, on ne peut trop insister sur ce point, agissent des agents ou robots algorithmes qui produisent, ' lisent ' et présentent des contenus instantanés dont la durée d'existence peut être très courte. La puissance de la paratextualité algorithmique exprime mais aussi amplifie et dépasse largement la notion de ' force illocutoire' agissant à la fois sur l'œuvre et sur le lecteur (Genette 1987: 15 suiv.) en ce que les performateurs et récepteurs ne sont plus nécessairement des êtres humains ou des communautés humaines, et en ce que les paratextes dynamiques peuvent agir sur d'autres paratextes dynamiques pour produire un surplus de sens. Cette explosion de paratextualité exprimerait donc une nouvelle hyperperformativité textuelle.

Dans un ouvrage récent, plusieurs auteurs (voir Desrochers et Apollon 2014) explorent et identifient certains de ces artéfacts algorithmes mutables comme des formes nouvelles de paratextualité numérique.

La thèse récurrente des diverses contributions de cet ouvrage est que dans l'environnement numérique la distinction fondamentale entre texte et paratexte, distinction d'ailleurs rejetée par Genette, et plus précisément, entre texte, péritexte, et épitexte tend à être remplacée par un nouveau conglomérat plus difficile à caractériser, parce qu'il est en évolution constante. Alors que le paratexte ' classique ' du monde des livres rend le texte ' présent ' au lecteur, on peut se demander, dans le cas des néotextes numériques qu'est ce qui est rendu ' présent ' et à qui, humain ou à quoi, agent algorithmique, ce rendu est-il présent.

Abstract

The debate on the notion of textual fixity deserves a critical treatment which may offer richer but potentially unsettling perspectives on the notion of textual fluidity. In a civilisation traditionally fixated on the textual object and on the aura of its materiality, textual fluidity tends to be seen as the converse of textual fixity, i.e., as the (very relative) presence or absence of variations in textual inscriptions. This paper endeavours to destabilise both notions, textual fixity and textual fluidity, by casting doubt on the importance of the determination of the materiality of documents on textual variation or lack of such, without, yet, rejecting totally such determinations. Digital *neotexts*, under the constraints of dynamic paratexts, actualise particularly well the complex relations between textual materiality and the production of meaning.

Références[2]

Anderson, K. 2012. The Mirage of Fixity — Selling an Idea Before Understanding the Concept. Blog article, 9 /1/2012, *the scholarly kitchen*. Accessible à l'adresse : http://scholarlykitchen.sspnet.org/2012/01/09/the-mirage-of-fixity/.

Apollon, D., Bélisle, C. et Régnier, P. (éds.) 2014. *Digital Critical Editions*, Series ' Topics in Digital Humanities '. Urbana, Chicago and Springfield, University of Illinois Press. Version française : *L'édition critique à l'ère du numérique*, Coll. ' Socio-économie de la chaîne du livre ‹. Paris : L'Harmattan.

Baron, S. A., Lindquist, E. R. et Shevlin E. F. (éds.) 2007. *Agent of Change : Print Culture Studies After Elizabeth L. Eisenstein*. Amherst (MA) : University of Massachusetts Press.

Barthes, R. 1984. *Le Bruissement de la langue : Essais critiques IV.* Paris : Seuil.

Busssotti, M. 2001. Écriture et caractères mobiles en Chine. *Textuel* 40 : 11-28.

Busssotti, M. et Landry-Deron, I. 2015. Impression du chinois et caractères mobiles (XVIIIe s.-XIXe s.) : les Buis du Régent de l'Imprimerie nationale. Intervention dans le cadre du séminaire mensuel de l'EFEO. Accessible à l'adresse : http://www.efeo.fr/index.php?l=FR&event=1494.

Carr, N. 2011. 'Books That Are Never Done Being Written', digital text ushering in an area of perpetual revision and updating, for better and for worse. *The Wall Street Journal* 31 (décembre 2011). Accessible à l'adresse : http://www.wsj.com/articles/SB10001424052970203893404577098343417771160

Carr, N. 2012. Words in stone and on the wind. Blog article, 3 février 2012, *Rough Type*. Accessible à l'adresse : http://www.roughtype.com/?p=1576.

Cerquiglini, B. 1989. *Éloge de la variante. Histoire critique de la philologie*. Paris : Le Seuil ' Des Travaux '.

Chartier, R. 2015. Matérialité du texte et horizon d'attente : concordances ou discordances ?. Conférence de R. Chartier, Séminaire Tigre, ENS, 7 novembre 2015. Résumé accessible à l'adresse : http://www.dhta.ens.fr/spip.php?article541.

Desrochers, N. et Apollon, D. 2014. Crossing Digital Thresholds on the Paratextual Tightrope. In Desrochers, N. et Apollon, D. (éds), *Examining Paratextual Theory and its Application in Digital Culture* : xxix-xxxix. Hershey, PA, IGI Global.

[2] Toutes les adresses URL vérifiées le 1er mars 2016.

Dijk, Y. van. 2014. The Margins of Bookishness. Paratexts in Digital Literature. In Desrochers, N. et Apollon, D. (éds), *Examining Paratextual Theory and its Applications in Digital Culture* : 24-45. Hershey (PA) : IGI Global.

Duranti, L. 2009. From Digital Diplomatics To Digital Records Forensics. *Archivaria* 68 : 39-66.

Eco, U. 1965. *L'œuvre ouverte*. Paris : Seuil, Collection ' Points '.

Eisenstein, E. 1979. *The Printing Press as an Agent of Change: Communications and Cultural Transformations in Early Modern Europe*. Cambridge : Cambridge University Press.

Eisenstein, E. 1983. *The Printing Revolution in Early Modern Europe*. Cambridge : Cambridge University Press.

Eisenstein, E. 1997. *The Printing Press as an Agent of Change*. Cambridge : Cambridge University Press.

Foucault, M. 1969. Qu'est-ce qu'un auteur ? *Bulletin de la Société française de philosophie* 3 : 73-104.

Gaver, W. W. 1991. Technology Affordances. In Robertson, S. P., Olson, G. M. et Olson, J. S. (éds.), *Proceedings of the ACM CHI 91 Human Factors in Computing Systems Conference. New Orleans, April 28 - May 2, 1991*: 79-84. New York, ACM. Accessible à l'adresse : https://www.lri.fr/~mbl/Stanford/CS477/papers/Gaver-CHI1991.pdf

Genette, G. 1987. *Seuils*. Paris : Seuil, Collection ' Points Essais '.

Gibson, J. J. 1977. *The Theory of Affordances*. In Shaw R et Bransford J (éds.), *Perceiving, Acting, and Knowing* : 127-143. Hoboken (NJ) : John Wiley & Sons Inc.

Goody, J. 1977. *The Domestication of the Savage Mind*. Cambridge UK, Cambridge University Press.

Jablonka, I. 2008. Le livre : son passé, son avenir. Entretien avec Roger Chartier. *La Vie des idées*, 29 septembre 2008. Accessible à l'adresse : http://www.laviedesidees.fr/Le-livre-son-passe-son-avenir.html

Jauss, H. R. 1978 *Pour une esthétique de la réception*. Paris : Gallimard.

Jauss, H. R. 1991. *Ästhetische Erfahrung und literarische Hermeneutik*. Frankfurt : Suhrkamp.

Kirschenbaum, M. 2008. *Mechanisms: New Media and the Forensic Imagination*. Cambridge (MA) : MIT Press.

Kristeva, Julia. 1969. *Sèmiôtikè. Recherches sur une sémanalyse*. Coll. ' Tel Quel '. Paris : Seuil.

Dord-Crouslé, S. 2013. Transcription du chapitre V. In Leclerc, Y. et Girard D. (éds), *Gustave Flaubert : Bouvard et Pécuchet. Transcription intégrale des brouillons*. Accessible à l'adresse : http://flaubert.univ-rouen.fr/bouvard_et_pecuchet/index.php.

Love, H. 2007. Fixity versus Flexibility in ' A Song on Tom of Danby ' and Dryden's *Absalom and Achotophel*. In Baron, S. A., Lindquist, E. R. et Shevlin E. F. (éds), *Agent of Change: Print Culture Studies After Elizabeth L. Eisenstein*: 140-155. Amherst (MA) : University of Massachusetts Press.

Mod, C. 2011. Post-Artifact Books & Publishing, digital's effect on how we produce, distribute and consume content. Blog article, Juin 2011, *@craigmod*. Accessible à l'adresse : http://craigmod.com/journal/post_artifact/.

Nichols, S. 1990. The New Philology. *Speculum* 65/1 : 1-108.

Ong, W. 1982. *Orality and Literacy : The Technologizing of the Word*. Londres et New York: Routledge.

Owens, T. 2012. The is of the Digital Object and the is of the Artifact. Blog article, 25 octobre 2012, *The Signal, Digital Preservation*. Accessible à l'adresse : https://blogs.loc.gov/digitalpreservation/2012/10/the-is-of-the-digital-object-and-the-is-of-the-artifact/.

Pichler, A. (éd.) 2015. *Wittgenstein Source Bergen Nachlass Edition*, Bergen. Accessible à l'adresse : http://www.wittgensteinsource.org/.

Poitou, J. 2009. Xylographie. Accessible à l'adresse : http://j.poitou.free.fr/pro/html/tkn/xylographie.html

Werner, S. 2012. Where Material Book Culture Meets Digital Humanities. *Journal of Digital Humanities* 1/3. Accessible à l'adresse : http://journalofdigitalhumanities.org/1-3/where-material-book-culture-meets-digital-humanities-by-sarah-werner/.

Williams, M. 2004. Analytical Intellectual Biography of Elizabeth L. Eisenstein. *IS 281 Historical Methodologies* 2004 (October 7). Accessible à l'adresse : https://pages.gseis.ucla.edu/faculty/maack/Documents/Chronological_20Bio-bibliography_20of_20Elizabeth_20Eisenstein.pdf.

Wollenberg, F. W. 1971. Genetische Darstellung innerhandschriftlichen Varianten. In Zeller H. (éd.), *Texte und Varianten : Probleme ihrer Edition und Interpretation*: 271-272. Munich : C.H. Beck.